A PROPHETIC TRAJECTORY

A Prophetic Trajectory
Ideologies of Place, Time and Belonging in an Angolan Religious Movement

Ruy Llera Blanes

berghahn
NEW YORK · OXFORD
www.berghahnbooks.com

Published in 2014 by

Berghahn Books

www.berghahnbooks.com

© 2014 Ruy Llera Blanes

Library of Congress Cataloging-in-Publication Data

Blanes, Ruy Llera, 1976-
  A prophetic trajectory : ideologies of place, time and belonging in an
Angolan religious movement / Ruy Llena Blanes.
      pages cm
  Includes bibliographical references and index.
  ISBN 978-1-78238-272-0 (hardback : alk. paper) —
  ISBN 978-1-78238-273-7 (ebook)
  1. Angola—Church history—20th century. 2. Toco, Simão Gonçalves,
1918–1983. I. Title.
  BR1447.25.B53 2014
  289.9'309673—dc23
                                                                    2013029904

British Library Cataloguing in Publication Data

A catalogue record for this book is available from the British Library

Printed on acid-free paper.

ISBN 978-1-78238-272-0 hardback
ISBN 978-1-78238-273-7 ebook

To Vanda, Leonor and Pedro.

To Simão Gonçalves Toko, an admirable man.

Contents

List of Illustrations   viii

Preface   ix

Introduction. On Prophetic Territories and Temporalities   1

Part I. Itineraries

Chapter 1. Trajectories: A Prophetic Biography, Part 1   39

Chapter 2. Trajectories: A Prophetic Biography, Part 2   64

Part II. Heritages

Chapter 3. Transmission: Word, Action and Mediation   107

Chapter 4. Trepidation: Spirits, Memories and Disputed Heritages   143

Chapter 5. Transcendence: Tokoist Diasporas   172

Conclusion   197

Primary Sources   205

Bibliography   207

Index   231

Illustrations

1. Simão Toko's house   2

2. *Estrela da Alva,* current symbol of the Tokoist Church,
   in entrance to church in Lisbon   41

3. Map of Simão Toko's vision of 1935   48

4. The Coro de Kibokolo in 1947   52

5. Simão and Rosa Maria Toko, recently married   56

6. Tokoist women in the Vale do Loge   67

7. Toko in the *matas*   77

8. The lighthouse in Ferraria de Ginetes, Azores   84

9. Toko revealing his scar after suffering heart surgery   91

10. Return of Simão Toko to Angola   93

11. Fragment of a letter by Simão Toko   109

12. Tokoist ceremony marked by clocks   120

13. Tokoists praying   121

14. Tokoist choir preparing to sing   129

15. Simão Toko, deceased   144

16. Tokoist Universal Temple   158

17. Celebration of the 'first Tokoist service in Lisbon'   173

18. Kimbanguist choir singing in a Tokoist ceremony   179

19. Tokoist church in Lisbon   181

20. Simão Toko's personal belongings in Ponta Albina   198

Preface

I first visited a 'Tokoist Church' – a Christian prophetic church of Angolan origin – in the neighbourhood of Vale do Forno (Odivelas, Lisbon)
in 2007. This book is the outcome of everything I've learned there ever
since. In September of that year I first got in touch with Simão Vemba,
then evangelist of the Tokoist Church, through a phone number given
to me by an Angolan Evangelical pastor. After a few informal meetings
in several malls and cafés in central Lisbon, Simão introduced me to
the church, where I eventually met the remaining community: its pastors, evangelists, choir leaders and singers, instrumentalists and regular believers. Sunday mornings – when they held their main weekly
service – became the central moments of meeting and reunion with a
community that through time would show me, in our conversations
and my participation in their liturgy, what it meant 'to be a Tokoist'.
My fieldwork since then took place in my visits to the cult space, especially on Sundays, but also on Saturdays and during the week after
work hours. If initially my meetings were motivated by requests for interviews and more or less informal conversations with different members, through time the pretexts that led me to the church became more
diversified, alternating between my participation in reunions and the
collaboration in activities and projects developed by the church. It was
through this joint work with the members of the church that most of
this book developed.

Initially, my interest in this church sprung from a research project
I was developing on Christian pluralism in Lisbon and the role played
by African migration in its current configurations. I was interested in
the way the Tokoist Church participated, as an 'African Church', in the
progressively pluralized and diversified Portuguese religious scenery,
in dialogue with broader processes of mobility and migration, secular-
ization and public space. My colleague and great friend at the Institute

of Social Sciences (ICS) in Lisbon Ramon Sarró had told me about an
'Angolan church' with similar characteristics to the more notorious
movement he was also starting to study, the Kimbanguist Church, but
nevertheless virtually unknown in the mainstream literature on African
Christianity. I was attracted by the possibility of looking at a different
version of Christianity to that in which I had specialized (Pentecostal
Christianity; see Blanes 2008a), and its similarity (and simultaneously
its distance) in regards to what I was reading in milestone literary references on African Christianity – in particular on 'Kongo prophetism'
(Sundkler 1948; Balandier 1963 [1955]; MacGaffey 1983).

However, as we will see throughout this book, the interrogations
and debates motivated by my research produced led down a signifi-
cantly different path from what was originally intended: the biography
and memory of the church's prophet founder, Simão Gonçalves Toko
(1918–1984), and through those, the concepts (ideologies) of time,
memory and belonging circulating among the followers of this movement. This shift in my orientation became an inescapability due to
the recurring revelation that was given to me in the church – that I
was standing before a movement in many ways deeply anchored in a
particular historical memory, in a collective past that transcended the
walls of the small space that housed the approximately one hundred
people I usually visited. The city of Lisbon itself offered more points of
interest from this perspective: by imposition of the Portuguese government, the prophet himself had lived for several years (in the 1960s and
1970s) in exile in Portugal; and the national archives in Lisbon host an
immense documental collection regarding this movement, mostly produced by the Portuguese political police (the PSP and later the PIDE)
of the Estado Novo regime (1933–1974) that is frequently mentioned
by the Tokoist believers not only of Lisbon but also of Angola. Thus,
among others, the PIDE and Portuguese Overseas Ministry archives,
both in the Torre do Tombo and the Arquivo Histórico Ultramarino
(Ultramarine Historical Archive), also became part of my research.

Meanwhile, the recognition of the amplitude and complexity of that
particular history led to an increasing curiosity on my behalf concerning the state of affairs in Angola. This allowed me to visit Angola on
five different occasions (2007, 2008, 2011, 2012 and 2013) for this research. In these visits, however, I was confronted with an unexpected
reality: that the Tokoist Church was fragmented into different, opposed
groups and allegiances that were claiming legitimacy and authority,
and disputing the heritage of the prophet founder. I began to develop,
with two of the most representative groups – the Direcção Universal
('Universal Directorship') and the Doze Mais Velhos ('The Twelve El-

ders') – what I will later call an 'ethnography of conflict', where I met
and interviewed the different leaderships and learned their visions,
opinions and positioning regarding their own history as a movement,
and the divergences and arguments they displayed within that same
plane. I visited headquarters, cult spaces and historical sites, and interviewed or conversed with some of the (old and new) protagonists of
the Tokoist history in this country.

This is, therefore, a book that works on multiple levels: it documents
the quotidian and ritual life of a small Angolan migrant community in
Lisbon, the labyrinthic depth of the historical archives in Lisbon and,
finally, the politics of religious conflict in Angola.

I would like to thank the following people who, whether consciously
or not, contributed to the making of this book. First and most obvious is the Tokoist community of Lisbon. I will mention here as many
as possible, and I apologize to those who for whatever reason are not
included. Simão Vemba, who was never an 'informant' or collaborator
in the academic sense, but rather a friend, enabler, problem solver and
professor with whom I learned Tokoist history and shared my theoretical and practical concerns and difficulties in the countless times
we met for coffee near his work place in Alcântara. I lost count of the
amount of doors Simão opened for me. I will never forget his sympa-
thy, mutual interest in church historiography and willingness to collaborate. Also, and especially, pastor António Gomes, who, as church
leader, authorized and guided my research with his observations, comments and timely exhortations. Other pastors and church members
also welcomed and encouraged my research: Pedro Segunda, Francisco Manuel Filipe, José António Malanda, António Macanda, Sebastião Ma'huno, Rui Paulo Caíla, André Canga, Vítor Santos Pedro,
Matcus Dias, Domingos Paiva, Ezequiel Ramos, Kelson Panzo, Sebastião João, brothers Noé, Fernando, Miqueias, Tobias, and sisters
Carolina, Tânia, Albertina, Antónia, Delfina, Berta and every family
that composes the group of Tokoists that attend the church at Vale do
Forno (my apologies to those I have unconsciously omitted). Other
Tokoists should be also mentioned: Ndongo Edgar, Isabel and Pedro
Daniel, who belonged to a different Tokoist allegiance and did not at-
tend services in the Vale do Forno Church. During my research, two
brothers who always had a kind word and a spare moment for me,
Vuvu and Xavier Branda, passed away; I cherish the memory of our
encounters and conversations.

It was through the church in Lisbon that I was also able to reach
other Tokoist churches in the European territory: Netherlands (Rotterdam) and UK (London). In these visits, I was able to build a broader

notion of the Tokoist experience in the diaspora, becoming aware of the difficulties they encounter when they try to develop and practice their faith. This, however, didn't stop them from welcoming me and taking me to their places of worship. To them, I offer my gratitude. In London, I also had the privilege of meeting one of Simão Toko's daughters, Ilda Rosa, who shared with me a more personal vision of the movement's history during the occasions we met for a coffee or a meal. This book is also dedicated to her in particular.

In my first visit to Angola in 2006, when this research had not yet officially begun, Augusto Nascimento, a researcher with decades of experience in the African continent, opened my eyes to a part of the world virtually unknown to me at the time, and showed me how to walk through it. I still remember vividly our endless strolls and conversations in and around the city of Luanda, under its scorching November sun. In two of my subsequent visits to this city, I was accompanied by Ramon Sarró, with whom I shared several fieldwork moments, performing joint visits to the Tokoist and Kimbanguist churches, and later comparing our own notes and impressions in our 'coffee breaks' in the Café Nicolas and Café Nilo in the Makulusso neighbourhood. I never stopped learning about anthropology, Africa, religion and the academy with him ever since. Two other colleagues from the Angolan academy were fundamental for this research, both in terms of technical arrangements, sharing fieldwork moments and, especially, of teaching me about the complexities of Angolan life. Their friendship and expertise on many topics discussed here were absolutely crucial for the success of this research. I am referring in particular to Fátima Viegas and Abel Paxe. Fátima's family (Luís, Evelyne and Paulo) were especially welcoming, helpful and encouraging during my visits. I would also like to mention other colleagues I met more recently in Luanda who showed great interest in my work: Aaron de Grassi, Jon Schubert, Claudia Gastrow, Ricardo Cardoso, Paulo Moreira and Gabriele Bortolami. Jon was especially helpful with recommendations to make my stays in Luanda comfortable. Murielle Mignot was always a welcoming, generous and friendly landlady during my stays at her house.

However, in Angola, many Tokoists were also pivotal in the task of historical and ethnographical reconstruction I engaged in. On behalf of the Doze Mais Velhos, I cannot but thank their leadership – namely, Vumambo David, Vasco Nzila, Sebastião Vuaituma, Manzambi Fernando and Mbala, who were always available to meet me on the several times I visited their headquarters in the Terra Nova, near the Congolenses market, and patiently answer my questions and naive concerns, sharing their own documentation and notes with me. António Neves Álvaro,

Maturino Nzila and more recently Paracleto Mumbela of the GCNET (Grupo Coral Nova Esperança Tocoista) have also been particularly important in the later stages of my work with their corrections and clarifications of previous versions of this text. Neves Álvaro in particular has become far more than a mere interlocutor, instead a great friend. On the other hand, the Direcção Universal was also highly enthusiastic, especially on behalf of its leader, Bishop Afonso Nunes, the Auxiliary Bishop Luzaísso Lutango, the director, Gabriel Nunes, Muanza Jorge and many others who were willing to share their time with me, both in Luanda and in Mbanza Kongo, Vale do Loge, Ntaia and Catete. In both cases, I genuinely hope I have met the expectations they had for this project. In a particular context of dissent such as this one, I am aware that it will be difficult, if not impossible, to produce a consensual narrative; but I will be relieved if they recognize the honesty and sincerity behind it. Other Tokoist believers from Luanda, such as Benção Quitunga, Elias Vemba, Paulo Vemba, Pedro Vemba, António Neto, the Casa de Oração group and others, were also pivotal in the construction of this book. Finally, two great scholars of the Tokoist movement, Joaquim Albino Kisela and pastor Melo Nzeyitu Josias, whom I met in Luanda and continued to converse with via email, were extremely helpful, enthusiastic and pedagogic concerning my work.

At an institutional level, this research was made possible thanks to the scientific and administrative support of the Institute of Social Sciences. Many colleagues there have shown interest and supported my research: João de Pina Cabral (who has always spared his time to hear me out), João Vasconcelos, Diana Espírito Santo, Simone Frangella, Tiago Saraiva, Nina Tiesler, Ana Stela Cunha and Nuno Domingos. The same happened with colleagues outside the ICS. Cléria Ferreira, also a scholar studying the Tokoist Church, was an enthusiastic supporter, with whom I exchanged information and debated points of view. José Mapril, Catarina Fróis, Anastasios Panagiotopoulos, Valerio Simoni, Anna Fedele, Vlad Naumescu, Arnaud Halloy, Joana Santos, Simon Coleman, Katrin Maier, Martha Frederiks, Nienke Pruiksma, Kim Knibbe, Clara Mafra, Claudia Swatowiski, Maïte Maskens, Joel Noret, David Berliner, Cristina Sánchez-Carretero, Anne Mélice, Keith Egan, Anthony Shenoda, Renato do Carmo, Nuno Porto, Fernando Florêncio, Jorge Varanda, Gerhard Seibert and many others. Also, this book would not have existed without the support of the Fundação para a Ciência e Tecnologia (FCT), that financed my postdoctoral project, as well as two other research projects coordinated by Ramon Sarró where I participated as researcher: 'The Christian Atlantic: Ethnographies of Religious Encounters between African, Brazilian and

Portuguese Churches in Lisbon' (2007–2010) and, more recently, 'The Politics of Hope: Churches and the Weaving of Society in Post-War Angola' (2010–2013). Another international project I participated in proved fundamental for my research: 'Recognizing Christianity: How African Migrants Redefine the European Religious Heritage', funded by the international consortium NORFACE.

The archival research was performed mostly in institutions in Lisbon: the ANTT (Arquivos Nacionais da Torre do Tombo), the AHU (Arquivo Histórico Ultramarino), the CIDAC (Centro de Documentação Álvares Cabral) and the IPAD (Instituto Português de Apoio ao Desenvolvimento) in Lisbon. In all these places, the help and kindness dispensed by the assistants was far more than I could have asked for as an anthropologist untrained in archival research; they were responsible for my making sense of the myriad of information before me.

My stay as a guest researcher between 2007 and 2010 at the Department of Anthropology of the University of Leiden, through the invitation of Professor Peter Pels, was pivotal for my grounding in the main theoretical debates in African studies – especially the bibliographical research I performed at the Afrika Studie Centrum in Leiden and the interaction with their researchers (Benjamin Soares, Rijk van Dijk, Stephen Ellis). To all, and to Peter Pels in particular, my gratitude. More recently, my presence as visiting fellow at the London School of Economics and Political Science, made possible by Matthew Engelke, also helped me expand and improve my theoretical approach through my exchange with several professors and students at the Department of Anthropology (Matthew Engelke, Deborah James, Fenella Cannell, Michael Scott, Stephan Feuchtwang, Tom Boylston, George St. Clair, Sitna Quiroz, Andreas Bandak). I thank Matthew in particular for his kindness, his introduction to the LSE and British academia and for his constant encouragement.

Finally, many colleagues read and helped me improve this book through their insights: Ramon Sarró, João Pina-Cabral, Diana Espírito Santo, Matthew Engelke, Michael Scott, Stephan Feuchtwang, Neves Álvaro. But, of course, none of this would have been possible if it weren't for Vanda, Leonor and Pedro, who patiently accepted and endured my absences. This book is for them.

On Prophetic Territories and Temporalities

It is mid-afternoon on 12 April 2011, and I'm about to leave the house of the late Simão Gonçalves Toko located in the Terra Nova, a neighbourhood in eastern Luanda. The neighbourhood is also referred to as '*os Congolenses*', due to the concentration of Bakongo (many of them former expatriates in the Lower Congo) living and selling in the local market. Toko's compound, located on what used to be an asphalt back street which has nevertheless been occupied by the market sellers and the occasional *zungueiro* (ambulant street seller) and flanked by rows of two-floored houses, somehow reminds me of the typical mid-century middle-class constructions in Portugal, with a front balcony facing a small patio at the entrance. On the front door, I notice – not for the first time – a sticker for Sporting Club Portugal, which also happens to be one of my favourite football teams.

I had been inside the house for most of the day, talking to a group of religious leaders, benefiting from their wisdom (as well as from their powerful air conditioning) and snacking on crackers and soda. Outside, the heavy, damp sun, the muddy water pools (a hard rain had fallen nonstop for hours the night before), the street market craze and the *candongueiros* (public taxis) that would take me to the room I had rented in the Mártires de Kifangondo neighbourhood awaited. It wasn't the first time I visited the house and the elders, but this occasion was special: I had brought with me a copy of a manuscript with the results of my research (and which would turn out to be this book you are reading), and we had been improvising a sort of focus group, where several aspects of my writing were invoked and discussed. Also, I was shown several 'historical photos' and we informally performed elicitations around them. As I stood up to say goodbye (I was to return to

Illustration 1. Simão Toko's house (second on the left), Terra Nova, Luanda, December 2007. Photo: Ruy Llera Blanes.

Lisbon soon after), I began to thank them for all their corrections and expressed my hope that they would find the final outcome of my work worthy of their respect – or that at least they would recognize the good intentions behind it. It was at that precise moment that Sebastião, one of the elders, replied: 'o pai já tinha dito que viria alguém de fora para estudar e escrever a nossa história' (Father had already told us that someone would come from outside to study and write our history). In other words, Simão Toko, the founder and leader of the movement, had already prophesied my research.

The Angolan Situation:
Forgotten and Reconstructed Histories

This book is about an Angolan Christian movement known as the Tokoist Church.[1] Its name comes as a result of the following of an Angolan prophet of Bakongo ethnicity, Simão Gonçalves Toko. Also known by his Kikongo name, Mayamona ('what has been seen'), Simão was born in Sadi-Zulumongo, a remote dwelling near Taia, in the commune of Maquela do Zombo (province of Uíge). In his youth, Toko studied in a local Baptist mission (Kibokolo), where he would eventually work as an assistant before migrating (at the age of twenty-four), like many other Angolan Bakongo of the time, to the nearest urban centre – Leo-poldville (today Kinshasa), in what was then the Belgian Congo – to find a job as Sunday School teacher and choir leader. In that city, after a miraculous event that took place on 25 July 1949 – the descent of the Holy Ghost before Toko and a group of his students and followers – he decided to create a reformist movement that took a stance against European political and spiritual colonization, as well as against the African traditionalisms of witchcraft and magic. The unrest provoked in Leopoldville by the events of 1949 pushed the Belgian authorities into arresting Toko and his followers, and, considering that they were all of Angolan origin, expel them into what was then the Portuguese colony of Angola. There Toko and his followers continued to face per-secution from the overseas branch of the Portuguese political police (*Polícia Internacional de Defesa do* Estado, or PIDE) for decades; sus-picious of their subversive potential, PIDE subjected them to prison, torture, forced labour and exile. This, however, did not provoke the end of the movement, which would resist and finally become, in the wake of Angolan independence in 1974, institutionally recognized as a church.

Thus, despite having its founding moment in the Belgian Congo, the Tokoist Church is today one of Angola's most important religious play-ers, notorious for its green and (predominantly) white garments and the symbol (an eight-pointed white star in a green background) they proudly wear on their suits and gowns every Sunday when they walk the streets and motorways, or ride their private cars or *candongueiros*, heading towards morning service.[2] In Luanda, for instance, it is com-mon to see these white and green gowns colouring the main road of the Golfe II neighbourhood in Southeast Luanda, heading towards the church's new mega cathedral – inaugurated in August 2012 – where tens of thousands of believers congregate and listen to the sermons of the current leader, Bishop Afonso Nunes. Not very far north from there, in the *musseque* (informal settlement neighbourhood) of Palanca, a smaller group, separated from the previous one, known as The Twelve Elders, also performs its Sunday service with a smaller, yet equally dedicated audience.[3]

This image of Angolans dressed in white garments walking the roads in the country's capital serves as an illustration of how the history of this particular church is aligned – albeit not very straightforwardly – with the history of the country itself. One could affirm that Tokoist history simultaneously feeds into, and offers an alternative (parallel) route to, the historiography of Angola as an independent nation, participating in one way or the other in the nation's milestone political moments, from the exiled emergence of a libertarian consciousness and independence to the civil war and the subsequent establishment of an authoritarian regime dealing in a particular way with its own past and diversity (Chabal and Vidal 2007). This historical insertion followed, as we will see, many and tortuous paths that lead into the current situation of institutional notoriety.

On the one hand, the Tokoist movement appears in an historical moment where, after centuries of trade-based and slave-powered colonialism with a primarily coastal implantation (Alexandre 1979, 2000; Birmingham 2000, 2006), the Portuguese metropolis increased its presence in the territory, seeking territorial, financial and ideological expansion (Freudenthal 2005; Bender 2009 [1978]). The height of this new imperialist policy – which materialized mainly for commercial reasons, after the Brazilian secession in the previous century (Marques 2010) which left Portugal with next to no resources to sustain its transcontinental project and combat internal poverty – took place mostly during the Estado Novo Regime (1933–1974), under which Angola and the other African colonies became a hypothetical 'new Brazil' (Marques 2010), inserted into Portugal's geographical and moral, ideological territory (Matos 2006) as prospective lands of opportunity. As Claudia Castelo (2007) describes, from the 1920s onwards Portugal began a 'civil occupation' of the Angolan and Mozambican territories, which took hundreds of thousands of continentals to the ultramarine provinces and developed major economic and scientific enterprises that dramatically changed the local scenery, especially in what concerned the urban growth of its major centres and the agricultural exploration of its rural areas (Carreira 1977).[4] Gerald Bender (2009 [1978]) saw this particular period as one where, along with a strong ideology of societal and racial miscegenation (known in the academic, political and cultural circles as luso-tropicalism),[5] the Portuguese enforced a system of colonial domination that used autochthon populations as enslaved labour force, in many ways resonant with the slave and penal colonization policies they were forced to abandon after the definitive international condemnation of slavery of the 1926 Slavery Act (see Ball 2005). Thus, the increasing political presence and pressure of the Portuguese in Angola also provoked a frictional state that progressively enabled the conflicting situation that exploded in the 1960s. For instance, if the relationship with the Bakongo and Lunda groups of northern Angola historically combined ancient slave trafficking, a posterior effort for political centralization and a late pragmatic, locally accepted commercial exchange (Thornton 1981; Hilton 1985; Henriques 1997), the installation of colonial enterprises using enslaved or poorly waged labour, such as Cotonang in Malanje, Diamang in the Lunda and other smaller agricultural ventures in the northwest, were seen by many as slavery in disguise, given the harsh working and living conditions to which many indigenous workers were subjected to (Rocha 2003; Ball 2005, 2006; Varanda 2011). In other words, if slave trafficking historically mostly served the purposes of economic enterprises, in the twentieth century Portuguese imposition of forced-labour policies implied an autochthon subjection into the socio-political hegemonic project of exploitation.

But, considering that it began within a community of northern Angolan Bakongo expatriates in Leopoldville, Tokoism also dwells in the interstices of two colonial endeavours – Portuguese and Belgian, which divided and colonized the physical and moral space of the ancient Kingdom of Kongo, construing, after the Berlin Conference of 1884–1885, a political frontier against a local tradition of transit, exchange and commerce within the Bakongo world, which traditionally only saw the Congo river basin as a momentary impediment for the north–south mobilities and circulations, prolonging or extending family networks and lineages (Vansina 1962; Wheeler and Pelissier 1971; Hilton 1983, 1985; Gonçalves 1985; Thornton 1991; MacGaffey 2008). This, along with the duplicated histories of dominance, violence and oppression written by both Portuguese and Belgian hands (Balandier 1965; Gonçalves 1985), provoked the progressive downfall of the old kingdom into a merely symbolic status. This does not mean, however, that it became a forgotten memory. In fact, as has been recently noted (Sarró, Blanes and Viegas 2008; Sarró 2009a), the memory of the Kingdom of Kongo is today very present among the Bakongo, and we can observe a contradiction between the political map designed by the colonial forces (and perpetuated by the postcolonial governments) and the mental map that the Bakongo remember from the ancient Kingdom of Kongo, which is often invoked as a genuinely African form of government, against the example of the colonial rule. Thus for many Bakongo, after a few isolated attempts,[6] the emergence of religious movements of protest (Margarido 1972), such as Kimbanguism or Tokoism, built new political coordinates to address such a contradiction (Gonçalves 1985). However, this epistemological frontier did not (and does not) prevent the Bakongo from circulating and exchanging through the border, a fact that remains politically contentious to this day (see e.g. Mabeko-Tali 1995; Brinkman 2008).

From this perspective, it is noteworthy that the emergence of the following of Simão Toko as a movement took place in 1940s Leopoldville, where other forms of expatriate Angolan association and libertarian spirit were evolving, both in response to Belgian and Portuguese colonialisms. Thus for instance, if as Georges Balandier described, religious movements such as Kimbanguism and Mpadism were concomitant to associations that later emerged as political contestations to the Belgian regime (1953, 1963 [1955], 1971), the city of Leopoldville also hosted several movements of struggle against Portuguese imperial interests, sponsored by several ideological movements – from communism to pan-Africanism and also libertarian grassroots Catholicism (Rocha 2003) – and became one of the focal points (Europe being the other) of Angolan nationalism.[7] Thus, Tokoism at the time was conceived as one of the several associativisms that congregated political sensibilities sharing the same goals: autonomy and independence, which ultimately justified the mistrust of the Belgian authorities and the ultimate expulsion of the Tokoists from the Congolese colony, and inaugurated the longstanding debate concerning the role of Tokoism in the emergence of a nationalist consciousness in Angola (see Ferreira 2012; chapters 2 and 3, this book). However, if the political-military movements dwelled in the Lower Congo, eventually proclaiming an Angolan government in exile,[8] Toko and his followers soon detached from the expatriate libertarian environment, as they were subject to repressive measures that placed them in the hands of the Portuguese authorities and henceforth in their politico-ideological system. In this line, these emergences reflected not one but several nationalisms developing in the Lower Congo, with different envisionings and tactics devised to seek independence (see Torgal et al. 2008).

By the time the Tokoists were repatriated into Angola (early 1950s), the Portuguese colonial authorities faced a particular catch-22. On the one hand, the moment was the historical culmination of the imperialist investment in Angola, with projects that involved massive human displacements from the metropolis and within the colony (Ball 2005; Castelo 2007), major agricultural, scientific and biomedical enterprises (e.g. Porto 1999; Varanda 2004, 2011) and transport and communication development (Heintze and von Oppen 2008; Esteves 2010). On the other hand, they dwelled in an environment of recurring and increasing political suspicion. This suspicion had many sources: the witnessing of the emergence of anticolonial movements and uprisings in neighbouring territories (Lower Congo, Katanga, etc.), and the increasing influence of communism in this region of Africa, promoted by the same people who fought the regime in Portugal (see e.g.

Neves 2006, 2008). But also the external pressure coming from the loss of the Asian territories (Goa, Díu, Damão) to India, the succession of political independencies in the African continent and in the territories surrounding Angola,[9] the anticolonial policy adopted by the United Nations and the consecutive declarations for self-determination in the African continent fed into a sensation of political instability that contrasted with the financial, political and ideological investment in Angola promoted by Lisbon. This in turn provoked the progressive installation of a political and policed regime, with the development of a complex network of surveillance, investigation and control activities, mainly exerted by the PIDE.

From an autochthonous point of view, the international support for the liberation movements organized in the Lower Congo regions grew, with the increasing presence of communist activists from Portugal, Cuba and elsewhere, as well from North American and European officials, who saw in Angola a new stage for the Cold War, and from other African leaderships, embarked in the newfound independency (Mazrui 2010). From this perspective, the region became a politically effervescent international stage, where several levels of political and economic interest were exposed, imposed and negotiated. But if the Lower Congo was an international stage for, among other things, Cold War politics, the main associations that fought the Portuguese also incorporated local ethnic logics that proved to be divisive and problematic for the common nationalist project: Bakongo (UPA-FNLA), Mbundu (MPLA), Ovimbundu and Lunda-Tchokwe (UNITA) (see Pelissier 1978; Heywood 1989; Messiant 1994; Henriques 2004; Pereira 2004).[10] Such movements, which began as exiled paramilitary organizations created to fight the Portuguese colonial system, later evolved into political parties, becoming the major protagonists of the independence period. From this perspective, social movements such as Tokoism were placed, voluntarily or involuntarily, against such a fragmentary map of ethnopolitical allegiances (Bittencourt 2000; Serrano 2008).

But instead of speculating over the wording we could choose to define Tokoism's place in Angolan independent history (from protagonist to spectator, victim or bystander), I prefer in this book to observe and debate the intersections that transformed Tokoism into a social, cultural and political agent in present-day Angola. In this line of thought, I will argue that there are many revelations and concealments in contemporary Angolan historiography that are directly related to its postcolonial political history. In the aftermath of the Carnation Revolution on 25 April 1974, a process of political transition began in which the main protagonists of the liberation war sought a consensus to form the first independent government. However, after a contested agreement signed in Alvor (Portugal) in January 1975, the MPLA party, led by Agostinho Neto, took cabinet and inaugurated a rule that lasted until this day.

The first years of Angolan independence were a vibrant mix of patriotism, libertarian ideals, communism and pan-Africanism, but, adding to the situation of militarized fraction between the different protagonists of the liberation wars, and struggling to build an endurable unity against the fragility of its borders,[11] the regime led by Neto quickly evolved into an authoritarian one, marked by a strong centralization of power (in response to the political fracture and ethnic plurality), an intense modernistic ideology (combatting previous, traditional or colonial leaderships) and a strong Marxist-Leninist ideology (Bittencourt 2008; Messiant 2008; Serrano 2008). But apart from the political fracture (Messiant 2008), the nation building enforced by the MPLA also responded to the recognition of Angola as a culturally and ethnically diverse country with no prior epistemological reference, a pre-colonial Angolan nation. From this perspective, independency and national sovereignty also involved the instalment of a project of national unity (Bittencourt 2010). Therefore, collective movements that did not abide by this project and presupposed alternative sovereignties – such as Tokoism, but also other religious movements like the Jehova's Witnesses – experienced major difficulties, adding a subsequent layer to their memories of suffering.

Religious Configurations and Reconfigurations in the Angolan Scene

Although there is no quantitative data to support it directly (see Viegas 2007; INAR 2010), there is in Angola a generalized opinion that the Tokoist Church is today, after the Catholic Church, *the* great Christian movement in this country, rivalling with other popular religious movements such as the Kimbanguist Church (with a stronger implantation in Luanda and Northern Angola), the Universal Church of the Kingdom of God (UCKG, with a more recent presence in Angola, but equally observing a fast growth), the Maná Church (eventually shut down by government decree in 2007), the Assembly of God and the Evangelical Baptist Church, among others. It is, within this comparative scheme, the only one publicly recognized as having an 'Angolan root' and one of the few that can claim to have representation throughout the whole Angolan territory, as well as in the Angolan diaspora in Sub-Saharan Africa and Europe.

From this perspective, the Tokoist Church occupies a particular place in comparison with other notorious contemporary African Independence movements. Historically, it became part of the same movement that led many African movements from prophetism to independency (Hastings 1996: 493–539), exemplifying like none other the concepts of autonomy and autochthony that guided the process of secession led by countless indigenous leaders in the late colonial period (see e.g. Sundkler 1948; Balandier 1953; Shepperson 1953; Barrett 1967; Turner 1967, 1969; Ranger 1968; Hastings 1974; Fasholé-Luke et al. 1978; Jules-Rosette 1979; Ojo 1988; Schoffeleers 1991; Comaroff and Comaroff 1992; Edgar and Sapire 2000; Sarró 2008a; Seesemann and Soares 2009). It is also inscribed within current, postcolonial expressions of 'southernized' transnational Christian movements stemming out of the African continent and into wider, transoceanic networks, protagonizing the 'changing face' of contemporary, third-millennium Christianity (Bediako 2000; Corten and Marshall-Fratani 2001; Sanneh and Carpenter 2005; Jenkins 2006, 2007; see also Sarró and Blanes 2009).

However, Tokoism also detaches *from*, and simultaneously speaks in a very particular way *to*, recurrent tropes in the contemporary literature on African Christianity – which seems to have been, to a certain extent, conceptually 'Pentecostalized' (see Engelke 2010) – and the anthropology of Christianity in general. I am thinking of current tropes that, although not exclusive, are recurrent in Pentecostal and charismatic discourse, such as those of political agency (Bayart 1989; Gifford 1995; Freston 2001; Ellis and ter Haar 2004; Anderson 2005; Maxwell 2005; Ranger 2008; Marshall 2009), spirituality, economy and power (Comaroff and Comaroff 1997; Green 2003; Werbner 2011), media and mediation (Hackett 1998; Meyer 2003, 2006; de Witte 2003, Pype 2012), conversion, healing and renewal (Meyer 1998, 1999; Asamoah 2005; Keller 2005; Klaver and van de Kamp 2011; Werbner 2011), etc. Many of these references respond more or less explicitly to a backdrop of 'African modernity', or its inevitability (Tonda 2005; Ferguson 2006). As I will try to demonstrate throughout this book, the Tokoist Church (and, by extension, Angolan religion in many ways) is a fascinating example for alternative ways of thinking about contemporary African Christianity, namely in what concerns ideas of temporality, territoriality, politics and belonging that do not necessarily embark in such narratives in the same vein.

But Tokoism also occupies a unique place within the Angolan religious scenery. Generally speaking, late colonial Angola was religiously characterized by a situation of tripolarity. On the one hand, we find the centenary presence of the Catholic Church in the territory, represented since 1940 by the Archdioceses of Luanda, but having worked for centuries in Angola and the Lower Congo through the presence, among others, of Dominican, Capuchin and Jesuit missionaries in the Kingdom of Congo (Gray 1983, 1999; Hastings 1998; Thornton 1998; Santos 2000; Almeida 2010). From this perspective, Catholicism is a creed with deep roots in Angola and the Lower Congo, since the first exploratory ventures by Diogo Cão in the Congo Basin (1482–1484), and found expression in the missionary work as well as in the official connections with the Portuguese colonial venture (Santos and Torrão 1993; Santos 2000; Schubert 2000).[12]

On the other hand, there is the presence, from the late nineteenth century (and in particular after the 1884 Berlin Conference), of Protestant missions of north-European or American origin, namely Baptist, Methodist, Presbyterian, Philafrican and Evangelical, among others, that progressively installed headquarters in the hinterland, promoting proselytist and educational projects, opening schools for the 'natives' in their missions (Péclard 1995, 1998; Birmingham 1998; Messiant 1998; Schubert 1999). And finally, there is the multiple local systems of belief ('animisms') against which both Catholics and Protestants fought amidst the 'civilizing mission' they found themselves embarked in.[13]

In this particular context, the process of imperial demise and consequent decolonization, and the appearance of local Christian movements such as the Tokoist Church,[14] implied a dramatic reconfiguration of the local socio-religious map that would eventually result in the postcolonial situation of 'religious proliferation' observed today (Schubert 2000; Viegas 2007). These movements were usually portrayed, in the literature of the time, as 'sects' and 'syncretistic movements' that incorporated a 'free interpretation of the Bible' (Gabriel 1978: 609) and 'naively amalgamated' it (Estermann 1965: 342) with traditional and pagan African elements (Santos 1969; Rego 1970). More recently, some authors debated the role played by protestant missions in the formation of 'autonomous religious subjects' or in the formation of anticolonial and anti-Catholic consciousnesses in this period (Messiant 1998; Freston 2001: 119–121).[15] In any case, the last decades of the Portuguese colonial project witnessed a process of transformation of the Angolan social and religious sphere that would be constitutive of the current situation of proliferation.

However, after Angolan independence in 1975, the new MPLA cabinet led by Agostinho Neto promoted a policy of intolerance and prohibition of religious affairs, discouraging public assembly and appropriating all assets belonging to the religious movements (namely

the Catholic Church, seen as the main 'partner' of the Portuguese colonial government).[16] The situation progressively shifted throughout
the 1980s, when the José Eduardo dos Santos cabinet promoted legal
recognition campaigns that, regardless of the state control they were
subject to, allowed for different religious institutions to become public
and set the scene for a progressively plural religious scenery in Angola
(Schubert 1999, 2000). If, in the first recognition campaign of 1987,
only the Catholic Church recovered its official status (and saw its assets
and properties returned), in the 1992 campaign, twelve other churches
were officially recognized – and among them, the Tokoist Church.

Thus, the 1990s were years of dramatic increase of religious institutions and manifestations in Angola – mostly due to the entry of foreign
churches, affiliated to the Pentecostal, Neopentecostal and Evangelical branches of Christianity (Freston 2005) – although not necessarily
so for the Tokoist Church, as we will see later on in this book. Cases
such as those of churches stemming from the transnational lusophone
space (the Maná or the UCKG churches, for instance) or working in
the southern African and Atlantic region (as the Igreja do Bom Deus,
for instance) reveal new societal logics, such as the development of a
transnational Southern Atlantic space of exchange with different trajectories and directionalities than those of colonial times (see Sarró
and Blanes 2009). In many ways, the current public situation of the
church today, described in chapter 4, can also be read as a reaction
to such movements and creativities. Today, in particular after the ec-
clesiastic participation in the processes of national reconciliation and
reconstruction (see Schubert 2000; Messiant 2008), and the creation
of the Instituto Nacional para os Assuntos Religiosos (National Institute for Religious Affairs, or INAR) in 2006, there is a persisting and
increasing awareness of the important role that religious entities can
play in the public space, which in turn is no longer circumscribed to
the symbolic space marked within the Angolan frontiers ('from Cabinda to the Cunene', as any Angolan would tell you), but is ramified in
the Sub-Saharan, Atlantic and lusophone space.

In this setting, autochthon prophetic religions such as Tokoism play
a highly symbolic and particular role, exemplifying how these sche-
matic interpretations of religious affairs only offer partial portraits of
their sociologic and spiritual reality. The vitality and transformation it
experienced in the post-independence and post-war periods, pushing
it to the forefront of the Angolan, Atlantic and lusophone postcolonial
religious field (where the Angolan diaspora is equally included), therefore deserve a closer look.

A Forgotten History

This initial exercise of apologetics and recognition of this particular religious movement, perhaps seeming somewhat exaggerated to you, is in fact a response to one of the most striking acknowledgements any researcher who deals with this church is confronted with: the fact that, in contrast with what happens with similar movements in this region of Africa, this church is very much unknown outside its country of origin and virtually ignored in international academic and media circles. In the international compendiums on African religious movements (for instance, Barrett 1968; Ranger 1986; Hastings 1996; Wauthier 2007), there is no reference to this movement, with the exception of David Barrett, who indeed describes (albeit synthetically) the church of Simão Toko as being the most important one in Angolan territory (1968: 27). This 'forgetfulness' contrasts, I argue, with the abundance of sources and pretexts for its study, and especially with the importance that Tokoists themselves concede to writing, publication and historical knowledge, and to leaving, in any possible way, a public imprint of their prophet founder's life and contribution, as a testimony of a concrete and exemplary 'way of being Christian'.

As I mentioned in the preface, in 2007, when I first heard about this church in Lisbon, I mentally categorized it as one of the many small African congregations that constituted religious minorities in the Portuguese and European territory, an expression of the will by many migrant believers of congregating 'their own way' (Blanes 2007). I also imagined it as being similar to the church my colleague Ramon Sarró was starting to study at the time, the Kimbanguist Church, perhaps due to the common prophetic eponym ('Simon', which is also present in other contemporary local prophets, as I describe below). At the time, I could not have imagined that behind the small group of approximately one hundred people attending the cult space in Lisbon, there was the movement of massive proportions I was to meet in Luanda in the subsequent years, and a church with a particular trajectory that was very different from the previous Congolese example, inserted within lusophone colonial and postcolonial history like no other in that territory.

There are more or less objective reasons that help us understand this 'forgotten history'. The first is, as just suggested, its historical, geographic and sociological proximity to modern 'Kongo prophetism',[17] where the figure of Simon Kimbangu (1889–1951) is notorious and prevalent, but where subsequently other prophets would appear, such as Simon-Pierre Mpadi, André Matswa or Lassy Simon Zépherin. From this perspective, the figure of Simão Gonçalves Toko became in a certain sense subsumed under Kimbangu's heritage and notoriety, as is also hinted at in the descriptions of the local religious scene set forth by Georges Balandier (1963 [1955]) and Wyatt MacGaffey (1983), who enhance the immediacy and impact of his legacy in subsequent movements that claimed direct or indirect lineage to the prophet.[18] This overlapping is therefore somewhat understandable, inasmuch as Toko's movement was born precisely in Leopoldville, amidst times of Bakongo nationalist effervescence, a few years before Congolese political independence – this will be an object of discussion later on in this book. Thus, the omission is to some extent expectable, even in the most important studies of prophetic and messianic movements in the region (Andersson 1958; Balandier 1963 [1955]; MacGaffey 1983). The same can be affirmed regarding broader research on prophetisms and independent religious movements in Africa (Balandier 1963 [1955]; Lanternari 1963; Sinda 1972; Ndiokwere 1981; Hastings 1996b; Wauthier 2007). The scarce references – usually as footnotes or last sentences in paragraphs – we find in this literature regarding Simão Toko's movement classify it as an offshoot or imitation of Kimbangu's original movement, one of the many that were inspired by his actions and legacy in the subsequent decades (Van Wing 1958: 608; Doutreloux 1965: 227; Barrett 1968: 27; Martin 1975: 100 and ff.).

Most of these references coincide in an analysis of Kimbangu within the trope of political reaction to colonial oppression. From this perspective, the problem of individual leadership and the political character of messianism became paramount, especially in the more notorious studies performed by Balandier (1963 [1955]) and MacGaffey (1983), who followed the imprint and legacy of the Bakongo prophet in local colonial and postcolonial society. Therefore, following this geopolitical rationale, Toko could easily be classified as one of the many local leaders inspired by (and eventually an imitator of) Kimbangu and his politico-religious stance – with the lateral curiosity of him being not Congolese but Angolan. But this explanation – that would be immediately discredited by anyone familiar with Tokoism – becomes too 'easy' to accept, as it is mostly based on the territorial and temporal coincidence or proximity between what is recurrently conceived in terms of an 'original' prophet and his 'photocopy'. There are, in fact, a few local references that do suggest a hypothetical influence of Kimbangu in Simão Toko's project (Cunha 1959: 31–32; Estermann 1965; Gonçalves 1967: 681; Rego 1970; Pélissier 1978; Grenfell 1998). However, the same sources, and other testimonies from the time, also point to other influences, such as the Watch Tower (the Jehova's Witnesses proselytist branch), with a growing influence in the region at the time, the Armée de Salut or even Catholicism as is pointed out by António da Silva Rego (1970: 35, 42). Also, as I describe later, this connection was more theoretical than anything else. These divergent reports, that did not in any case prevent the collage between the Tokoist movement and notions of syncretism or Kongo prophetic independentism, do begin to reveal the complexity behind its theological construction, and simultaneously the ideological motivations behind the descriptions. From this perspective, as I partially conclude in chapter 1, the history of Tokoism is also one of transcendence of the conceptual straightjacket imposed by the traditional circumscription of 'local (Bakongo), colonial messianisms'.

This forgotten history may also be explained by another factor: the intrinsic features of the available exogenous literature on this movement, mostly produced in colonial times and by people in one way or the other connected to the Portuguese regime, either as political and religious agents or as academics researching religious phenomena in the territory within a strategy of 'counter-terrorism' (Gonçalves 1967: 693). This production, despite some noteworthy exceptions or nuances, coincides in a very unflattering portrait of Simão Toko and his movement, with abundant references to an 'amalgamation of disparate elements that rebel against Cartesian logic' (Estermann 1965: 332; my translation). The narrative that inaugurates these tropes is authored by Joaquim da Silva Cunha, at the time professor at the Instituto Superior de Estudos Ultramarinos (Higher Institute of Overseas Studies) and later minister of defence and overseas in the Marcelo Caetano cabinet, who was very much involved in the installation of the PIDE political police in Angolan territory. In 1959 he produced an extended and detailed account of the Tokoist movement when it was still in its early stages. Having interviewed, under the aegis of the PIDE vigilance activities, Simão Toko and some of his main followers (such as Pululo José and Luvualo David), and using testimonies, letters and secondary reports on the movement's services and activities,[19] Cunha put together a biographical portrait of Simão Toko, describing him as an introspective, hesitant, confused and insincere person, although with some persuasive capacities and political ambitions (1959: 29 and ff.). A few years later, the Catholic priest and ethnologist Carlos Estermann invoked Cunha's work to describe Tokoism as a doctrinally confusing 'nebulous sect' (1965). In contrast, José Julio Gonçalves, from the Missão para o Estudo da Missionologia Africana (Mission for the Study of African Missiology), distanced himself from the demeaning psychological profiling and instead interrogated the unexpected success of this movement (1967). Eduardo dos Santos, author of an

extensive volume on religions in Angola published by the Junta de Investigações do Ultramar (Board of Ultramarine Research), also wrote
from a distance, but only dedicated three pages to Tokoism, highlighting the prophet's subversive, 'agitating' and 'racialized' ideas (1969: 469
and ff.).

From the 1970s on, we begin to see counterpoints to the demeaning
portraits. Historian António da Silva Rego, for instance, sought to contextualize the appearance of Tokoism with the 'Bakongo paradigm',
insisting in his connection with the three other homonym Bakongo
prophets of the time (Kimbangu, Mpadi and Lassy) and suggesting a
common political consciousness connected to a nostalgia of the old
Kingdom of Kongo (1970).[20] At the same time, the Portuguese sociologist (living in Paris) Alfredo Margarido, perhaps inspired by Georges
Balandier's theories on the 'colonial situation' (1963 [1955]), inaugurated a reflection on the socio-political context that facilitated the Tokoist message of resistance, questioning the role played by the church
in the Angolan liberation movements (1966, 1972). The same opinion
can be found in the work of Douglas Wheeler, a North American historian of Angola, who placed Simão Toko's movement amidst the process
of Angolan revolution (1971: 152–155; see also Marcum 1969).

However, despite the change of paradigm, even after the end of the
colonial era, the literature regarding this movement remained scarce.
From this perspective, the years of insurgency and, later, civil war in
Angola, as well as the difficulties associated with conducting research
within an authoritarian regime, may also explain the absence of a
systematic study of the Tokoist and other religious movements in the
pre- and post-independence periods. We find a few exceptions with
researchers from the French (Pelissier 1978), British (Grenfell 1996,
1998) and North European (Hansen 2006) academies, as well as from
a few Angolan (Gonçalves 1984, 2003; Manzambi 1995; Viegas 1999;
Matumona 2009; Paxe 2009) and Brazilian (Ferreira 2012) social scientists. Two major themes, already present in the work of Antonio da
Silva Rego and Alfredo Margarido, intersect most of these references:
the place of Simão Toko's movement in the genesis of Angolan nationalism and its insertion within the Bakongo cultural matrix. I will explore both issues throughout this book.

In any case, as many Tokoists ceaselessly pointed out to me along
the way, there are also internal reasons that help explain this forgetting. The hostility that they suffered from three different political regimes throughout the decades produced, in many Tokoists, a defensive
instinct that became in many cases a withdrawal from the 'outside',
the concealment of their own religious affiliation and the mistrust re-

garding the *coisas do mundo* ('things of the world'). In many of my conversations in Luanda, some Tokoists would recall that there were, over the years, many internal campaigns envisaging the 'erasing of history', motivated by internal disputes and the disagreement regarding the public pertinence and opportunity of the kind of knowledge that was being produced and represented by the Tokoists (see chapters 3 and 4). This form of withdrawal also explains in a way the argument of this book, inserted within a process of reconstruction and oriented towards the representations and discourses (in many cases, explicitly political and ideological) produced by the Tokoists as self-referential justifications within this forgotten history.

A Reconstructed and Territorialized History

Many Tokoists I met during my research are knowledgeable of the references quoted above mentioning their leader, and the literary production they have embarked on can be seen, in many ways, as a reaction to the paradigm of forgetfulness or personal demeaning of the prophet. In the last years, they have produced their own biographies (e.g. Agostinho n.d.; Quibeta n.d.; Melo 2002; Kisela 2004; Nzila 2006) and directed their own documentaries, where they illustrate their own versions of historical facts,[21] their own historiographical production regarding the prophet's life and works and their religious and social implications in Angola and the world. But this movement of self-production isn't just a call to remembrance; it is also, as we will see, an epistemological rupture with two orders of knowledge: a Western knowledge and historiography (see Goody 2006), and a Euro-centric Christian theological history. Amidst wider movements of epistemological recovery of African knowledge and philosophy (see Horton 1976; Mudimbe 1988; Cox 1998), the proposals set forth by Simão Gonçalves Toko and his followers will also imply a process of contestation and response to given intellectual proceedings and paradigms, through their own initiative and production. 'We always start from the past', Pedro Segunda, one of the pastors of the church in Lisbon, once told me. Since then, I have witnessed how Tokoists have been performing their own 'reading of history'. In February 2009, when we were celebrating the ninety-first anniversary of Toko's birth in the Tokoist Church of Lisbon, its leader, Pastor António Gomes, stated in his sermon:

> Today we are celebrating the great joy, the day of birth, February 24, 1918. Perhaps our anthropologist, Ruy, if he pursues his research a little

further, will tell us: when that child was born, in 1918, what was happening? Or even before he was born, what was out there, what was the world experiencing in that moment? Perhaps the distance is not that great. When we talk about the end of the World War that was destroying the world, in that context, in that confusion, in that uncertainty, when a child is born, then.... As we know, this war didn't only take place in Europe, it struck all corners of the world, even Africa. That is why our researchers, with time, they will tell us. They will discover many things. That is why we open this space, so that people investigate, find out new things. Many things will surface. My dear brothers, today we conclude this great joy, the birth of that shining star that opened the path that today our people, the chosen ones, are following: the steps of Our Lord Jesus Christ. (Excerpt of sermon, Tokoist Church in Lisbon, February 2009)[22]

Pastor Gomes's words were revealing of two desires: the desire to investigate and discover and the desire to follow a path, a trajectory.[23] From this perspective, as we will see, the Tokoist Church reveals a particular path that distances it, throughout its history, both from the territorial (Bakongo, Angolan) paradigms and from the political (anticolonial) prisms reflected in the aforementioned literature, and incorporates a particular theology and identitary discourse that simultaneously engages with ideas of Angola-ness, Africa-ness and universalism – and where the idea of prophetic leadership is imbued with sets of meaning that push it away from the classic conceptual paradigms (see conclusion). Interestingly enough, that departure is produced over the years through two concomitant and mutually related movements: Toko's personal and spiritual biography and the trajectories followed by him and his followers in the historical process of institution and development of this particular religious culture.

Both vital movements – through territories and biographical memories – are indicative of an enhanced, and simultaneously complex, historical consciousness among the Tokoists, to whom the senses of 'belonging' and 'being' imply the acceptance of a particular historiography. Memory is omnipresent in their spiritual knowledge and ethos, and it is through acts of memory that certain moments of the past 'become present' (see chapter 3), ultimately producing an after-the-fact attribution of charisma. This is visible, at first glance, in the recurrent invocations of the prophet's life that operate in different levels and spheres of action: in the archival work and the biographical production mentioned above, but also in the testimonies of the *mais velhos* (elders) that participated in the Tokoist history and personally interacted with the prophet; in the church liturgy that crystallizes the prophetic knowledge in the time and space of ritual action (from codified conduct to hymns and prayer modalities); in the church sermons that repeat and contextualize Toko's words and wisdom; in the church tabernacles, where certain information pertaining to him is revealed through acts of charisma and possession; in the mementoes or histori-cal objects and documents that many believers hold and cherish; and in the study and production of knowledge that allows for, among other things, the biblical exegesis by comparison with the prophet's life and words, or the interpretation of historical facts according to a particular prophetic knowledge. From this perspective, what seems to be at stake is simultaneously an ethno-theology (Scott 2005, 2007), a mythopraxis (Lambek 2007), a poiesis (Lambek 1998) and an organization of the past, as Pierre Nora would put it (1989) – different ways of approach-ing the past, according to a particular idea of history (Collingwood 1994).

But this is also verifiable in the 'updating' of memory, or the way how, through the historical formation of generations of Tokoists, the proph-et's memory shifts and repositions according to differing postures, motivations and expectations regarding history and the world (see Sarró 2007: 263 and ff.). I am referring specifically to a very common problem among prophetic and messianic movements: transformation within the generational leadership transition process, in particular af-ter the death of the original prophet founder (see Blanes 2010, 2011a). In the case of the Tokoist Church, this will become a fracturing and (re)structuring problem, as we will see in the last chapters of this book. The conflict that broke out in the church after the passing of Simão Toko in 1984, which fractured the church into several opposing groups that disputed legitimacy and authority, created a situation where his-torical consciousness and research are objects of scrutiny and appro-priation. History, in certain contexts, is a battlefield where Tokoists of different allegiances, acknowledging the 'power in the story' (Trouil-lot 1995), strive to produce proofs and make their points. The texts and biographies produced both from within and without the church (including the pages you are reading right now), become, in a certain sense, unfinished narratives, objects that feed into the permanent, on-going debate.[24]

Nevertheless, these methods of memory are also revealing of a fun-damental theological configuration in what concerns Tokoist belief: a reformist spirit that is supported by the concept of *relembramento* or 'remembrance' (Blanes 2009a). As Domingos Pedro Macanda, an elder evangelist from Luanda that was visiting in Lisbon, told me, Simão Toko did not *found* the church; in fact, he *remembered* it, returning to us the original church of the apostles that had been meanwhile corrupted (8 August 2010). Dofonso Manzambi Fernando, an elder from the church in Luanda, also spoke about Tokoism as 'a revision of events passed' (Álvaro 2011). This concept of remembrance, described in more detail in chapter 3, configures in many ways the core of To-koist theology. Its Portuguese translation denounces this complexity (unattainable in the English concept of 'remembering'), as it conju-gates the act of *lembrar* ('to remember') with the prefix *re-*, which adds repetition to the action. *Relembramento* would thus evoke a 'double remembrance', which for the Tokoists implies a double moment of memory and revelation.

But, through the sedimentation of historical experiences, this mem-ory also configures an ideology of suffering (Blanes 2009a) that stems from the remembrance of the different episodes of persecution suf-fered by the prophet and his followers in the foundational moments of the church, but is also reminiscent of Christian theologies of suffer-ing and sacrifice (see Castelli 2007). Thus, this memory also produces 'itineraries of suffering' – temporalized landscapes (Ingold 1993) that are identified by the Tokoists within their self-location in the world. But, as is common in prophetic movements, the memory of suffer-ing also implies an exercise of 'situation' in the present,[25] a teleology and an eschatology of hope. One could affirm, as historian Reinhardt Koselleck (2004) does, that remembrance and memory are part of the same exercise that combines experience and expectation, looking for-ward, hope. Hirokazu Miyazaki speaks about a 'production of hope' as a method of knowledge formation that determinates a posture facing the world (2004). In this regard, Tokoists, through these processes of 'remembering' and 're-remembering', are also embarked in a process of production of hope that aids them in 'making sense' of their current situation, no matter how heterotopic it may seem. This production could also be seen as an intellectual act of transformation of heteroto-pia into utopia.

This production is also, from an ideological and experiential point of view, intrinsic to prophetic and messianic cultures that stand upon two fundamental notions: martyrdom and providence. This comes down to an argument I heard time and again during my fieldwork: "he [the prophet] sacrificed himself for us for a reason." From this per-spective, messianism can be understood as a form of 'acquiring con-sciousness' and historical positioning, the recognition of a context that enables a 'master pedagogy' (Faubion 2001), i.e. a set of ideological, narrative, poetic and experiential dispositions that teleologically and providentially evolve into a particular (millennial) expectation. There are, therefore, different notions of temporality involved that are diver-

gent (Carvounas 2002), punctuated (Guyer 2007) and conjugated in a
non-linear fashion: the consciousness and expectation of 'messianic
moments' against the perception of history as a positivistic progression, as Walter Benjamin had suggested (1968).[26]

The notion of providence appears therefore as what Vincent Crapanzano (2004) would refer to as an imaginative horizon, a marker of
the kind of temporal perceptions (Hodges 2007; Naumescu 2011), and
consequent ontologies, that we encounter when we become aware of
the different modalities of Tokoist experience. In other words, we are
before a prophetic temporality that is mediated by multiple notions
of memory, sacrifice and expectation. But we are also before senses of
temporal incongruence (Miyazaki 2003) when we observe the different
claims of the past and providence that are at play, and refer to different
ontologies (Scott 2007; Naumescu 2010, 2011). In any case, it explains
the continuous need for fulfilment (Miyazaki 2000), the need for re-
covering and updating memory that is so present among the Tokoists.
In other words, Tokoist belief (or rather, its public expression) also
becomes a formulation of a pursuit of certainty (James 1995).

The most immediate outcome of this is a book balanced between
experiential and political representations of Tokoist belief. This book is
also the product of the unfolding of different methods – forms of knowledge that, unmasking 'time's arrow' or its immediate linearity (Hodges
2008), incorporate different temporalities and different ways of grasp-
ing them, i.e. relying on remembrance and historiographic prophetic
wisdom (chapter 3), 'living in 1984' or announcing new millennial eras
(chapter 4), among other things. Again following Miyazaki's rationale,
here I take hope as a particular stance of a certain knowledge that
pertains and affects ideas of time. Likewise, I see the connection between memory and hope as what Fredric Jameson (2005) would call
an 'archaeology of the future', the political constitution of an utopian
thinking according to specific perceptions of history.

Such configurations make up for what I have been describing here
as a 'prophetic temporality', a complex, multi-layered experience and
organization of time that is neither modern nor postmodern, as it does
not prefigure its own end (see Jameson 2003). Time thus becomes a
focal point here, especially if we consider its conceptual and ideological configurations. As many authors have pointed out, there are
several 'qualities of time' (James and Mills 2005) that may vary, in a
Braudelian pespective, from abstract configurations to specific notions
of civilization (Feuchtwang and Rowlands 2010), tradition and stability (Boylston 2012), transmission (Naumescu 2010), cognition (Gell
1992), semantics (Koselleck 2004), ontology (Hodges 2008), epistemol-

ogy (Fabian 1983), etc. (on this see also Munn 1992). These approaches reveal the complexity and multiplicity behind what often appears as a simple trope: the past is behind us, and the future lies ahead.

From this perspective, the notion of modernity itself, as a culmination of 'historical linearity', became the object of debate and critique (Comaroff and Comaroff 1992; Faubion 1993; Knauft 2002a; Meyer and Pels 2003; Sahlins 2004). Here, I follow Stephan Feuchtwag and Michael Rowlands when they suggest that there is more involved in the process of historical acknowledgement than simply 'detecting multiple and rival historicities' (2010: 118). What needs to be tackled, therefore, is what they refer to as the 'teleology of modernizing projects' (ibid.), in its conceptual, theoretical and empirical manifestations – as has been brilliantly rehearsed by Bruno Latour (1991). As Bruce Knauft (2002b: 1) asks, what is effectively entailed in the process of 'being' or 'becoming' modern? What are the movements and directionalities involved, and to what extent do they imply the assertion of particular narratives or meta-narratives? It would be impossible to come up with one straight answer for these questions. They do, however, stimulate awareness against the 'omnibus assumption' (Knauft 2002b: 3) that the concept of modernity often produces in anthropology.

In this respect, a pertinent case in point are the recent debates within the anthropology of Christianity (Cannell 2006; Engelke and Robbins 2010) that have focused precisely on the issue of time and its epistemological and heuristic implications, directly or indirectly looking at the idea of modernity as a problem. After John and Jean Comaroff's proposal of thinking of African colonialism and mission through concepts of agency and transformation (1991), the work of Birgit Meyer, although not necessarily new (see Engelke 2004), provoked an important paradigmatic movement by thinking of the relationship through notions of modernity and (epistemological, ontological) rupture, unearthed by processes of religious conversion. In her case, she referred to the impact of Pentecostal churches in 1990s Ghana, the transformations operated through the massive processes of religious conversion to this branch, especially in what concerned issues of local tradition, history and culture (1998, 1999). This language of conversion and transformation, albeit already present in other ethnographies of Evangelical Christianity (for instance in Stromberg 1993; Csordas 1994; Crapanzano 2000; Harding 2000; Mafra 2002), placed theology and its practical implications in the believers' experience, at the centre of the analysis. In many cases, a 'conversion to modernity' (van der Veer 1996) seemed to be at stake, where the process of spiritual transformation entailed the individual and collective insertion into a particular flow of time (on this see necessarily Hefner 1993; van der Veer 1996), where ideas of Western-ness, globalization, transformation and power would circulate.

These rupturist theses would later be resumed and debated by other anthropologists, who would question more broadly the relationship between belief and cultural continuity – oriented towards the more philosophical problems of morality (Robbins 2004, 2007), praxis and discursive formations (Engelke 2009, 2010) and especially the rapports between subject, change (conversion) and modernity (e.g. van der Veer 1996; Keane 2002, 2007; Peel 2000; Cannell 2006; Barker 2007; Tomlinson 2009; Engelke 2010; Coleman 2011). This insertion into modernity often appears as an externally imposed inevitability, an adoption of a linear narrative that opposes (and ultimately constructs) notions of tradition and progress (van der Veer 1996; Robbins 2004), in an association that has proved proficient in most literature on Christian movements around the world (see Cannell 2006). In Meyer's work, this distinction becomes quite evident, placing the Ewe she worked with in the following temporal conundrum: should we convert to Pentecostalism and thus be modern, or in turn remain traditional (see Meyer 1998, 1999)? In a way, it detects the seduction that the idea of modernity itself exerts in places like Africa (Ferguson 1999; Tonda 2005). But what happens if there is such a context where 'modernity' does not seem to appear as a concept with currency among those with which we, as anthropologists, work (see e.g. Scott 2005)? Or where the 'modernity of Christianity' is actively contested (e.g. St. Clair 2011)? In the case of the Tokoist Church, what is often at stake with the cultivation of memory is precisely the refusal of the 'forgetfulness of modernity', as Pierre Nora (1989), Jacques Derrida (2005) and Paul Connerton (2009) have pointed out.

As I describe in chapter 1, despite exogenous descriptions in the opposite direction (Cunha 1959; Estermann 1965), Toko's movement was seen in its early stages in Angola as an 'anti-traditionalist' movement, namely in what concerned the rejection of witchcraft and 'devilish spiritism' (Agostinho n.d.). From this perspective, through its reformist spirit, Tokoism could easily be catalogued beside the many 'modern' anti-witchcraft movements described in the late colonial Africanist literature (see Richards 1935; Marwick 1950; see also Geschiere 1997 [1995] and West 2005 for a critique). But, as we will also see, Toko did not engage in a specific rhetoric of modernity, but instead in one of revelation and historical acknowledgement, overturning the master narrative of conversion and modernity. In this regard, what is necessary, I feel, is the critical detection of the diverse Christian temporalities

(Naumescu 2011) and the possibility of their political, ideological and experiential conflation, distinction or competition – from born-again ruptures to Pauline messianisms, everyday millennialisms, prophetic remembrances and eschatologies (see e.g. Robbins 2001; Engelke 2009, 2010; Marshall 2009).

Thus, the problem, from a messianic and prophetic perspective, where ideas of familial and communitary continuity, stability and re-assurance concerning the past are linchpin (see chapter 3), is the epistemological weight that some of these approaches place on religious conversion as an epistemological device, and the insufficient way they deal with contexts that show different qualities of time, multiple materialities and temporalities (see Engelke 2009), or with ideas of tradition or modernity that diverge from the 'familiar narrative' that has been built in the academy (Keane 2007: 7) – contexts where history has become epistemologically 'abundant' (Orsi 2008). In the first place, I am referring to an empirical context (Angola, Congo, Portugal) where Christianity and transformation have walked together for centuries, becoming part of the local history, and where the really dramatic process of conversion, in what concerns memory, subjectivity and identity, was the political transformation from a colonial to a postcolonial society, turning the idea of modernity into something devoid of its original content (Ferguson 2006: 176 and ff.) and spatialized into specific territories of inequality and dissent (see, in this respect, Latour 1991).

In the second place, this multiplicity, in the way I describe it in this book, is the result of a process that is ultimately political, where the 'relational epistemologies' (Bird-David 1999) presented are a result of a 'struggle for coherence' on behalf of the different sectors and ways of 'being Tokoist', leaving little room for a unified 'Tokoist theory of modernity'. Thus, the crux is a broader understanding of 'movement' and 'transformation' that includes both processes of personal and spiritual transformation, and reactions to historical conjunctures, relationships with the land, intellectual projects and dialectics of negotiation and resistance. From this perspective, when talking to different Tokoists about history and memory, I wouldn't engage in discussions about 'modernity', but rather about 'the past', 'the future' and its continuities and disruptions. In this particular regard, the theological concept of remembrance was, from a political point of view, a way of bypassing modernity and redefining its alter ego – tradition (see chapters 3 and 4).

But the modernist seduction also brings about another apparent conceptual inescapability: the insertion of Christianity into particular stances of globality and globalization, where it seems to be commonly assumed that Christianity is a pervading element in the transnational dynamic and debates that connect 'the modern social' at a global scale (see Engelke and Robbins 2010). It is not difficult to agree with that; however, I do argue for the epistemological relevance of the local (i.e. the land, a certain geographical notion, a frontier, etc.; see Christian Jr. 1989) in the understanding of Christian practice. From this perspective, 'modernity' can come to mean many different things, and either acquire centrality and transcendence or be relegated to mere irrelevance. Michael W. Scott, for instance, has brilliantly reminded us how there is such a thing as 'autochthonous histories' (2007: 163 and ff.), where the land becomes central to the ontological constitution (topogony) of Christian believers in the Solomon Islands. Similarly, I will argue that Tokoist belief and ideology is equally engrained in particular sites and territorial identitary circumscriptions that have produced particular narratives concerning the church's place in the world.

From this perspective, we are also facing a 'prophetic territoriality', one that projects meaning unto the land, creating and circumscribing spaces of spiritual agency and political contention. The processes of mobility involved in its historical constitution have provoked, as we will see, dramatic transformations within the Tokoist Church, which successively overcame different territorial belongings (see Blanes 2009c) and geographic epithets – Zombo, Bakongo, Angolan, African, etc. As I will argue throughout this book, time and place are connected in the Tokoist experience in such a way that challenges the mainline interpretations that construe prophetism as a 'regional phenomenon' – be it Bantu (Sundkler 1948), Kongo (MacGaffey 1983), Nuer (Johnson 1994), Amazonian (Queiroz 1965; Clastres 1975; Clastres [1993] 1975; Musumeci 2002), Melanesian (Lanternari 1963; Scott 2007), etc. From this perspective, Tokoism could be seen as a de-territorialized and re-territorialized prophetism that reconfigured notions of temporality, being and belonging through this process of geographic mobility. And, as we will see, this reconfiguration was operated through political and ideological stances, or what Scott called 'ethno-theologies' (2007: 301– 327). I therefore see the connection between mobility and the land as a creative process (Leach 2004), but also a necessarily unstable one.

I also take on two fundamental understandings concerning prophetic territoriality and its connection to notions of time. Firstly, I tackle the connection to place as the movement against the modernist sense of amnesia or 'end of history' (see Jameson 2003; Fasolt 2004), as discussed by Pierre Nora in his *lieux de mémoire* (1989) and Paul Connerton's recent reflections on the 'topographies of forgetting' (2009). I incorporate Robert Orsi's suggestion to study the 'abundant histories'

ing them into tracing the genealogies of significance that made certain African prophets 'revealing' (1995: 1–26). Within this line of thought, we can argue that the forgetfulness of Tokoism could also be a collateral effect of the classificatory problems that the different writers and academics encountered in their analyses of African prophetism and religious independentism.

In what concerns this region of the world, there is an intellectually profitable conceptual lineage that, if it has not helped us pin down a stable definition, has certainly produced an intellectual agenda that remains relevant and challenging to this day. Georges Balandier's suggestion of the 'revelatory character' of Bakongo messianism (and the prophet Simon Kimbangu, in particular) is, in this context, salient. Building upon the precursory reflections of Maurice Leenhardt (1902) and Bengt Sundkler (1948) on Ethiopian and Bantu religious leadership, Balandier addresses the problem of cultural contextualization of independent prophetic individuality – a problem inherent in the posterior work of scholars who also worked on prophetism in the Congo region, such as Effraim Andersson (1958), A. Doutreloux (1965), André Droogers (1980), Joseph Tonda (2001) and, especially, Wyatt Mac-Gaffey, who discussed 'Kongo prophetism' in terms of 'cultural roots' (1977) and 'religious commissions' (1970). MacGaffey sought to explain the cultural role of prophets such as Simon Kimbangu (1887–1951) as a Christian version of the Bakongo *ngunza* or religious leader/healer or prophet – in correlation with other roles, such as chief (*mfumu*) or magician (*nganga*) (1970) – produced within processes of "political allocation" (1983: 78). Many authors explained the socio-political claims and concomitant development of historical consciousness within independent African religious movements – from Ethiopianism and Zionism to 'Kongo' prophetism and apostolic movements, and so on – from this perspective (see Barrett 1968 for a review). In other words, from the idea of an 'oppression paradigm' (MacGaffey 1983: 1) that seemed to reduce prophetism to a political problem. This approach, however, revealed itself as being somewhat restrictive (Sarró 2008a: 3), and does not account for persisting issues in the contemporary approaches to the subject: the persistence and revival of such prophetic movements in postcolonial and contemporary times (see Sarró and Blanes 2009); their 'survival' and regeneration after the removal of the 'charismatic element' or the succession of the prophet into second and third generations of religious movements (Fernandez 1973), eventually translated into forms of routinization; and finally the emergence and negotiation of novel forms of leadership, such as those stemmed from Pentecostal and Neopentecostal movements, for instance (Mary 2002).

Placing these discussions on commissions and allocations in temporal perspective, and within a particular historical constraint, necessarily pushes us to invoke the problem of leadership and authority
– a key issue in terms of understanding prophetic biography and the
intersection of charisma and memory in the construction of 'church
history' framed in terms of what Max Weber would call disruption (see
below), but that others have debated in terms of (often generational)
innovation (Droogers 1980) or iconoclasm (Sarró 2008a), for instance.
This was a recurring theme in the study of Kongo prophets, inevitably focused on the political agency and social dissemination of such
leaderships within specific historical moments – the transition from a
colonial to a postcolonial context. From this perspective, Simão Toko
would not escape such configurations, as he too was often seen as a politically active religious leader. However, throughout this book we will
also see Toko as what Dozon (2006) called a prophetic *contretemps* or
reversal, a leadership that emerges as a reaction against the historical
moment, exploring new avenues of temporal configuration. If he was
seen equally by the different interlocutors as a 'rupturist' and a 'tra-
ditionalist' in this particular moment and territory, through concepts
such as remembrance and New Jerusalem, Toko proposed an alternative route to such classifications. The question here is precisely what
became the outcome of such proposals in the diacrony of generational
transition (explored in chapters 3 to 5).

Thus, another problem, at least for someone preoccupied with stabilizing definitions, becomes particularly clear when we acknowledge
that such conceptual lineages and reproductions are not exclusive to
the academia, occurring within similar intellectual activities. In what
concerns the leadership of Simão Toko, there is no consensus among
his followers regarding his personality, personhood and public profile.
As we will see in chapters 4 and 5, there is an on-going disputed legacy
that not only questions the certainty of its historiographical knowledge
but also the very perception of Simão Toko as a leader. This occurs
precisely due to what is described in chapters 1 and 2: the histories of
temporal and spatial transcendence provoked by the prophetic trajectory of Simão Toko. Thus, one needs to search for other concepts and
configurations to understand the place of the prophet founder within
his own movement and his followers. Here, I take on the notion of
charisma and its conceptual ambivalence, intersecting social, political,
psychological, historical and aesthetic dimensions of religious experience. In the particular case of the Tokoist movement, charisma is not
only used as a trope to understand and classify the prophet's personality and leadership qualities, but also as theological configuration of

spiritual experience and activity, directly connected to the notion of remembrance, as I explain in chapter 3. It thus encapsulates personal, political and spiritual dimensions simultaneously.

From this perspective, there is also something inherently temporal about the idea of charisma. Charismatic qualities (psychologies), pulsations (spiritual gifts) and agencies (leaderships), in a sense, inaugurate a category of experience in anyone for whom the idea of charisma becomes relevant: that of temporal acknowledgement and expectation, embodied in senses of memory, hope, expectation and certainty. This at least is what stemmed from Max Weber's classic formulation of charisma as a 'removal from the sphere of the ordinary' by which certain individuals would be 'treated as endowed with supernatural, superhuman, or at least specifically exceptional powers or qualities' (1947: 358–359). This treatment of the individual on behalf of a collective of followers engages in a certain idea of (utopian) 'expectation' – under the guise of hope and/or dread (Feuchtwang and Mingming 2001: 13) – one where that exceptionality serves a specific purpose of advancement.

Weber, thinking from the perspective of religious and political authority, had understood this in his recognition of the 'disruptive' character of charisma, as an agent of renewal or innovation often subject to subsequent processes of routinization and bureaucratization (Eisenstadt 1968). From this perspective, charismatic leaders can also be understood as tricksters (Hansen 2001), agents of disorder and contestation, destruction and creation within moments of crisis (Feuchtwang and Mingming 2001). But for this to be possible, of course, we must also accept that the charismatic leadership is based on interpersonal relationships, on 'group mentalities' (Lindholm 1990), 'generalized activity' (Scott 2009: 295) or, in fact, quasi-Durkheimian 'charismatic communities' of leadership and following, involving rhetoric (Csordas 1997), persuasion and acceptance, and aesthetic repertoires.

Thus, charisma appears here as a 'relationship' rather than an 'attribution' – an empirically grounded, contextualized approach that has been explored by anthropologists in particular regimes of Christianity, such as Evangelicalism (Coleman 2004; Csordas 2009). This leads to a questioning of the univocality of traditional conceptual foundations that surround charisma: is leadership necessarily charismatic, and does charisma necessarily evolve into political leadership? What are the emic and etic notions of authority invoked in the conceptual constitution of charisma? What kind of concepts and categories emerge from this ambivalent epistemological process? This book will delve into such complexities.

But, interestingly enough, there is also a creative friction between emic and etic configurations of Tokoist leadership. One example of how such descriptive categories floated between different fields took place in the 1960s. One of the few publications concerning Tokoism at the time was an article published by Carlos Estermann, a German Catholic priest who travelled to Angola on missionary work with the Spiritans and who later became known for his ethnological surveys in the colony spanning several decades and topics (see e.g. 1983). In 1965 Estermann published an article in the journal *Garcia de Orta* (from the Junta das Missões Geográficas e de Investigações do Ultramar), where he discredited the movement and its leader, accusing him of creating a fanatic, dangerous sect that presented itself as Christian when in fact it was closer to traditional African spiritist belief (1965: 342).[28] In a letter written in 1970 by Toko to Lando André, a follower living in Luanda, he commented:

> I have with me some books that the world has written about me, and where we can find truths and lies about everything I did in Angola and the former Belgian Congo.... One such book was written by Father Carlos Estermann.... In this book it is written that I am a false prophet, enemy of the Church of Christ, enemy of the Catholic Church, enemy of God, enemy of Jesus, etc etc. For that reason, and to stop dragging men through paths of lies, I ordered that the church be closed down.... I have no religion, I am just as I was born, the Church of Christ is inside my heart. God will punish me for my evil deeds, but will not punish me for preaching his word. (25 April 1970)[29]

From this perspective, if Toko was aware that there was an external production concerning his person and creation (as he was when he announced the future coming of researchers like me), he was not insensible to the framing that was being built. His 'battle' thus became one of preservation, justification and explanation, both outwards towards a general audience, and inwards towards his own following.

The Book

This book is intended to address the dialectic between the overarching concerns by the Tokoists regarding history and time, and the way social sciences have dealt with the problem of collective memory and interpret alternative ways of 'making history'. It is, therefore, a book written as much for academics as for the Tokoists themselves, looking for a 'creative knowledge' (Bakhtin, in Shalins 2004: 4) through the dialectic between the different points of view and discourses. It thus becomes 'participated' and 'mutual' – in the sense suggested by Johannes Fabian (1995) and especially as is debated in João Pina Cabral (2013) – exploring the affinities and frictions produced in the different positionings within the conflictual process, constitutive of what Viveiros the Castro would call an 'enemy's point of view' (1992), but beyond academic attempts of discovering analogies and systematic conclusions that would attempt to 'make sense of' what we study. Through the confrontation of those positionings and consequent argumentations, it also explores the misunderstandings and equivocations that are, as Fabian stated, inherent to ethnographic practice (1995).[30] Without wanting to seek any particular sense of 'relative' or 'objective truth' in this exercise of writing ethnography, I do however believe that there is a 'positive gain in knowledge' (1995: 41) that occurs when we address incompatibilities, incongruences and misunderstandings, which challenges the face value of discursive and ideological dimensions of ethnographic production. I therefore use the notion of ideology not so much as an 'authoritative meaning' (Asad 1993) but rather as the intent and the will to make certain 'meanings authoritative'.

This book starts with 'itineraries', presenting a 'spatialized biography', a portrait of Simão Toko's life through the different voices that commented on it, the places that witnessed his presence and the processes that identified heritages and patrimonialized the paths he covered, contributing towards the meaningfulness of the church's formal designation: 'Church of Our Lord Jesus Christ in the World.' It is, in a particular sense, a 'sensory biography' (Desjarlais 2003) through which the Tokoist followers identify temporalities, places and meanings – or transform memory into history (Nora 1989). It is also the substance, the 'archive' or commencement, as Derrida put it (1995) from which Tokoists build different repertoires of knowledge, materiality, orientation and practice. Here, I follow Stephan Feuchtwang and Wang Mingming (2001) and Cristina Sánchez-Carretero and Peter Jan Margry (2011) in the focus on the 'grassroots' dimensions, i.e. the social processes by which an identification between history (or memory) and belief occurs (Feuchtwang 2001) within the negotiation of problems of individual leadership, authority, etc.

I thus propose an approach that combines ideology, knowledge and experience, alternating between the existential and political dimensions of Tokoism.[31] In order to do so, I propose the notion of 'trajectory' – a path followed by someone or something – that, in a way, collapses perceptions of time and space through the agency imposed by the thousands of people that participated in the process of 'institution' or transformation from a spontaneous following of a local leader into a formal, public religious entity. With agency I am thinking more specifically of identifiable contexts and protagonists of acts of consciousness, memorialization, dispute and ideology construction.

The first two chapters of the book constitute therefore the matter upon which these agencies are built and imposed, their referential axis. Together, they reconstruct a prophetic biographical narrative, the prophet's trajectory, the episodes and processes that fed into the notion of 'history' that circulates within Tokoism – from the remote village of Sadi-Zulumongo, in a distant commune in northern Angola, to places as diverse as Leopoldville, Luanda, the Namibe desert, the Azores islands, Lisbon, etc. These places, and their memory, became part of a Tokoist moral geography (Taylor 2007), but also of a process of re-territorialization and identitary belonging that transformed Tokoism into its current stance, a particularly complex phenomenon, introducing different narratives and ideologies of movement and belonging. I refer here to processes of involuntary mobility (prison, exile, etc.), as well as to explicit processes of mobility and agency (mission, etc.) that produced concomitant (but not necessarily convergent) alignments with the historical and political situations they witnessed.

The third chapter exemplifies, through three different materializations, the way that prophetic trajectory became a heritage, translated into very specific acts: performing liturgy, singing, praying and prophesying. These acts are identifiable constitutive axes that construct the difference between Tokoist praxis and pragmatics and other religious and Christian expressions. Likewise, these trajectories also reveal a historical process of transmission and negotiation, where the meanings were debated and defined within dialectics of prophetic leadership and charisma, and mediated by the problem of absence and presence. Here, I describe how writing and the exchange of letters produced a particular way of doctrinal development that constantly alternates between dynamics of profusion and reclusion.

If the third chapter focused on material processes of transmission and stabilization, the fourth chapter, as an inverted mirror, detects ideological and discursive processes of destabilization; it returns to the problem of prophetic heritage, but from a different perspective: the way it was appropriated, disputed and ultimately fragmented after the physical disappearance of the prophet, that provoked the unearthing of motivations and positionings that were, until then, subjacent. I describe how the prophet's memory became an object of debate and public contestation within internal attempts to 'survive prophecy' (i.e. survive the disappearance of the prophet founder and corresponding generational transition). Here, another type of agency and subjective perception becomes explicit: the dimension of spiritual agency in political dispute and the establishment of temporal narratives.

Finally, the fifth chapter arrives to my empirical point of departure, describing the current expression of the transformations explained in the previous chapters, observing a particular version of Tokoism from its epistemological periphery, i.e. its diaspora. Through the eyes of the Lisboan Tokoists, I portray one of the most dramatic processes of territorial transcendence known in the history of the Tokoist Church, which illustrates the vicissitudes of its newfound universalism through movements of expansion and contraction.

Notes

1. The official designation of the movement is Igreja do Nosso Senhor Jesus Cristo no Mundo, Relembrada em 25 de Julho de 1949 pela Sua Santidade o Profeta Simão Gonçalves Toco ('Church of Our Lord Jesus Christ in the World, Remembered on 25 July 1949 by His Holiness the Prophet Simão Gonçalves Toco'). The naming 'Tokoist Church' or 'the Tokoists' has been used throughout the years in diverse contexts as a form of designation, often producing some discomfort in some members. However, it is the most common designation in the church, so I have decided to keep it here. Also, it is common to find among the different sources and writings the family name 'Toko' spelt with a *k* or *c* ('Toko' or 'Toco'). Here I will keep to the most common usage in English speaking references ('Toko'), which is increasingly common also in Angola.
2. Estermann (1965); interview with Afonso Nunes, *O País Online* (10 November 2009).
3. Below and in chapter 4 I explain the development of these different 'Tokoist groups'.
4. Prior to this moment, Angola was also used as a penal colony to where Portuguese criminals were deported (Keese 2003; Bender 2009 [1978]: 199 and ff.; Bastos 2009). Subsequently, the urban scenario of cities like Luanda became demographically complex, segmented, class-based and racialized (Torres 1986; Mourão 2005).
5. The concept of luso-tropicalism was coined by Brazilian intellectual and politician Gilberto Freyre in his writings on the history of Brazil and Portuguese colonialism. See e.g. Castelo (1998) and Bastos, Almeida and Feldman-Bianco (2002) for a critical debate.
6. In 1914, an unsuccessful revolt led by Álvaro Buta represented the last autochthon attempt on behalf of the Kingdom to combat the Portuguese political domination of the territory. In the same year, the Kingdom was formally dissolved. See also Wheeler (1969).
7. Brazzaville, the capital of the French colony on the other side of the river, was obviously experiencing similar movements, such as André Matswa's

Société Amicale des Originaires de l'Afrique Équatoriale Française (Balandier 1963 [1955]: 396 and ff.).

8. The Governo Revolucionário de Angola no Exílio (GRAE – Angolan Revolutionary Government in Exile), founded in 1962 by the then military
organization FNLA (see below) and subsequently recognized by the Organization of African Unity.

9. The Republic of Congo (Leopoldville) would become independent in 1960,
while the Katanga region experienced violent turmoil and attempts of secession; Zambia in turn would become independent in 1964, while Namibia remained under South African administration.

10. The UPA (Union of the Peoples of Angola) was founded by Holden Roberto in 1957, and was later rebaptized FNLA (National Liberation Front
of Angola). The MPLA (People's Movement for the Liberation of Angola),
a merger that stemmed from the Angolan Communist Party (PCA), was
in turn founded by Viriato da Cruz in 1956, and the UNITA (National Union for the Total Independence of Angola) in 1966 by Jonas Savimbi and
António da Costa Fernandes. These were the main but obviously not the
only political associations that emerged in this period; they did however
become the most prominent.

11. In the first years after the declaration of independence (1980), the Angolans fought off, with the aid of Cuban forces, an attempted invasion on
behalf of the South African army. If the United States of America, Cuba,
Zaire and the Soviet Union we already in the field supporting the MPLA
and UNITA, South Africa also revealed its intentions in the Angolan territory, after supporting the FNLA in its attempt to prevent the MPLA from
declaring independence in 1975 (in what would be later remembered as
the Battle of Kifangondo).

12. The Lower Congo region was the first, but obviously not the only, to be subject to Catholic missions. For instance, the central Planalto and southern
regions of Angola also experienced an important influx of Spiritain missions since the nineteenth century (Santos and Torrão 1993; Dulley 2010).
This connection however should be understood as being complex and mediated with the history of the Catholic Church in the Estado Novo regime
in Potugal, which saw different moments of approximation and distance
(see e.g. Rezola 1999; Almeida 2008). See below for the Angolan case.

13. See Gonçalves (1960), Santos (1969), Santos and Torrão (1993) and Santos (2000). Contemporary sources, such as the PIDE archives, refer to the
existence of other non-Christian religious movements in late colonial Angola, such as the Baha'i or the Islamic community. On this see also Santos
(1969).

14. The PIDE archives also mention the existence of several other movements,
classified under 'sects': from the Kimbanguist Church to the Église des
Noirs, 'Lassism', the 'Alice Movement' and the 'Ethiopian and Zion sects'
or the 'Vapostori [Apostolic] sect'. From these, only Tokoism could be considered autochthon to Angola.

15. I deliberately move away from, following the suggestion by Neto (2011),
the dichotomization that places the Catholic field as 'allied' and the Protestant as 'oppositional' to the colonial project. The scenery, as is now known,

was far more complex, and the 'formation of consciousnesses' also took place in the Catholic missions (ibid.; Rocha 2003).

16. This despite the fact that, as Didier Péclard reminds us, the main political protagonists of Angolan nationalism – Agostinho Neto, Jonas Savimbi and Holden Roberto – bore a religious background and education (1998b).

17. I invoke the concept of 'modern Kongo prophetism', following Wyatt Mac-Gaffey (1983), in order to distinguish this twentieth-century prophetic culture from other historical phenomena such as the Antonian or Kimpa Vita movements (Thornton 1998; Mboukou 2010), Appolonia Mafuta (Thornton 1998; Young 2007) or the following of Francisco Kassola (Sinda 1972). However, I do not necessarily propose an epistemological separation between them. For a history and debate on Bakongo messianism and prophetism, see, among others, Andersson (1958), Balandier (1963 [1955]), Sinda (1972) and MacGaffey (1983).

18. I was also able to observe this, for example, when I met members of the Mpadist Church on a trip to Mbanza Kongo, near the border of the DR Congo (October 2008).

19. The vast majority of this material can be found in the PIDE archives in the Torre do Tombo, as I explain in chapter 1. I was able to consult most of the sources invoked by the author for this book. From this perspective, most of the posterior references quoted here also rely on first-hand material obtained by the PIDE in the Tokoist movement against the will or knowledge of the believers, or on Cunha Silva's pioneering work.

20. This idea is still very present in contemporary Congolese religious movements, such as Kimbanguism (Sarró, Blanes and Viegas 2008), among others.

21. I am referring in particular to two documentaries, *Vida e Obra de Simão Toko* (1997, directed by Joaquim Kisela) and *Simão Toco, O Senhor da Paz* (2009, directed by Francisco Rebello). Also, other recent initiatives could be mentioned, such as the creation of Facebook pages, blogs, websites and Youtube feeds by Tokoist believers and researchers.

22. My translation. Likewise for all the subsequent quotes of letters, documents, interviews, etc., in this book.

23. This book, which began to emerge as an idea in my head around that time, is also an answer to that personal request by Pastor Gomes, who therefore 'inserted' me into this process of narrative exchange and historical reconstruction.

24. As I hinted in the preface, during my fieldwork in Angola I worked with the two most representative factions of the church, the Direcção Universal and the Doze Mais Velhos, with whom I attended services and performed interviews. I also visited and engaged with members of other groups, such as the Casa de Oração, 18 Classes 16 Tribos (Mundial), Lundi Mbongo, Fikambi Kambi, etc. Thus, part of what we see here is a result of an 'ethnography of conflict', where I met opposing arguments and points of view within the Tokoist universe. Obviously, it was not my intention to produce a verdict on the Church's problems, but rather to understand their place and consequences within the contemporary Tokoist experience and notions of temporality.

25. Tokoists often refer to each other as 'brother co-sufferer'.
26. The expression of this conjugation takes place, for instance, in the invocation of the 'prophetic fulfilment', that in these case is always found to be 'in the process of confirmation', avoiding 'failure' – thus producing a permanent sense of actualization, expectation and permanence, but also of ambiguity within the ideology and experience of prophetic faith (Sarró, personal communication; see Festinger, Riecken and Schachter 1956; Tumminia 2005).
27. There are obviously definitional and linguistic aspects involved, as these terms obviously do not refer to the same thing. However, it is also true that in many contexts 'prophet', 'messiah' and 'millennial confirmation' appear conflated.
28. The PIDE archives in the Torre do Tombo reveal that Estermann, like Silva Cunha before him, kept correspondence with the police, and the information collected and analyzed by him was used in their strategic decisions.
29. All translations from Portuguese texts or primary sources in this book are mine.
30. I must stress, however, that the points of view presented here, albeit representative of the main political and experiential stances, are not exclusive or represent the totality of 'Tokoist experience', since there are other minoritary Tokoist churches, movements and tendencies that I haven't explored to this date.
31. In contrast with Foucault, I do not see experience and power as separate or irreconcilable dimensions (see Mittermaier 2011: 18).

PART I

ITINERARIES

CHAPTER I

Trajectories
A Prophetic Biography, Part I

> 'Here, we walk slowly and look onward, to the place from where
> our endless liberty will come; but who among our brothers, sisters,
> nephews and nieces will be able to resist the satanic temptation that
> will soon accumulate?'—letter by Simão Toko, 4 April 1974

In contrast with what happens in other African Christian movements – such as the Kimbanguist Church (Nkamba), the Zion City Church (Moria) or the Redeemed Christian Church of God (Redemption Camp) – the Tokoist Church does not have a 'New Jerusalem' or terrestrial holy city to where its believers cyclically head to in pilgrimage. Frequently, as in the case of prophetic cultures, these places assume a fundamental role in the believers' ideology and religious experiences, since it is there where 'testimonies' and proofs of faith can be found – i.e. the remains of the prophet founder, sites that witnessed miraculous events, etc. – and it is through their constitution as destinies of pilgrimage that many religious experiences are built and negotiated. One could say that holy cities provoke 'sacred geographies', networks of religious significance imposed onto a certain site (Townsend 1987: 596). Thus, place and territory become part of a moral geography (Basso 1996; Thomas 2002; DeRogatis 2003; Taylor 2007) from which spaces of memory and celebration are distinguished (Allerton 2009). Landscape, thus, becomes recruited for the construction and interpretation of history (Taussig 1987: 286).

In the case of the Tokoist Church, however, there are several places that bore witness to miraculous or impacting events that have become part of the church's history – Vale do Loge, Catete, Leopoldville, the Azores, etc. – and the mortal remains of the prophet rest, since 1984, near his place of birth, Taia (or Ntaia), in Maquela do Zombo (Uíge), a few miles off the border with DR Congo. But these places have not, as of yet, experienced processes of sanctification, sacralization and urbanization as in the cases mentioned above (see e.g. Mélice 2011; Sarró and Mélice 2012). This does not mean, however, that place and space aren't significant in the Tokoist culture and theodicy, nor that these places aren't sites of remembrance, celebration and appropriation. There is, in fact, a clear perception of a 'vital trajectory', of movement through time and space (Ingold 1993) that produced concomitant sensations of memory and territorial belonging through the location of specific sites that eventually became 'spiritual' (Allerton 2009). For many Tokoists, the different places that witnessed the prophet's route and have become spiritualized are, so to speak, steps in an open path that is in the process of reshaping. This path was inaugurated on February 1918 on the occasion of the prophet's birth – the day when, according to the Tokoists, the 'shining star' began to guide the Africans towards salvation (Melo 2002; Nzila 2006). A star that is today the central symbol of the church, the *estrela da alva* ("star of clarity").

From this perspective, the 'pilgrimage' for the Tokoists is the path itself, the course that the prophet travelled, and not its final destination. It is the walking that produces the experience (Ingold and Vergunst 2008; Ingold 2010; Egan 2011), although in this context 'walking' must be understood both literally and metaphorically, as a trajectory through time and space that made the church what it is today and configured certain expectations regarding its future routes. 'We will take the church with us wherever we can', said pastor Pedro Segunda in a public sermon that celebrated the sixteenth anniversary of the church in Lisbon and compared it to the suffering and persecuted community of Antioch (7 September 2008).

As we will see throughout this and the next chapter, the story of Simão Toko and his followers is one of constant mobilities that determined and reconfigured the ecclesiastical institution's ethos throughout the decades – or what has been called in the church a 'geo-history' (Álvaro 2011). These mobilities, however, do not refer to direct intentional movements between point A and point B, but rather to a complex set of phenomena and events that took place throughout their lives, where mobility is rather constituted as a vital experience, a process of self-positioning in the world, an orientation, a sense of belonging. It is here, for instance, where we find several dynamics of 'involuntary mobility' (Blanes 2009c, 2011b) such as deportation, expulsion or exile; or dynamics of 'detained mobility', such as prison and clandestinity. These mobilities are not only incorporated in the church's collective memory through the 'history of suffering' that circulates in the church, in a sort

Illustration 2. *Estrela da Alva,* current symbol of the Tokoist Church, in entrance to church in Lisbon, 2007. Photo: Ruy Llera Blanes.

of itinerary of pain that is constantly invoked in the Tokoists' doctrinal constructions, but also produce a consciousness and subjectivity where the notion of 'captivity' (as an external imposition of restricted or inexistent mobilities – see Nashif 2008) becomes central in the self-configurations within what is often referred to as a 'martyr church' experience. From this perspective there is, in Tokoism, a providential understanding of history that encapsulates, through Simão Toko's vital trajectory, both historical consciousness and expectation – the idea that sacrifice and prophetic martyrdom are part of a temporal inevitability: the future victory of Christ.

Together with this memory of suffering, one can also perceive dynamics of 'updating' that prevent memory from crystallizing or resting in certain places – i.e. 'places of the past' – but rather play them against the 'acceleration of history' (Nora 1989: 8) that produces the distance between knowledge and perception. This updating, which is in itself a process of 'heritagization', is operated in the different ideological configurations that these places that became significant for the church – from the Bakongo territory to Angola, Africa and 'the world' – adopted throughout history. These different sets of meanings eventually conflated into a body of knowledge that is simultaneously a 'theory of emotional movement' (Fernandez 2003) to which the identitary discourses and definitions that the Tokoists manipulate are attached.

What we will see in this chapter and the next is a biographical reconstruction of Simão Gonçalves Toko's life through its spatial and vital trajectory, which began and ended in the *sanzala* (small village or agglomerate of houses) of Sadi-Zulumongo in the Uíge region, but also crossed the Kibokolo commune, the Bembe, Leopoldville, the Loge valley, the Namibe desert, the island of São Miguel, Luanda and other sites. This is, therefore, an instrumental exercise, inasmuch as it is through it that we will recognize the 'methods of memory', the conversations and projections observed within the church and described in the subsequent chapters. It is to this prophetic biography that the Tokoist believers turn to amidst their providential constructions and contemporary political disputes.

This biography is composed of diverse sources and materials that incorporate different degrees of controversy. There are many testimonies compiled internally by the church, performed by both Simão Toko and the believers that followed him from day one, and some of them were included in the four notorious books published by members of the church in recent years (Agostinho n.d.; Quibeta n.d.; Melo 2002; Kisela 2004; Nzila 2006). These publications, regardless of their particularities, construe, more or less explicitly, biographies of the prophet. In addition, two documentary films have also been produced by people within (1997) or close to (2009) the church.[1] But the most extensive set of information regarding Simão Toko's life is found not in Angola, but mainly in two historical archives in Lisbon that bear witness of the 'by-product' of the PIDE[2] activities in this country from

1950 to 1974: the Torre do Tombo and the Arquivo Histórico Ultramarino. In these archives, several different files and volumes pertaining
to the movement and its leader, disclosed in 1994, contain diverse sets
of documents – from internal police reports and communications to
proto-ethnographic investigations that attempted to classify the movement to (and especially) material belonging to the Tokoists and with-
held by the PIDE for their investigation.[3] And finally, there is the set
of academic research I describe in the introduction to this book that
partly deals with these primary sources, as well as my own research
– that included interviews and conversations with people who remember and research Toko's itinerary and is placed in a cumulative plane
regarding them.

   This is, as one can imagine, a heterogeneous body of material that
conjugates diverse sources – as diverse as the motivations that produced them. From this perspective, this biographical reconstruction
cannot set aside the political motivations behind the different produc-
tions: if, for the Portuguese political police, it was about researching
and 'asserting' the 'terrorist character' of the movement and controlling its activities amidst their own regime of policing, securitization
and repression, for the authors who collaborated with the regime and
produced the first notes on Tokoism, the issue at stake was provid-
ing an intellectual, scientific layer to the colonial policy and ideology,
enhanced through the incorporation of a Catholic perspective (see
mainly Cunha 1959; Estermann 1965; Gonçalves 1966; Santos 1969;
Gabriel 1978). In both cases, despite these motivations, the methods
and the partiality with which they built these portraits of Simão Toko
and his followers – the will to 'understand' the phenomenon they were
facing – produced a set of texts with an impressive level of description and detail. On the other hand, if for the Tokoists in general the
key issue was of contesting and producing an alternative account of
history through their own eyes, we find within the movement, as we
will see later on, different and frequently opposed 'regimes of truth'
(in the Foucauldian sense of the term) concerning certain aspects of
the prophet's biographical narrative, and also (and especially) different
acts of archaeology and remembrance within contemporary politics
and ideologies (explored in chapter 4 of this book). There is, therefore,
a double reading of biography: a public, externalized, presentational
one, intended for a wide audience; and an internal one, disputed and
subject to processes of concealment and revelation, located 'behind the
official story' (Scott 1990). In this regard, there is a difference that has
to be established between what is 'revealed' through my ethnographic
practice and what remains concealed, both from the public eye and my

own. Despite the constant feeling of 'Ogotemmelian revelation' I got every time I worked with these sources and interlocutors, I also and increasingly got the feeling that I was just touching the tip of the iceberg, the part that was decided to be relevant enough to disclose to me. This was obviously related to the internal transcripts that the Tokoists manage in their tabernacle, to which I refer in chapter 3.

However, it is also true that these heterogeneous narratives coincide in one common trait: the 'struggle for coherence', the need to produce a biographical narrative that adjusts to the motivations that bind it. Theoretically speaking, this recognition may seem problematic to some authors, who point out that biography is, more than an act of memory, an 'art of memory' (Cole 2001), a narrative construction that does not necessarily bind to 'objective' facts. Such was the case, for instance, of Pierre Bourdieu, who saw the biographical exercise (and in particular the typical life histories) as a commonsensical intellectual exercise, 'smuggled' into the social sciences (1986). In other words, the recourse to biography could reveal itself as a fiction, an illusion, as life or family histories imply narrative dispositions that transform memory into lineal, trajectorialized and coherent stories, incorporating a beginning and an end, elaborated from a specific interest of motivation that does not necessarily take into consideration the complexity of social life. From this perspective, the attempts to 'make sense' that we find in biographical narratives, the attempts to 'transform life into a story' (Bourdieu 1986: 70) would be none other than intellectual artefacts (1986: 71).

This particular critique would be taken up again a few years later by John and Jean Comaroff, who contested the 'historical imagination' produced by ethnographers in the biographical constructions they elaborated, closer to Western bourgeois models invested by particular notions of subjectivity and historical consciousness than to native intellectual exercises, illustrative of the 'imposition' that the Western anthropologist/ethnographer poses unto the interlocutors and narrators he/she seeks to perform them (1992: 27 and ff.). This kind of epistemological hegemony (see Santos and Meneses 2009) therefore implies, from this point of view, a hardly innocent and partial way of accounting for social life.

However, what Bourdieu and the Comaroffs do not accept is precisely what I find more challenging from a heuristic point of view: the fact that biographies are perceived as socially distributed 'narrative constructions' which, as a result of the need to 'make sense' and attribute coherence, become persistent and impacting (Antze and Lambek 1996), both in contexts such as the one I am focusing on here and in many others, be they religious (such as hagiographies and martyrologies) or secularly oriented (such as autobiographies, curricula vitae or confessional testimonies). Ultimately, if we were to take Bourdieu's and the Comaroffs' argument to the limit, it would deny any possibility of academic historicity and biographization (see Palmié 2002) other than that produced by Western imposition. For people such as the Tokoists, what is at stake is not just a reaction against the historical backdrop of the epistemological hegemony that imposes a certain narrative and conceptual modality unto them, but also, and especially, the agency and power they can obtain from those narrative regimes – the consciousness of that history and the possibility of taking the role of accepting, correcting or contesting it (Balandier 1963 [1955]; Sahlins 1981, 1985). Thus, biography incorporates a necessary dimension of power and creativity.

On the other hand, from a heuristic point of view, biographical regimes, as methods of memory, do not necessarily have to correspond with subjectifying and univocal registers such as those that Bourdieu and the Comaroffs have in mind (the life history, the diary, the memoirs, etc.). There are other biographical modalities that persist precisely given their social, shared, created and disputed character, constitutive of particular 'modes of inscription' (Comaroff and Comaroff 1992: 26). Such is the case, for instance, of prophetic biographies, which reveal how particular religious movements emerge from the intersection between individuality and sociality, motivated by dynamics of leadership and charisma (Werbner 2011; see Blanes 2011a for a debate).

Thus, the biography presented in continuation can be seen as a proposed narrative, composed by multiple voices and points of view. It is a 'relevant' narrative, as it is fundamental for the Tokoist ethos, and produces a tense, disputed legacy.

Northern Angola, 1918–1942: A Shining Star

On 24 February 1918, nine months after the first apparition of Virgin Mary in Fátima (Melo 2002; Kisela 2004: 20–21), in the same year of the World War I armistice, a little boy was born in the remote village of Sadi-Kiloango in the commune of Taia (or Ntaia), Maquela do Zombo, Uíge province, in northern Angola. The mother, Ndundu Nsimba Toko, also bore a little girl, but the baby did not survive the labour work (Quibeta n.d.: 19). The little boy was given the name of Mayamona, which in Kikongo means, quite prophetically, 'what has been seen' (Agostinho n.d.: 34; Quibeta n.d.: 19–20; Kisela 2004: 23). His father, Ndombele

Luvumbu Ditopo, was a local farmer and, after working as foreman in the Belgian Congo, became the *soba* (local traditional authority) of the Nampemba clan. It is said that when Ndombele was on his deathbed, young Mayamona was taken to his side by his uncle, Capitão Finda, to say goodbye. When he arrived, Ndombele ordered that Mayamona be removed from his side, crying 'don't you know that death is very shy?' (Kisela 2004: 24), and requested that the family take good care of him, 'because he will be a great king' (ibid.; Quibeta n.d.: 21).

Tokoist sources describe Toko as a 'different' boy, with above-average mental capacities, who experienced several miraculous events in his childhood. In one such event, Mayamona and his older cousin, Domingos Quibeta, were crossing a river, and Quibeta saw Mayamona falling into the water and being dragged by the currents. He desperately looked around the margins for hours, to see if he could find him or his body, but to no avail. When Quibeta was about to quit, he saw young Mayamona emerge from the water and move towards him. When they met, Mayamona apologized and revealed that he had to go away to respond to the call of the Creator in the bottom of the river (Kisela 2004: 25–26).

Domingos Quibeta took charge of Mayamona's education, teaching him Kikongo and Portuguese, and then decided to send him off to the Baptist Mission of Kibokolo,[4] which eventually happened in 1926. Before entering the mission, Quibeta decided to change Mayamona's name to Simão (Portuguese for 'Simon') Gonçalves (as given name) Toko (his mother's surname). At this point, another miraculous event, remembered by the Tokoists as a revelation of what was to come, takes place: when Simão was heading to the Kibokolo mission with Domingos Quibeta and Maurício Kiala (an elder who worked as deacon in the mission), a torrential rain started to fall to such an extent that everyone began to fearfully pray for their lives. At this moment, they heard a loud voice saying: 'Maurício, Maurício, Maurício, as soon as you take this child, you will never catch rain again until you die.' From this moment on, it never rained upon Maurício again (Agostinho n.d.: 36; Quibeta n.d. 23–24).

Simão remained at the mission until 1933, fostered by missionaries Edward Holmes, Arthur Enock Guest and George Hooper, working as a servant (in Guest's house) and revealing himself to be an exemplary student: 'He became a good student, and in class he always stood out above the rest', recalled William Grenfell, head of the mission at the time, to a PIDE inspector (Letter, c. 1957). However, as some sources reveal, on 2 October 1928, at the age of ten, he abruptly abandoned the mission and escaped – for reasons which remain unclear – to Leopoldville, where he sojourned until 1929, when Enock Guest went looking for him.[5] Despite Guest's efforts, Toko did not want to return to Kibokolo, and in 1930 he left to Thysville (today Mbanza Ngungu), where again he attended the Baptist Missionary Society (B.M.S.) school. In 1931 he finally decided to return to Kibokolo, where Guest baptized him on 1 August on the Lussenguele river (Kisela 2004: 29).

Two years later, when he finished primary school, considering his outstanding school performance, the missionaries decided to send him to Luanda, where he would attend, at the mission's expense, secondary school at the then Liceu Salvador Correia (today Liceu Mutu ya Kevela). As he had no relatives in Luanda, he stayed in the house of Reverend Pedro Agostinho Neto (father of António Agostinho Neto, future first president of independent Angola), from the Methodist Episcopal Church of Luanda. It is said that in those days Toko and António were good friends. However, as we will see later on, this relationship would deteriorate considerably.

In any case, during his stay in Luanda, Toko combined his studies with a more active role in terms of evangelical work, and was offered, among other things, the responsibility of teaching a Sunday school class (the Classe de David – see letter by Simão Toko, 4 April 1973). At this point, a first episode of spiritual mediation takes place. Toko recalled:

> In 1935/36, at the Luanda Methodist Episcopal Mission, I fell sick. I was almost dead, some boy and girl friends were crying, and I was on the lap of my spiritual Mother, the mother of my sister Lúcia Alberto da Silva. … As they cried, I couldn't listen, but I had a vision. I was climbing a mountain and saw a light, white and yellow, and saw a beautiful city; then, I heard a voice saying, 'It's the future New Jerusalem.' I wanted to go down the other side of the mountain, that separated the world and the city, but then a tall man, Elijah, appeared. He said, 'Simão, where are you going?', and I replied, 'I want to see that city.' 'Not now, you will see it in the future.' 'But I don't want to go back to the world', I said, but he answered, 'You have a lot to do in the world.' I resisted but he then kicked me, as if he were kicking a ball, and screamed: 'Go back! You will see it in the future, if you keep the faith!' I began to struggle, and rolled down the mountain like a ball. At this point, I heard the moaning of my colleagues, who shouted, 'He opened his eyes!', etc. (Letters by Simão Toko, 15 March 1973 and 4 April 1973).

This encounter with the prophet Elijah, remembered in the epistles written by Toko in 1973, reveals an ontogenic process of gestation and spiritual development he experienced in his youth: 'The service that awaits, as was told to me on the top of that mountain, is what we are doing today, working in the Lord's harvest', he added (4 April 1973). In the epistles, Toko drew a map of what he envisioned, dividing the terrestrial world, the mountain he sought to traverse and, finally, the celestial world, the New Jerusalem.

In the map, and in Toko's imaginative landscape, the mountain represents the path to be followed by Tokoists and all Christians in order to arrive at New Jerusalem – here understood as 'salvation'. This apocalyptic vision shows how young Simão began, since 1935, to idealize a religious trajectory and eschatology from a particular biblical interpretation.

In 1937, after concluding secondary school, Toko returned to Maquela do Zombo and to the Kibokolo mission, this time to work as an assistant to the missionaries. One year later, he would be transferred to the Bembe mission, where he started working as a full-time teacher. In the Bembe, his work was immediately recognized and accepted by the inhabitants of the neighbouring villages and *sanzalas*, but it began to conflict with the Baptist leadership. According to the Tokoist histo-

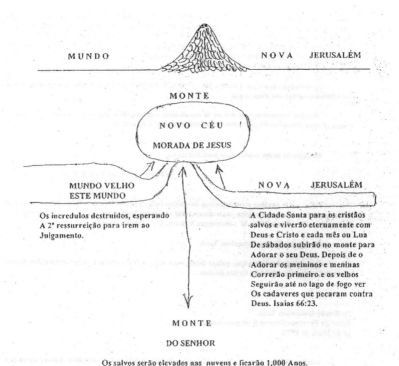

Illustration 3. Map of Simão Toko's vision of 1935 (letter by Simão Toko, 11 May 1973), transcribed by unknown author. *Source:* Ruy Llera Blanes's personal archive.

rians, Toko began to contest the fact that the *pretos* (blacks) were not allowed to reach the same education levels as the whites, which he understood to be a form of intellectual subjugation; nevertheless he finally succeeded in extending teaching lessons to the locals (Agostinho n.d.: 44–45). Shortly afterwards, he asked for an increase in his salary under the pretext that he was to prepare his marriage with Molly Vicente Sadi, daughter of the Kibokolo mission secretary, and support his future family.[6] Seeing his request denied, and finding his work in the mission concluded, he decided to leave the Bembe and headed towards Leopoldville (letter by Simão Toko to the Bembe Mission, 1942; Grenfell 1998: 211). Years later, Toko explained what happened:

> There was a misunderstanding with the missionaries, because I was earning very little money, and didn't have enough to take care of myself. So I asked for a leave to go to the Belgian Congo and work, in order to earn more money. They gave me the leave, and when I arrived to the Belgian Congo, to Leopoldville, as the society is the same, the Baptist Missionary Society, the missionaries there asked that I stay in the Belgian Congo; so I stayed and helped the missionaries there. (Interview Simão Toko to Portuguese Television, RDP Açores, c. 1974)

On the missionary side, however, there was a different understanding:

> Toko became unhappy with his work, because he left the mission without authorization. He arranged marriage with a young girl from Kibokolo, and a six-month leave was given to him. But he never came back nor wrote to explain his decision of leaving the mission. (Statement by William Grenfell, c. 1957)

However, it is also known that shortly before leaving to Leopoldville, Toko decided to organize a farewell party, inviting students, local elders and mission leaders. At the party, he appeared wearing a sisal bag and singing a Kikongo hymn that said: 'The turncoat has worn a bag, the turncoat has worn a bag, the turncoat has worn a bag.'[7]

Leopoldville (Belgian Congo), 1942–1950: A Bakongo Prophetism

At only twenty-four years of age, Simão Toko decided to leave his home and migrate to Leopoldville, to 'do some shopping for my marriage' (letter by Simão Toko, 11 November 1971). The choice of his destination is not surprising, as the demographic and economic exchanges between northern Angola and the Lower Congo were very intense

(Pereira 2004: 54 and following), to the extent that in the Leopoldville–
Brazzaville axis – a vibrant region that acted as a magnet of many regions for Bakongo (Balandier 1952; Margarido 1972; MacGaffey 1986;
Vellut 1989; MacGaffey and Bazenguissa-Ganga 2000) – the community of migrants coming from the Maquela do Zombo region, as one
of the largest foreign communities in the area, were known as Zombos
(baZombo) and were notorious in the city for working mainly in commercial activities.

After working as an apprentice watchmaker, painter, public registrar
and secretary in several mutual help associations,[8] Toko decided to create an association of his own, called Nkutu a Nsimbani (later known
as Associação Mútua Cristã do Planalto do Zombo – Christian Mutual
Association of the Zombo Plateau), with the goal of aiding Zombo expatriates in the Belgian Congo, building schools and offering medical
support (Grenfell 1998: 211–212). Due to financial misunderstandings,
the Association wouldn't last very long; however, it did motivate some
speculation regarding eventual connections with the ALIAZO (Aliança
do Povo Zombo, or Zombo People's Alliance) political movement,
which would later become the PDA (Angolan Democratic Party; see
Kisela 2004: 34). In the meantime, Toko lived off the charity of friends
and, allegedly, by selling his paintings – portraits and religious motifs
(Marcum 1969; Grenfell 1998) – in the streets of Leopoldville.

In any case, as we see in his words above, Toko also continued to
collaborate as a catechist with the Baptist missionaries in the Itagar
mission by teaching at a Sunday school. There, considering the on-
going tradition of creating local choir groups according to the geographic provenance of the members, Toko was invited (in April 1943)
to lead his own group, composed by Maquela do Zombo folk, called
the Coro de Kibokolo (in honour of the mission where he studied
and grew up). In one of his epistles, he remembers the moment of
creation:

> In 1942, when I returned to my land, I went to Matadi and reached Leo-
> poldville, currently Kinshasa. There, Our Lord said to me: 'Go and herd
> the sheep that have been lost because of the grass and the pleasures of
> this world.' Read Revelations 3:2 and Matthew. Some of you know the
> work I have done in Leopoldville beside you. On April 5th, 1943, in the
> home of Daniel Nsuamani on Loa Street number 55, I took twelve young
> boys and formed a choir. From that choir the Church of Christ in Africa
> was reborn. (In Agostinho n.d.: 49)

The success of the choir was such that it granted a higher notoriety to
Toko around the Protestant circles of the Lower Congo, and Toko was

often invited to participate in religious events of other churches in the region. From 13 to 24 July 1946, the Coro de Kibokolo was invited to participate with their hymns at the International Protestant Missionary Conference that took place in Leopoldville. Toko was also invited to intervene, along with two other 'native Christians' – Gaspar de Almeida and Jessé Chipenda Chiúla[9] – in the conference activities, to addressing the audience for a few brief minutes. The conference convenors had prepared beforehand what the pretos should say: Jessé would ask for an increase in instruction, education and progress for Africa; Gaspar, for the 'equal opportunities and the same access to money as the white man'; and, finally, Simão Toko would discuss 'the power of the Holy Ghost in Africa' (Agostinho n.d.: 54 and ff.; Quibeta n.d.: 71 and ff.). Toko would explain the sequence of events in a letter written in 1966 to the Tokoists in Maquela do Zombo and Taia Nova:

> Summarizing. In 1946, there was a Protestant Missionary Congress, with missions from all over the world in Leopoldville, and where people from diverse races such as black, white, mestizo, etc. came together.
>
> Many things were said about the Africans' general education, the increase in civilization, law, etc., and finally, the increase of the light of Christ's Gospel in a few years. I was also invited to participate in the Congress. I saw and met many blacks coming from different parts of the world, some we couldn't even understand because they spoke their native tongues, and we had to resort to an interpreter to talk to a brother from another land. I also met black brothers from North, South, East and West. Some of them I already knew. Others had been my teachers in Primary School. I remember being put in charge of receiving their clothes and taking them to the laundry; I didn't charge anything for it, since I didn't want my fellow countrymen to spend their pennies in a foreign land. All clothing expenses were taken care of by me. God is my witness.
>
> Before the conference ended, I think three days before the end, two pretos were chosen to say prayer to God. The first one prayed to God to increase instruction, education, progress, law and the unification between whites, blacks, etc. That black man was called Rev. Gaspar de Almeida, from the Evangelical Episcopal Mission of Luanda, who is currently in prison.
>
> The second black was told by missionaries Dr. Tucker from the Donde mission in Huambo – Nova Lisboa, who has already passed away, and Dr. Brecht, from the Philafrican Mission of Caluquembe, not to say much in his prayer, but just ask God for the Holy Ghost, in order to convert the African people that were in darkness and sin, because without the power of the Holy Ghost Africa will remain the same, and that prayer could not be performed by a foreign person. It had to be performed by one of the

Africans chosen by the missionaries that brought God's gospel to Africa. That second African prayed and just asked for the power of the Holy Ghost in Africa and the increase of God's word. That black man is called Simão Gonçalves Toko, the outcast. (Letter by Simão Toko, December 1966)[10]

Toko's participation in this event motivated, at the time, several comments among those present – especially because when his choir was asked to perform a hymn, the leader instructed his singers to sing a different hymn from what had been agreed on with one of the organizers (Rev. Salmon): '*Vena ye zulu dia mvumami*', as it appeared in the Baptist Missionary Society Hymnal (n° 295), which revealed a more political content than was expected and desired by the organizing committee.[11]

Meanwhile, possibly influenced by these events and the success of his choir and Sunday school classes, Toko decided to take his leadership role to a different level. Upon meeting some Watch Tower missionaries in Leopoldville, he asked them for Christian books to read and share with his students and singers.[12] He then decided to take on a new venture: to translate the books to Kikongo, so they could be read and understood by the locals. This initiative clashed with the ideas of the Baptist missionaries, who reprimanded and reminded him that the

Illustration 4. The Coro de Kibokolo in 1947. *Source:* Ruy Llera Blanes's personal archive.

reading of the Jehova's Witnesses' books, banned by the Belgian Congo authorities, was 'false teaching' (Grenfell 1998: 212–213).

However, this did not prevent Toko from continuing what he progressively established as a 'mission'. His contact with other religious movements (both local and missionary)[13] may have helped him devise a path and a strategy – a vision that many external commentators would deny from the start (Cunha 1959; Estermann 1965; Henderson 1990) – inspired and supported by *nzambi* (God) and *nkanda nzambi*, the book of God (Grenfell 1998: 212). Meanwhile, Toko continued his work in the Baptist Sunday school, where he kept on translating and teaching the books he collected to an ever-growing assistance:

> The books I ordered from America – I even wrote a letter to them, to the reverends, and they promised to send me the books that explain the Bible. … They sent a few books, in French and Portuguese. And we started reading those books, the books that explain the Bible. We started reading, and the Christian folk at the Baptist Mission became interested. The crowd kept growing, flocking in from other churches, and there was no room left at the Mission church, there would be people listening from the window, it was full of people. (Interview Simão Toko to RTP, c. 1974)

In the meantime, in October 1947, Simão Toko created the *Anciens Éleves,* a parallel group to the Coro, composed of Zombos who already knew how to read and write. The group would conduct religious research, reading and translating the Bible, and also working with a book called *Luz e Verdade* that Toko had found in the rubbish bin in his previous visit to Luanda. There was also another book known as *Vita Velela* (Holy War) that was used by the elder members of the group. The group combined catechism with more conventional education, where the students would also learn Portuguese and English with a professor from Luanda hired by Toko. Toko told them at the time: 'Prepare yourselves, because one day we will work on our land.' As André, one of the youngsters who participated in this group, told me, each of the members of the group paid for these classes only what they could afford.

The appeal of Toko's autonomous and reformist message, committed to turning the Bible into an 'intelligible object' for his followers, seemed evident. In July 1949, his status as a local leader is confirmed when he is invited to lead a delegation of the Coro de Kibokolo (253 people), precisely to the homonym mission where he had studied to participate in the celebration of the jubilee of the fiftieth anniversary of its foundation (Agostinho n.d.: 51).

In that same month, another episode took place which would close the 'prophetic circle' initiated in 1946 at the Protestant Missionary Conference and would landmark the 'institutional' foundation of Toko's movement. On 24 July, at a time when Toko was already somewhat distanced from the Itagar leadership, he decided to convene with thirty-six of his followers at 159 Mayenge Street (on the *quartier indigène* of the city) in the backyard of Ambrósio Kinavuidi's house, where Toko lived. The goal was to 'ask God if he had heard the prayer that was directed to him on 1946' (letter by Simão Toko, December 1966). And so it was that in the middle of the night, they 'heard a great noise and saw a light' (ibid.), a 'strong wind was felt' (Cunha 1959: 32; Grenfell 1998: 214), people began to shake, speak in tongues and quote passages from the Bible, namely Acts of the Apostles, chapters 1 and 2 (Cunha 1959: 32). The Holy Ghost had descended. At that moment, the prophet recommended that everyone open the Bible and read Joel 2:28.[14] A few moments later, everyone left Toko's house and began to pray and chant in the streets all night long. 'Finally, it dawned and people from different tribes appeared at my house to listen to the word of God. The city of Leopoldville really shook' (letter by Simão Toko, 8 November 1971). The following day, Toko reconvened with his followers, this time in the backyard of *velho* (old) Timóteo's house (155 Kitega Street), and told them: 'Tell your brothers that we have received the power of the Church of Our Lord Jesus Christ in the World'; the doors were then opened for a proselytist movement.

Word spread and the house at Mayenge Street became a 'tabernacle' where people appeared seeking to know more about what had happened. Vumambo David, who was in Leopoldville at the time, told me, 'That's when people, even those who had not been there that night, began hearing about it, others started acting as if they were crazy, and headed towards the dirigente's house at Mayenge' (interview, 19 October 2008).

Having heard about what happened, the Baptist missionaries summoned Simão Toko and scolded him, forbidding him from talking about the salvation of Africa and translating books into Kikongo – namely, the forbidden ones. This was the moment that provoked Toko's final separation from the mission, after which he began to organize meetings in his house – where he would, soon later, experience another Pentecostal event (Cunha 1959: 33).

As word continued to spread, many – Angolan and Congolese – approached Toko to see what was happening. The weeks that followed appear today as somewhat confusing, with reports of miraculous events and accusations of disobedience to the authorities and even of criminal activity on behalf of the local authorities. In August, Toko married Rosa Maria Toko, also a Zombo migrant, who had studied at the Baptist mission and followed the prophet's classes and teachings. The ceremony took place on the 22nd – at the same spot where the Holy Ghost had descended – on the 'First Tabernacle of the Church' (Agostinho n.d.: 88). A short time later, on 9–10 September, at a meeting at Kitega Street, Toko clarified to his followers what was happening and delivered his message: 'this is not about the end of the world, but the changing of things' (Agostinho n.d.: 56; interview with the Doze Mais Velhos, 19 October 2008).[15] In any case, what seems certain is that, as Toko had said, 'the city of Leopoldville really shook', and the local newspapers reported on the impact of these events among the baZombo (*Courrier d'Afrique*, 10 January 1950; *L'Avenir Colonial Belge*, 11 and 12 January 1950).

Thus, a few months after the descent of the Holy Ghost, on 22 October 1949, Simão Toko and eighty-two of his followers were arrested and accused of disturbing the public order. The complaint originated from the Baptist missionaries, who accused Toko of proselytizing with forbidden books and 'making politics' (Cunha 1959: 33). Toko was then sent to the Olfitra prison (then serving as a detention centre), where hundreds of his followers would later voluntarily turn themselves in (interview with the Doze Mais Velhos, 19 October 2008; *Courrier d'Afrique*, 13 January 1950) in order to be closer to their leader. Once there, a sentence was pronounced deciding for the expulsion of the group to Angola, taking advantage of the fact that they were all Angolan Zombos.

In the meantime, foreseeing the persecution that lay ahead of him in the following years, the *dirigente* announced to his followers the institution of a group of Doze Mais Velhos ('twelve elders') that would remain in charge of safeguarding his message and assume the work towards a future church in his absence.[16] This would become the first 'institutionalized', internally recognized entity within the following of Simão Toko.

The Belgians had an idea.... They had the idea of transferring only Simão Toko and his wife. But then Simão Toko thinks about the elders that had been arrested with him, but also on those that weren't arrested. He organized things and said: 'As soon as I am arrested, you keep away and do your prayers.' But with this he also thought, 'Well, from here I will also have to form a group of elders, out of those with more courage and willing to accept to die if necessary.' He calls for three elders.... And then he advises: 'The Belgians want to send my wife and me to Angola. If this group remains, we will build a church in Angola. You three, look for

Illustration 5. Simão and Rosa Maria Toko, recently married. *Source:* Ruy Llera Blanes's personal archive.

nine other elders. And ask them if they want to die or not.' From then on, they started to look around and talk to people, explaining.... And that's how the Twelve Elders were completed, on the 22nd of November of that same year. (Interview Vumambo David, 19 October 2008)

Thus, when their leader was in jail, the Doze Mais Velhos contacted the Belgian authorities, writing a letter to pressure them into freeing Toko. But, on top of receiving a negative answer, the elders were also arrested, and many other Zombos then voluntarily gave themselves in and 'offered' themselves to be deported after their leader (interview Doze Mais Velhos, 19 October 2008) – which finally took place on 28 March 1950.[17]

Toko and the first group of followers were then taken to the border with Angola. On that day, as many Tokoists now recall, he stated before the officers that escorted him: 'I am going to Angola, to my land, and soon you will also go back to your land' (interview Doze Mais Velhos, 19 October 2008).[18]

Notes on Prophetic and Territorial Paradigms

At the moment in which he was taken to the border between Angola and the Belgian Congo, Simão Toko was not much younger than myself as I write this book: thirty-one years of age. Thus, the events described here reveal a process of intellectual and spiritual formation in a young man that would conform the backdrop of the subsequent institutional formation that I will describe in the next chapter.

In this process we observe a conflation of spiritual narratives that detect a prophetic quality in the young boy and student, who experiences a series of premonitory miraculous events that would configure this 'prophetic trajectory'. The dream vision he had in 1935, one of three he had in total (letter by Simão Toko, c. 7 April 1973), determined the coordinates through which the church would travel: 'I will feel great sadness if my brothers, sisters, nephews and nieces you do not keep your faith and see that mountain in Jerusalem. Brothers and nephews from the North and South of Angola, this is the voice that is crying out among you, you will listen to it if you want to' (ibid.).

But it is in Leopoldville that the process of institution ultimately took place, to an extent that led Toko into an irreversible process of autonomization. His contact with other religious movements and leaders, both missionary and local, was decisive, especially taking into consideration the effervescing times of religious proliferation he witnessed:

the plural presence of Catholic and Protestant missionaries of diverse creeds (Baptists, Jehova's Witnesses, Salvation Army, among many others – see e.g. MacGaffey 1983) and the Atlantic connections that bore them (Thornton 1998b); the enduring presence of local 'religious commissions' (e.g. Andersson 1958, 1968; Van Wing 1959; MacGaffey 1970, 1983; de Craemer, Vansina and Fox 1976); the new religio-political configurations that emerged in the late colonial context (Andersson 1968; Balandier 1963 [1955]; MacGaffey 1983); and also the memory of local prophetic lineages that established historical continuities between past and present religious leaderships (see e.g. Droogers 1980; MacGaffey 1983; Thornton 1998; Sarró 2008a; Matumona 2009).

From this perspective, the establishment of a continuity (and consequent submission) of Tokoism with the Kongo prophet paradigm performed in the references discussed in the introduction was to some extent understandable. In the available literature, there is some debate as to what kind of influence Kimbanguism may have exerted over Simão Toko (see Cunha 1959: 33; Rego 1970; Grenfell 1998; Matumona 2009).[19] And in fact the 'ideological exchange' was more than probable, given the coincidence in many of Kimbangu's and Toko's proposals. Also, it is known that Toko had met at some point with Joseph Diangienda (Martin 1975: 100; Grenfell 1998: 212), the son and continuer of Kimbangu's work during his thirty-year incarceration in the prison of Elisabethville (today Lubumbashi) before his passing in 1951. Other testimonies from both Tokoists and the PIDE refer that, after the events of July 1949, many Leopoldville locals approached Simão Toko thinking that he was in some way related to 'the things of Simon Kimbangu' (PIDE Report, 5 April 1955).[20]

James Grenfell also notes that there were some cases of Kimbanguists converting to Toko's movement (1998: 212). This idea is corroborated by the Tokoists themselves, who recall that a woman called Madalena Quengue, of Kimbangu's kin, had heard the prophet tell his followers before his arrest in 1921: 'As soon as you hear of a young man coming from Angola and carrying the same word, follow him.' That young man was Simão Toko, and Madalena Quengue followed him (interview Doze Mais Velhos, 19 October 2008).[21] Thus, despite the continuous distinction that is mutually operated within Tokoism and Kimbanguism, there was in fact an establishment of a spiritual continuity between both prophets, particularly in what concerns the messianic ideology that was involved.

In any case, to ask questions about the 'Kimbanguism' of the Tokoist ideology in itself would be reductive and misleading. We must open the scope and consider its continuity with a wider set of ideological and spiritual paradigms that were taking place in the Lower Congo, spreading through the cracks of the colonial system.[22] Apart from Kimbangu and Toko, many other prophets sought to spread their message in these times and territories, associating spiritual content and emancipatory speech. Such is the case of the abovementioned Simon-Pierre Mpadi, André Matswa and Lassy Simon Zéphyrin, to name the most notorious (Andersson 1958; Balandier 1963 [1955]; Sinda 1972; MacGaffey 1983). Also, outside the Lower Congo, other prophetic contestation movements were noted in the Lunda region in the 1930s (Margarido 1972) and also back in the nineteenth century (Wheeler 1968). These religious leaders, despite their individual differences, did share a few particularities: the apprenticeship in (and posterior emancipation from) Protestant (Baptist, Salvation Army) or Catholic missions, and the subsequent development of an autonomous religious institution that is placed as a contestation of a status quo – namely, the colonial system and missionary imposition (see Wheeler and Pelissier 1971: 152–155) and the general perception of, and reaction to, oppression (Lanternari 1963). From this perspective, what seemed to be at stake was a 'theory of agency' where these leaders invoked words and deeds through a political conceptualization of religion that was typical of the colonial situation, as suggested by most specialists in these topics (among many others, Balandier 1963 [1955]; Bernard 1971; Pélissier 1977; Gonçalves 1985; Mbaya 1991).

In his first and more ideological public interventions, Toko does seem to have absorbed, in his travels to Leopoldville, this political stance in his theological configurations. On the other hand, it is also evident that the local (extremely pluralized and dynamic) missionary field acted as a catalyst (Andersson 1958: 240 and ff.). As we saw, a decisive moment in Toko's trajectory to this point was his contact with other Christian (and namely Protestant) realities. After the 1946 conference, Toko became progressively interested in the eschatological elements of the Bible, and made several contacts with foreign missionaries, against the Baptists' will. Here, the role of the Jehova's Witnesses and its missionary branch (the Watch Tower) in Toko's on-going theological reflection was decisive. His example, as well as Kimbangu's, seems to confirm the generalized suggestion that Protestant missions were instrumental in the 'decolonization of consciousnesses' that motivated the liberation movements in countries like Angola and Congo (Pélissier 1977; Messiant 1998; Freston 2001).

However, from a Tokoist perspective, what we see here precisely is a detachment from Protestant missionary culture, which the leader himself conceived as oppressive and part of the colonial endeavour. Subsequent events in Angola, described in the next chapter, will make this point clearer. We also witness a process of theological formation that becomes, in a certain sense, de-territorialized, as it begins in the Uíge and Luanda, but then materializes in the Lower Congo. As Wyatt MacGaffey would suggest in his study on Kimbanguism, there was indeed a 'plural context' against which such religious leaders operated (1983: 83–102). But the particular itineraries that feed into that plurality often reveal stances that, in a way, question the regional envelope under which they are presented. Toko's contact with different, 'foreign' Christian cultures (in Luanda, in Leopoldville and especially amidst the 1946 conference) already denoted that his exclusive insertion into the territorial prophetic paradigm was an intellectually reductive act.

However, if this argument makes sense from a leadership and theological point of view, it may not be so at the grassroots, following level, where the Kongo circumscription remains significant and powerful in many ways – regardless of what Toko himself devised and taught – especially in what concerns the political identification of the ethno-theologies discussed in the introduction (see chapter 4). As I collected in several conversations in Luanda, many Bakongo were initially attracted to Tokoism because they identified certain spiritual practices within the church (i.e. the work in the tabernacle) with local traditions such as the so-called *casas mavenge* or local practitioner houses. Others, like some Kimbanguists or adepts of the Kidista movement,[23] saw in Toko the continuation of the prophetic lineage started by Kimpa Vita. But on the other hand, not all Bakongo related in the same manner to their common royal and prophetic history; as Luena Pereira (2004) suggests, the baZombo seemed to be in fact more concerned with commercial activities than with the restoration of the ancient Kingdom of Kongo (see also Ferreira 2012: 16).

In any case, what can be ascertained from an ad hoc, diachronic point of view is that these intellectual formations absorbed different ideologies and political stances through which a 'prophetic category' is developed – i.e. a specific, theologically grounded form of leadership and following. But what we will see in the following chapters is a process of historical imposition that culminated into what began as an involuntary transcendence of certain localized (namely Bakongo) traditions. Ultimately, it may have been this movement of transcendence that pushed Tokoism away from the Bakongo prophetic paradigm, which provoked its (academically) 'forgotten history' we discussed in the introduction.

Notes

1. Obviously, there are countless other documents, textual or audiovisual, that circulate between the followers of the church and cannot be classified as 'publications'.
2. As mentioned above, the PIDE was the political police that acted under the aegis of the Estado Novo (1933–1974) regime, both in Portugal and its colonies, where it began its activities in the 1950s (see Mateus 2004; Blanes 2013), focusing on counter-espionage, surveillance and repression against alleged revolutionary movements. Although the PIDE officially lasted from 1945 to 1969 (when it was replaced by the Direcção Geral de Segurança [DGS]), the secret police activities lasted until 1974, the year of the Carnation Revolution and the demise of the regime. See Pimentel (2007) and Domingos and Pereira (2010).
3. This disclosure was performed through a decree (nº 16) published by the Portuguese government on 23 January 1993, under a new communication and privacy act. In brief, what we find in the Torre do Tombo and Arquivo Histórico Ultramarino collections can be classified in three groups: confidential reports and correspondence between the different delegations and sub-delegations of the PIDE in Angola, and transcriptions of interrogatories to Tokoists or reports by local informants, etc.; diverse materials such as newspaper or magazine reports, transcriptions of foreign press, etc.; and, finally, materials belonging to Angolan Tokoists intercepted by the PIDE, mainly letters exchanged between the leader and his followers during his years of exile in the Azores (1963–1974), probably the most extensive set of materials of these collections. These letters appear in their original versions (handwritten in Portuguese or Kikongo) or translated and transcribed by PIDE agents or collaborators. This obviously raises issues on authorship and veracity, considering the counter-espionage in course and the knowledge, on behalf of the Tokoists, that the letters were more often than not intercepted and read by the PIDE; on the other hand, as the PIDE would suggest explicitly in their correspondence, there is the possibility that some of these letters were forged by the police (see chapter 4). Finally, these documents were all object of a purge under a privacy act; and it is also possible that some documents have been stolen for unknown reasons. All this makes the ethnographer cum historian's work all the more difficult.
4. The Baptist Mission of Kibokolo had established in the Uíge region in 1899, by initiative of North American missionaries Thomas and Gwen Lewis, and John Pinnock. At the time Toko arrived at the Kibokolo, the mission was at its most vibrant stage, housing over a thousand members (Grenfell 1998: 210). Besides Kibokolo, the Baptists also established missions in northern Angola in the Bembe and São Salvador (today Mbanza Kongo) regions. For more on the Baptists in Angola, see Samarin (1986) and Grenfell (1996, 1998).
5. According to some Tokoists, the search for Toko in Leopoldville was such that it even implied the arrest of several children of Angolan origin in the city. But still the boy was not found (Quibeta n.d.: 26).

6. The wedding would eventually be cancelled by Molly's initiative, when Toko was already in Leopoldville, after she heard rumours that he was not living a 'dignified life' in that city (letter by Simão Toko to the Bembe Mission, 1942).

7. In Kikongo: 'O mavilukidi o vwete e nzole, o mavilukidi o vwete e nzole, mavilukidi o vwete e nzole' (Agostinho n.d.: 45). This was seen as an announcement of a future inversion of the current state of things. It is said that by that time, Toko also sang hymns in Kikongo where he summoned the Africans to 'open their eyes' (ibid.), in what can be understood as a progressively public contestation to the work of the missionaries.

8. As Marcum (1969), Wheeler and Pelissier (1971), Pelissier (1978), Gonçalves (2003), Pereira (2004) and others describe, at the time there were several (cultural, co-operative) associative movements active in the Lower Congo and in particular among the Angolan expatriates. Some of these associations, like NTO-BAKO, ABAKO and Ngwisako, would later incorporate a political agenda and actively participate in the genesis of the liberation movements in Angola.

9. Interestingly, all three participants would later become key figures in the postcolonial religious scenery in Angola. Jessé Chipenda, who had also studied with Toko in Luanda, would become an important pastor in Central Angola, in what is today known as the Igreja Evangélica Congregacional de Angola (Angolan Evangelical Congregational Church). Reverend Gaspar de Almeida would later become the leader of the Igreja Metodista Unida (United Methodist Church).

10. There is an obvious and unexplained discrepancy between the previous paragraph and what is stated in Toko's quote, where he seems to ignore the presence of the 'third black man', Jessé Chipenda. The same happens when he is interviewed by the Portuguese television circa 1974. In other letters, however, he would include Jessé (see, for instance, letter by Simão Toko, 11 November 1971).

11. 'Vena ye nsambil' azikuka, ye nkunga mia luyangalalu kansi o wete wa ngimbila, ke wakanini moneka yo' (There is a peaceful heaven and the power to rule with no tears; but as we will see, that glory, that time hasn't yet arrived. There is loving the most perfect God, the joyful hymns, but the glory of singing them has not yet arrived) (Agostinho n.d.: 52).

12. The books in question were *A Criação* (The Creation), *O Gozo do Povo* (The Joy of the People) and *Rejouissez-vous oh Nations* (Rejoice Oh Nations), as well as the *Sentinela* pamphlet. In fact, in 1949 Toko would write a letter to the Watch Tower's central offices in New York to request those books (Margarido 1972: 39; Grenfell 1998: 212). See below.

13. Kimbanguism, as I mentioned in the introduction, is a case in point. I will return to this at the end of this chapter.

14. 'And afterward, I will pour out my Spirit on all people. Your sons and daughters will prophesy, your old men will dream dreams, your young men will see visions' (New International Version). This verse, as we will see in the next chapter, is fundamental for the understanding of Tokoist praxis and theology.

15. This phrase was presumably spoken in French – 'C'est pas la fin du monde, mais c'est le changement de la terre' – possibly because Toko was not speaking exclusively to a Zombo audience.

16. This group was composed by Tumissungo Cardoso, Ndongala David, Nsuka André, Dombaxi André Malomba, Daniel Finda, Kiteba João, Canga Pedro, João Baptista Félix, Mavembo Sebastião, Sala Ramos Firmon, Cula Daniel and Daniel Nsuamani. They are still active today, led by the descendants of the original group, as well as others who also left Leopold-ville at the time (see chapter 4).

17. Some testimonies suggest that around three thousand self-claimed Tokoists were expelled from the Belgian Congo in these months (letter by Simão Toko to the Kibokolo BMS, 4 April 1956; interview Doze Mais Velhos, 19 October 2008).

18. According to Agostinho, not all Tokoists were expelled; some remained and continued to evangelize in the Lower Congo as well as in the Congo-Brazzaville (n.d.: 201).

19. Local Leopoldville newspapers of the time also wondered if the events surrounding Toko were some sort of a 'Kimbanguist rennaissance" (see *Courrier d'Afrique*, 10 January 1950; *L'Avenir Colonial Belge*, 12 January 1950). As Kimbanguism was at the time forbidden by the Belgian authorities, this could explain their preventive reaction concerning Tokoism.

20. Cunha Silva claims that when he asked Toko about what he knew of Kimbangu, Toko replied that he had heard about him bringing the dead back to life and that he was arrested by the authorities due to the missionaries. Silva, however, suspects that Toko was not revealing everything he knew at the time (Cunha 1959: 31).

21. Madalena would later be arrested and deported to Angola, where she would die years later.

22. The Congo gained independence in 1960, after a decade of active resistance on behalf of politically organized groups such as the ABAKO (Alliance des Bakongo), led by Joseph Kasa-Vubu, the future first president of the then Republic of Congo (1960–1965). In this decade, several regions in northern Angola also witnessed unsuccessful local uprising attempts on behalf of workers in the Portuguese labour camps and factories (see introduction; Freudenthal 2011).

23. A movement that sprung from the following of Manuel Kidito in the Kingdom of Kongo.

CHAPTER 2

Trajectories
A Prophetic Biography, Part 2

In the previous chapter we described the process of spiritual and political formation that preceded the 'founding moment' of the Tokoist movement that took place in Leopoldville in 1949. Those events inaugurated a movement towards an institutionalisation of what was until then a spontaneous following. They also inaugurated the conjunction that would define the Tokoist ethos in the subsequent decades: political repression, religious resistance.

Angola, 1950–1963:
Colonial Deportation and Ethnic Transcendence

January 1950; on the border between the Belgian Congo and Angola, at the frontier post of Noki (south of the Congolese city of Matadi), dozens of Zombo, among whom stands Simão Gonçalves Toko, are crossing the river Congo by boat to be delivered to the Portuguese government by the Belgian Sûreté. The Portuguese authorities, previously warned by the Belgians, are waiting for this group of 'potential terrorists'. In the correspondence between both countries, one could read:

> … Considering that the Angolan natives, whose names follow, practice and manifest their desire to continue to practice the rites of a hierarchical mystic-religious doctrine that preaches the coming of a new order under the reign of a new Christ, overthrowing the current authorities and powers, to take their place and do justice reign. (Dispatch by the governor of the Leopoldville province, L. Morel, 8 December 1949; my translation)[1]

The first group of 82 people is thus delivered to the Polícia de Segurança Pública (PSP),[2] who then seeks to 'solve the problem' and simultaneously prove the potential danger of these people in what concerned the security and identity of the colony – in a historical moment where, after the United Nations declaration (1945) of the universal right of self-determination of all peoples, the African continent began to witness political and military uprisings, in many cases with the spiritual and/or material support of independentist religious movements (Hastings 1974). In the Portuguese case, in October 1951 Angola would evolve, after the revocation of the 1930 Colonial Act, from 'colony' to 'province', and had already experienced occasional separatist attempts in the previous decade (see Wheeler and Pelissier 1971: 160 and ff.). As described in the introduction, the Portuguese authorities were also being pressured by the international community to recognize Angola's right to self-determination, which contradicted the country's own Luso-tropical imperialist stance (Heimer 1973; Bender 2009 [1978]; Pelissier 1978; Newitt 1981; Birmingham 2004; Messiant 2006; Castelo 2007). It is therefore within a context of progressive securitization that the Angolan delegation of the PIDE is created, with the goal, among other things, of centralizing and channelling the circulation of information, and the development of relationships with foreign police corporations for the exchange of intelligence (Mateus 2004: 24–25). Within this framework, religious movements like the Tokoists, the Kimbanguists or the Jehova's Witnesses became point-blank subjects for authorities eager to identify and configure enemies (Blanes 2013).

In what concerned the *tocos* (as it often appeared in the police correspondence) in particular, there were several suspicions associated to them. Namely, the idea already conveyed in the Sûreté's correspondence that there was a backdrop of political and revolutionary ideals in such movements. An anonymous report delivered at the PIDE in 1957 studied the 'system of infiltration of communism in the province of Angola', focusing on the so-called *seitas* (sects). It was suggested that the infiltration of communism, as part of a project of general revolt led by the 'technicians of the World Communist Revolution', was mentored from the Belgian Congo and used as the main vehicle for the aggregative capacities of movements like Nzambi Ya M'Papa (The God of Father Simão Toko) – which, interestingly enough, used at the time a red, five-pointed star as their symbol, proudly worn by followers on their clothes or chests.

Therefore, the strategy assumed by the PIDE concerning this specific group was one of 'correcting the process of subversion that the sect had been following' (PIDE Report, 8 May 1966). They decided to divide the group into smaller groups and distribute them through the different *colonatos* (colonies) – labour camps the Portuguese authorities kept throughout the territory – as part of the policies of colonial population and agrarian production (Bender 1973; Clarence-Smith 1985; Ball 2005, 2006; Esteves 2010), a policy euphemistically referred to as fixation of residence (*fixação de residência*).[3] The same would happen with the Tokoists that would be subsequently arrested in Leopoldville and deported to Angola, which eventually reached the thousands. The vast majority of these groups would be pushed into agriculture, industrial or public construction work under the order of *cipaios* or foremen with a mandate from the colonial administration, and under the vigilance of the *chefes de posto* (local official representatives), who also acted as informants for the PIDE. Others would endure detention and prison in the São Nicolau camp or Baía dos Tigres prison in the southern regions of the colony. The Uíge region would welcome the first big group (including Simão Toko) in the Vale do Loge, a valley located near the Bembe municipality. Subsequently, other groups were sent to Ambrizete (Zaire province), Luanda, Benguela, Porto Alexandre (today Tombwa), Baía dos Tigres and Moçâmedes (in the Namibe region) and also São Tomé and Príncipe (Margarido 1972; Grenfell 1998). Finally, smaller groups of men and women would be dispersed in countless other villages throughout the territory (Kisela 2004: 52–61). Simão Toko himself would eventually experience several residence fixations, beginning in the Bembe:

> We arrived at Angola, and each one of us followed his own path according to the government's decision; I requested to be sent for agriculture. The state gave my brothers and myself a plot covered with thicket at the Vale do Loge, northern Angola so we could cultivate coffee, and a Colonato was formed. The whole area is of 32 kms in width, and there was no path or roads to get there, but still we worked on that valley. The Tokoist population was of around five hundred families, and it looked like a white man's village. Everyone was happy, despite the hard work to earn our daily bread. This valley was in the Bembe region, where I had taught, and it was 200 kilometres away from my home. As you know, I left the region at the end of 1950. Thus, 1950-1942 means less than eight years that passed. The villagers of the land that knew me from the five years I had spent teaching there, were thrilled and very soon many of them, Protestant and Catholic, converted to our church. It was a big event. The word spread throughout all northern Angola. (Letter by Simão Toko, 8 November 1971)

This sojourn in the Vale do Loge would prove to be pivotal in the history of the Tokoist movement. In first place, because it was in the valley that one of the largest groups of Tokoist deportees was concentrated; and, as we see from Toko's letter quoted here, it was thanks to their work ethics, organization and solidary spirit that they would transform, throughout a decade, the *colonato* into one of the most productive agrarian enterprises of the region, with the exploration of coffee and also the plantation of palm trees (*Jornal do Congo*, 5 October 1960).[4]

It was also at the time of Toko's sojourn in the Bembe that other, spiritual events took place. One of the most defining ones would take place on 17 April 1950, when the leader was on his way to Caconda (Huíla) for a mission and stopped to spend the night in Catete (Bengo, about 30 kms east of Luanda). At night, the heat was such that Toko woke up, attacked by mosquitoes. He decided to leave the house to catch some air and take care of his physiological needs. He moved forward in the dark, towards some bushes that were beside the house, and suddenly saw a shining light beside a tree nearby. He ran towards the light to see what it was, and found himself before a tall white man, dressed in a khaki outfit, surrounded by a strong light. The man spoke to Simão, asking him: 'Do you know who I am?' 'Jesus Christ', replied Simão, but the apparition responded: 'No, I am not Christ, Christ is my son.' Toko fell on his knees and the man continued: 'I will put something inside you, that you will not know or understand' (letter by Simão Toko, 8 November 1971). Young Toko insisted that the man reveal what that

Illustration 6. Tokoist women in the Vale do Loge, 1950s. *Source:* Ferrão 1957.

could be, but the apparition began to lose clarity and disappeared. After that encounter, remembered today as the 'encounter with the Good God in Catete', Toko resumed his mission in Caconda and soon returned to the Vale do Loge.[5]

This event would then become part of a charismatic and prophetic sequence that would end a short time later in the Vale do Loge. After returning from Catete to the valley, Toko congregated a new group of elders to pray and summon God so that the ancient prophets would return and help them in the task of spiritual salvation (Pedro 2008; see chapter 3). From this moment on, the Vale do Loge became, apart from a historical site, a spiritual place for the Tokoists. In its sceneries, one can recognize mounts and prairies travelled by Toko, who in turn attributed holy names to the landscape: Mount Sinai, Mount Zion, River Jordan, etc. (interview Doze Mais Velhos, April 2011).

However, after ten months in the Bembe, and because he would not cease to preach and 'provoke agitation' among the local communities (Cunha 1959: 54), the *dirigente* is then transferred to the *colonato* of Caconda, where he would work as bricklayer and also tractor-driver's assistant.[6] Here, many Tokoists recall, he was object of an attempted murder on behalf of the foreman who managed the colony (known as Palma): under the pretext that some wild grass was obstructing a tractor's engine, he ordered that Toko remove it. When Toko went below the tractor, foreman Palma pulled the tractor forward and crushed the prophet's body, ripping it into four pieces. But immediately his body recomposed and Toko stood up and cleared the dust off his clothes (Agostinho n.d.: 65–66; Quibeta n.d.: 41–43; Kisela 2004: 65). Other murder attempts followed (Quibeta n.d.: 42) – but to no avail.

Finally, after sojourning in the small villages of Jau and Cassinga, Toko settled in as an assistant worker in a lighthouse in the Ponta Albina – on the Baía dos Tigres (today Tombwa), the last populated spot before entering the Namibe desert in southernmost Angola. At the lighthouse, Toko lived with his wife, Rosa,[7] his daughters, Ilda and Esperança, and his nephew João Sivi, who helped him in the lighthouse maintenance tasks. The compound also housed the lighthouse keeper Firmino da Silva (originally from São Tomé) and his family, as well as a small group of servants. A member of the Angolan Military Commando that visited him in those years described the setting as being 'quite isolated – a stretch of sand –, two hours away, following the telephone line posts, from Porto Alexandre' (PIDE report on trip to Ponta Albina, c.1957).

Despite the isolation and dispersion to which most Tokoists were voted, the residence-fixation measures were not as effective as would be witnessed years later. The Tokoists were forced into compulsory labour, but nevertheless were able to pursue their faith more or less clandestinely in the places where they sojourned.[8] Perhaps resting on the confidence that the caesarean strategy of *divide et impera* was the most adequate, the PSP and later the PIDE did not exert, in this initial stage, a strong (or at least effective) control upon the church members, convinced that the fixation measures and a routine surveillance would be enough to pursue their goal of controlling and extinguishing the movement. But the Tokoists were still able to perform their religious services in the shadow of the night, and the leader was still able to communicate with his followers through the letters he wrote that were collected by believers who secretly travelled the endless sand dunes that separated Ponta Albina and Porto Alexandre (where a nucleus of 'fixated Tokoists' also lived). Then, from the Porto Alexandre, the letters would be copied and distributed by hand throughout the territory, despite the fact that 'sometimes they caught the letters. For instance, I was in the post office and saw the letters, and often the PIDE caught the letters. ... And we got the letters after the PIDE had seen them. ... We received the letters he wrote which were already checked by the PIDE' (interview Sebastião Vuaituma, October 2008).

The lighthouse keeper himself took charge that Toko and his nephew would not contact the other servants, and also intercepted the letters he received, forwarding them to the Capitania (captainship) of Moçâmedes (PIDE report on trip to Ponta Albina, c.1957). This, in any case, did not prevent Toko from communicating with his followers, and that the different places of fixation become themselves places of proselytism and evangelization. As the PIDE would eventually recognize in their internal reports, 'the removal of Simão Toko did not prevent him from managing, through correspondence, the sect's business and from being seen by most of his followers as an indisputable leader' (PIDE report, 8 May 1966).

In these years that the prophet remained proscribed in the Ponta Albina, another event took place that would be defining of the trajectory devised by Toko and the decisions he was forced into taking, in terms of constituting an 'independent church' in the Angolan territory (see Cunha 1959: 33–41). In 1955, John Cooke, an emissary from the Watch Tower (the evangelizing branch of the Jehova's Witnesses) arrives at Luanda (see Pinto 2012). Considering that Toko had contacted the Watch Tower's central offices to ask for reading material when he was still in the Belgian Congo, there was a natural expectation on behalf of the Jehova's Witnesses that they were dealing with a group of 'natives' willing to convert. However, upon his arrival to Luanda, Cooke realizes that the group's reception is not what he had imagined: upon visiting the nuclei of Tokoists in Luanda's Bairro Indígena, he observes how many of them were unaware of the Jehova's Witnesses' existence, nor were they willing to join the religious organization (letter by John Cooke, 25 February 1955).

Cooke then decides to embark to southern Angola. He contacts a group of Tokoists fixated in Moçâmedes, led by João Mancoca, André Macota and Sala Filemon. In a letter written on 20 March 1955 to the Tokoists in southern Angola, the three local leaders summon that everyone should welcome Cooke and accept his words, inasmuch as 'his way of preaching the Good News of the Kingdom is no different from that of Simão Toko'. This message was not, however, entirely successful, and most of the believers refused to make a decision before listening to (or reading) the prophet's opinion.

After several diligences with the Portuguese authorities, Cooke is finally authorized, on April 1955, to interview Simão Toko and ascertain of his will to join the Watch Tower.

> Arriving at Sá da Bandeira, three government officials waited for me; they took me to the hotel and then to the Local Administration to talk to Simão. He looked surprised but was very happy. We spent the rest of the day and the next morning talking and discussing several issues. ... Simão added a few words to the letter you gave me in Portuguese as recommendation to the dispersed groups. Here they are: 'Likewise, I reciprocate my sincere greetings to all my beloved brothers in faith, especially those brothers in Christ of the Society of the New World (The Bible Watch Tower Society), and I agree with what the brothers in the Baía dos Tigres wrote. I am your brother in Christ.' (14 April 1955; letter by John Cooke to João Mancoca, 21 April 1955)

However, the situation quickly and unexpectedly changed. After the interview, Cooke fails to come to terms with one of the figureheads of Simão Toko's following in nearby Baía dos Tigres, Luvualo David – who was part of the first group to be deported from the Belgian Congo – and this motivates a counter-reply by Toko, who then circulates the following statement: 'our religion is not that of the whites, it is ours, of the Africans; if a white man shows up, you can welcome him, but if he wants to give orders, he is not welcome any more' (PIDE report on interrogatory to 'Three Dissident Natives from the Watch Tower', 11 May 1955).

Toko's announcement surprised Cooke, who was still convinced that he was about to convert a group of Angolan natives. A short time later, in June of that same year, Cooke is forced to leave the country due to the expiration of his visa, but this reaction by Toko would have certain consequences. Part of the group of Tokoists based in Baía dos Tigres, led by João Mancoca (who had also been in Leopoldville in July 1949), disagrees with Toko and provokes a dissidence by joining the Jehova's Witnesses. Luvualo David would then write a letter to this group, asking them: 'Are you sure the white man can serve as a good guide to show the black man the way to Salvation? He who looks after the interests of the white man is a traitor and will never be able to tell the truth before the others' (2 June 1955). Toko himself would eventually reply to Mancoca:

> I hereby acknowledge your letter from January 1st, 1956. I thank you and inform you of the following: ... from here on you are advised not to send me your correspondence any more, as you are all grumpy people and I don't want to hear from you any more; ... I don't want to see your evangelical newspapers nor hear about your business and common interests.... You are hereby warned. (Letter by Simão Toko, 8 February 1956)[9]

At this point, it becomes clear that, despite the influence that the Watch Tower books may have exerted in Tokoism's intellectual formation, the leader did not want to follow that missionary entity, but rather use its literature as an instrument for his project of religious utopian emancipation. It is also clear that the affirmation of an African and racialized ethos becomes explicit. In comments read in the correspondence of both the Jehova's Witnesses and PIDE there is a growing idea that they are before a 'racist' and 'xenophobe' movement (e.g. report from the governor of Moçâmedes, 26 July 1956). As a Catholic priest would note months after the Tokoists arrived at Angola, 'in their singing, in their prayers, Tokoism proclaims both the expulsion of the white man, his subordination to the black man and the liberation of the African continent, performed by a Saviour to be sent soon by god, in the person of Simão Toko' (report by Father Alberto Dandu, 7 June 1951). However, in contrast with what was evident in the Lower Congo, the 'Africanity' of the Tokoist ideology was no longer necessarily or exclusively relying on a Bakongo perspective, but rather to a progressive racial conscience that associated emancipation to the spiritual (and political) liberation of the pretos, where the vector of Portuguese colonialism and 'Angola' as a national project would become increasingly pivotal.

Furthermore, the territorial dispersion of the Tokoists promoted by the Portuguese authorities would have fundamental consequences in the posterior doctrinal and theological structuration of the Tokoist movement, which would thus involuntarily transcend its initial Bakongo framing (Ferreira 2012: 33–40). Throughout the 1950s and

1960s, the initial group that originated from Leopoldville would be joined by a new generation of adepts from other ethnicities, thanks to the evangelizing endeavours of the deportees. Reports from the Portuguese political police of the time describe how several villages from north to south of Angola were visited by individuals spreading the word about an Angolan prophet who would spiritually and politically release them from colonial and missionary oppression. This spreading of the Gospel was also performed door to door by dozens of followers of Simão Toko, who reached out to the communities neighbouring their camps; Kisela describes one such case in the Kalukembe, for instance (2004: 67–68). But the Tokoist example of resistance against colonial authorities also served as an impacting example for many Angolans, who sought in Tokoism a native response to the situation of oppression they were experiencing. Furthermore, the hundreds of deportees, many of them young men and women, would eventually marry and father new generations of Tokoists in the places of fixation.

Thus, new, multi-ethnic 'Tokoist centralities' would emerge in the most populated nuclei of 'fixated Tokoists', such as Ambrizete (Zaire), Vale do Loge (Uíge), Luanda (Bairro Indígena, Terra Nova), Benguela and Caconda (PIDE report, 2 February 1966). In a report delivered on February 1966, the PIDE would acknowledge the existence of 'formal' Tokoist nuclei in the following regions from north to south of the province:

Zaire: Ambrizete, Musserra

Congo (Uíge): Carmona, Damba, Sanza Pombo, Macocola, Songo, Maquela do Zombo and Povo Taia, Alto Cauale, Negage

Cuanza Sul: Amboim

Luanda

Benguela: Lobito, Catumbela, Benguela, Chicuma, Gubal, Baía Farta

Huambo: Nova Lisboa

Huíla: Caconda

Moxico: Luso, Teixeira de Sousa

Moçâmedes: Baía dos Tigres, Santa Rita, Porto Alexandre

Of these places, Luanda, the Vale do Loge (and later Ntaia Nova – see below) and Benguela became known within the church as the three 'centralities' through which the movement developed. In Luanda, for instance, the group of repatriated Tokoists occupied were fixated in one, new neighbourhood, the Bairro Indígena, which is now also known today as the *Congolenses*, given the ethnic origin of their original inhabitants.[10] They became one of the major loci of church activity in the subsequent decades, and welcomed Simão Toko in his sojourns in the city in between his periods of exile.

This territorial multiplication and ethnic complexification experienced by the movement would eventually provoke an attempt towards a bureaucratic reformation of the movement's organization, progressively self-envisioned as an ecclesiastical entity (Ferreira 2012).[11] This reorganization was based on a division of the modes of representation and local management into internal entities called classes, and took place in particular in the city of Luanda, where the cult spaces multiplied throughout the preceding years. According to instructions left by the leader before leaving for exile in 1963, these classes would act as parishes with defined areas of influence in the capital, pertaining mainly bureaucratic and administrative functions.[12] In a first stage, these classes were divided within the four cardinal points: north, south, east, west; however, they quickly grew into composing the current eighteen classes (all referring to names of neighbourhoods in Luanda): São Paulo, Caputo, Cemitério Novo, Cazenga n° 1, n° 2, n° 3, n° 4 and n° 5, Rangel, Rangel Marçal and Zangado, Calemba, Cassequel, Maianga, Golf, Mota, Ilha do Cabo, Classe Central and Mulemba (Agostinho n.d.: 223). A few years later, in the 1970s, a new organizational reform took place: the subdivision of the church membership into 'tribes' (*tribos*) through which members with the same 'cultural affinities' (Agostinho n.d.: 223; Paxe 2009), sharing the same language, land of origin, habits and customs would congregate and interact. This process of 'classification' and 'tribalization', albeit mainly administrative, geographical, cultural and spiritual, reveals the growing need, on behalf of the church leadership, of dealing with the process of internal pluralization. The notion invoked was that of the 'communocratic character of the African man' (Agostinho n.d.: 224), which suggested a notion of political union and connected to biblical historiography: 'the sum of all tribes forms the Church of Christ united into one nation, in this case Angola – it forms the Angolan Church. In the past, the Church of Christ also had its tribes, the well known twelve tribes of Israel, as is read in the Bible, Number 1: 1–16. Today, thus, the Church of Christ in Africa also has its own tribes' (Agostinho n.d.: 225).

From this particular perspective, despite the continued insinuations on behalf of the Portuguese authorities and authors of reports on the Tokoist Church, which blatantly accused Toko of *feiticismo* (witchcraft), the movement offered a particular stance concerning 'African tradition', from the standpoint of a biblical framework. Alfredo Margarido described how Toko built his theology from the rejection of the *mundo dos velhos* (world of the elders), associated with 'tradition' and which he considered in many respects accessory to white hegemony (1966: 88). On the other hand, Jose Gonçalves noted in 1967 that Toko was object of frequent attacks on behalf of traditional authorities, who accused him of instigating the younger generations' rebellion against the *usos e costumes* (habits and customs; 1967: 685), refraining them from wearing the traditional clothing and from participating in dances and 'fetishist acts' (ibid.). In this regard, the descent of the Holy Ghost in 1949 is also frequently seen within the church as a rupture and liberation from a specific tradition. One of the church's most notorious hymns, 'Rei dos Céus Andará' (The King of the Heavens will Walk) sings:

> God visits Africa
> Its shadows He dissipates
> Evil actions he will destroy
> Jehovah will walk
>
> Witchcraft he will eliminate
> Human commerce he will abolish
> Illicit unions he will invalidate
> Jehovah will walk[13]

The advocacy of an Africa in rupture with its cultural and political history was explicitly present in the discourses, decisions and singing promoted by the Tokoists, who promoted a new Africa in their own terms. This rupturism was also a consequence of Toko's conviction that intellectual formation and technical apprenticeship were fundamental aspects of communitary growth and spiritual salvation: just as he had previously emancipated through reading and translation, so should his followers be predisposed for learning and personal and professional improvement, having in mind a near future of spiritual and political liberation (Margarido 1966, 1972; Grenfell 1998).[14] On the other hand, it also reflected the particular characteristics of late colonial urban Angolan society, where some *assimilado* (assimilated) Angolans had access to education and work conditions denied to 'native Angolans' – Tokoists included, many of whom were still attempting to free themselves from the slavery conditions they were forced into (Agostinho n.d.: 131–132). From this perspective, many Tokoists promoted communal solidarity, discipline and personal perfection, in particular those who attended the Baptist and Salvation Army schools (Margarido 1966). In this line, historian Cléria Ferreira (2012: 25 and ff.) also detects continuity with Bakongo ideologies of belonging, relatedness and collective identity, namely in what concerns the expression of networks of solidarity and association.

But exogenously, ignorant of this ethical framework, the PIDE agents at the time were more concerned with the movement's subversive potential:

> Simão Toko's sect movement is anti political religious. It follows the doctrines of its predecessors Simon Kibango [sic], Simon Mpadi; Simão and his disciples are individuals who are enemies of the State and all its officials, of the doctors, missionaries (both Catholic and Protestant) and all those who work for them. You must hear them preach and sing. They say the time is coming when they will reign through all Africa. The whites will be submissive and will serve them. (PIDE report, 1956)

Several dispersed accounts from the Tokoists also seem to confirm this posture. For instance, some members who had been delocalized in southern Angola remembered how Toko would challenge the colonial regime in small, quotidian actions, such as changing the lyrics of the Portuguese national anthem, sung everyday at the hoisting of the flag in the administrative stations.[15]

Simultaneously, several documents of this period referred to Simão Toko's movement as the 'religion of the star' (PIDE archives, Torre do Tombo), in reference to the fact that the symbol chosen, in July–August 1949, to identify and represent the movement was a four-pointed star on a red background – each of the points symbolizing the four voices of the choir (soprano, contralto, basso, tenor). At the time, the emblems that carried the symbol were called, in kikongo, *detembo* (star) or *dimbo* (sign) (PIDE report, 5 April 1955). Interested in this symbology, Silva Cunha questioned several Tokoists on the meaning of the star, but would only receive ambiguous and contradictory replies; but Toko himself would explain that 'the star showed that Africa had received the light of God' (1959: 61).[16]

However, soon after the events of July 1949, the leader would recommend that the star change to an eight-pointed, white star on a red background, to be worn as a badge in the believers' lapels. Finally, after 1974, the symbol stabilized to the current eight-pointed star on a green background. One explanation for this change referred precisely to the political connotations of the symbology invoked. As Papá Vuaituma explained to me in Luanda, 'the star was red, but it meant "spiritual warfare", according to the hymn we sang, we fought against the world. ... It was a symbol of spiritual warfare. But the colonialists said we were communists, because of the red colour. That's why they dispersed us, they thought we were political' (19 October 2008). Thus, the transition from red to green would be explained with the end of the struggle for Angola's (spiritual and/or political) liberation that would end in 1974, where red represented the blood shed by the Tokoists throughout the process, and green the Christian hope of triumph of the Kingdom of Christ on earth (Agostinho n.d.: 26–27).

As this last example suggests, concomitant to this ideological transition, there was also within Tokoism a growing consciousness and political positioning, somewhat imposed by the historical circumstances. Namely in what concerned the process of Angolan liberation, begun in 1961 by several the MPLA, the UPA-FNLA and UNITA, exiled in the Lower Congo and Dembo regions (Wheeler and Pelissier 1971). Following the revolt in the Baixa of Cassanje (4 January 1961) and the failed uprising promoted by the MPLA in the São Paulo prison in Luanda (one month later), the conflict deflagrates through guerrilla actions and consequent colonial response that took place in the northern regions of the colony. The culmination of this was the massacre of thousands of civilians (both native and colonialist) and the flight of thousands of Angolans to the *matas* (woods) and the Lower Congo (Marcum 1969, 1978).

In October of that same year, Toko is brought by the colonial authorities from Ponta Albina to the Uíge, where he is asked to perform public summons asking the escaped natives to return home to their villages and thus restore 'normality' (PIDE information, 24 September 1962). With this strategy, the Portuguese, aware that they could no longer disdain Toko's public impact as a local leader, attempt to instrumentalize his notoriety in order to pacify the region and simultaneously reaffirm their political project, placing the prophet in the battlefield and confounding the different independentist movements (*Courrier d'Afrique*, 4 August 1962).[17] His leadership and mobilization capacities become evident, but cannot dissipate some suspicion on behalf of the authorities concerning his real motivations, in a moment of increasing tension. This despite the fact that Toko apparently placed himself publicly in the Portuguese side in the conflict. For instance, in August 1962, Toko is driven to the frontier village of Kimpangu, in the Congo, to address the Angolan refugees with his loudspeaker and summon them to return to their country. The PIDE sub-inspector that filed the report of this visit recalled how in the day prior to their arrival an unsuccessful sabotage attempt on behalf of UPA and PDA (Angolan Democratic Party) members took place:

> In the meantime, Simão Toko spoke to his adepts. Our arrival provoked mistrust and made his adepts question him why there were so many

Illustration 7. Toko in the *matas*, 1962. *Source:* Ruy Llera Blanes's personal archive.

whites – to which he replied that in his country blacks and whites lived in harmony, and thus the fact that he was escorted by white men should not be surprising. At that moment, we were able to witness the affection and devotion that the Congolese Tokoists dedicate to Simão Toko; it appeared that they could not believe he was there among them. (PIDE report, 28 August 1962)

We can thus sense the environment in which Toko moved, dealing with the suspicion of some and the adoration of others. Many of these believers, the so-called *regressados* (returnees) that had run away to Leopoldville, eventually returned (PIDE report, 22 November 1962). Around a thousand men, women and children returned from Kimpangu and the neighbouring villages of Baza Sosso and Malele alone (PIDE extraordinary report of the Maquela Station, 9 August 1962).

Already in Ponta Albina, Toko had stated to a local newspaper that he was 'content' and 'lived happily': 'I am in good health and am a government official like any other, as I have my wage, my family support allowance and I have my deductions for my retirement.'[18] Around this time, he releases a public statement, where he explains: 'According to a piece I read in the newspaper *A Província de Angola*, about terrorists singing a song in my name, I tell you the man in that song is not me, because they worship another Simão from their land, called Simão

Timão' (interview to the Portuguese media, October 1961).[19] In a report sent to the CITA (Centre of Information and Tourism of Angola)
in August 1962, Toko could not be more explicit:

> Angola belongs to the white and black natives, sons of Portugal, living
> here in Angola, under the protection of the Portuguese Nation; it does
> not belong to the blacks and whites hidden abroad. Holden, Pinnock and
> all the other parties fooled by the foreigners who gave them weapons,
> bombs, fuses, mines, etc., are all thieves and want to steal a land that
> doesn't belong to them. (Simão Toko, report on a trip to Northern An-
> gola, 20 August 1962)

In another letter written on September of that same year to the general
governor of Angola, he declared himself 'one hundred per cent Portuguese, until the day I die' and willing to collaborate in putting an end
to the massacres perpetrated by the UPA (letter by Simão Toko, 24 September 1962). And in March 1964, after the earthquake that shattered
the island of São Jorge in the Azores and caused hundreds of deaths,
the leaders of the church in Luanda, following the *dirigente*'s orders,
wrote to the council administrator of the city, lamenting the events
and offering the sum of twenty thousand escudos to help the 'brother
victims' (15 March 1964).

But on the other hand, just as we had seen in previous attitudes,
during this period one could also observe references to Toko's politics
of 'peaceful resistance' to the colonial project, instructing his followers
to not collaborate with the whites, in an attitude described as 'refined
xenophobia' (PIDE-DA report, 12 February 1966). This is revelatory
of the different 'truths', often contradictory among themselves, that
circulated at the time: on the one hand, Toko and his followers as well-
behaved, solidary colonialist supporters; on the other, as misbehaved,
racist anti-colonialists. In March 1961, a group of Angolans repatriated
from Cabinda to Negage were placed under custody of the Portuguese
authorities for allegedly being followers of the Tokoist movement.
Their luggage was scrutinized and in it the authorities found a 1961
agenda notebook (of the brand Ambar) with the following verses written in Kikongo:

> In the year 1482 they entered our land.
> With their strength they entered our land.
> We want to stand up, may God help us; they have been here too long.
> When they entered our land, the elders of times past would say that the
> land was good, but now they ruined it.
> (Carmona District Subsection report, 9 June 1962)

In the months that followed Toko's deportation out of Luanda, the concern regarding the movement's subversive potential aggravates: the rumours in this direction increase, facilitated by the growing tension within the colonial regime and by the Tokoists' 'lack of collaboration'. A PIDE report reproduces the words of an informant, who stated that Toko was allied with the UPA and was preparing to 'make a scene' on the Island of Luanda at any moment, threatening the pretos who would not join him in his mission and in the independentist cause 'will be killed' by his 'army' (PIDE procedure, 10 December 1962). In another report, it is stated that Toko visited the Damba region (Uíge), where he had shown an 'explicit hostility regarding the whites' and announced that the 'religions of the whites' (Catholic and Protestant) had 'their days in Africa counted' (SCIIA report, 11 July 1962).[20] In another note, an informant confided about 'a secretary from Simão Toko's party who would often go to the Congo to bring terrorists and hold meetings in a mission, at the Bairro Indígena' in Luanda (PIDE information, 26 September 1969). Yet another information reaffirmed the growth of Toko's movement in the Bairro Indígena quarters, with the arrival of new members from outside the neighbourhood and Luanda, and meetings were being celebrated at night and during the weekends; one of the followers had been caught drunk and singing the UPA hymn, and another one had sworn that 'the twenty-eighth would be the day when Simão Toko would gather his troops' (PIDE information, 3 October 1962).

The regime's disconcertment regarding Toko's 'true' ideological allegiance was evident, as in the following report that describes the 'preoccupying' increase of Tokoist activities in the Benguela region:

> The situation is fastidious, as the leader of the sect, Simão Toko, has recently collaborated in the task of bringing expatriate Angolans to their homes and previous situations, and is willing to give patriotic lectures. It is likely that the notorious enthusiasm and frequency of these meetings, now performed publicly, is not just because of their religious purposes but also political, given that the sect is explicitly racist, and does not admit any white follower. (Report of the Lobito Subdelegation, 5 November 1962)

The apparent contradictions between Simão Toko's speech and that of his followers – which, according to the PIDE reports, alternated between collaborationist subservience and terrorist conspiracy – should nevertheless be read within the context of repression and rebellion in the Angola of the time, as an expression of resistance or resilience (Paxe 2009) to a hegemonic imposition where, alongside a public subordination to colonial power, one could find several other and complex forms of resistance that contradicted, in those complaints by the PIDE agents, the public transcript (Scott 1990) of Toko's official statements.[21] We thus find different forms of resistance, not necessarily pointing in the same direction and with variable degrees of strategy involved in them: a political, public resistance developed by the leaders and Toko, who fought for his own ideals, but was confronted with the fact that he became a leader of masses, in many ways responsible for the destiny of thousands of people; a quotidian resistance, reflected in the more or less spontaneous reactions of Toko's followers, amidst the processes of vigilance, suspicion and accusations they were object of; and an ideological resistance, motivated by the conviction that, sooner or later, a societal change would occur in the territory. From this perspective, one of the most remarkable forms of Tokoist resistance was precisely an idea of 'secrecy' associated with what Tokoists 'knew' and 'concealed' – the knowledge of future events that would take place in Angola and the world (Estermann 1965). This secret, as an inherent part of Tokoist spirituality,[22] did not cease to feed incomprehension and suspicion into the authorities, which sought to understand and simultaneously impose a particular vision of the 'problem'. One such 'secret', for instance, was 'the [Tokoist] elders make believe that they can see the future and know the date when Salazar will give Angola back to the black natives' (PIDE report, 25 April 1966). The outcome of this was an 'impressive mutism, presenting an unbreakable ingenuity and humility that makes the investigation on their procedures and intentions extraordinarily difficult' (PIDE report, 12 July 1962).

Another act of resistance referred to the obvious ambiguity with which Toko publicly instructed his followers, teaching obedience to the authorities and respect to national sovereignty, but simultaneously promoting 'excessive zeal'. According to James Grenfell, the Tokoists were known in the *colonatos* for their work capacity, will to learn and impeccable behaviour, which for instance transformed the Vale do Loge into a successful coffee plantation (1998: 219). But they also refused open exploitation, such as the payment of taxes that they deemed unfair (ibid.). It was, from, this perspective, a peaceful, non-militarized form of resistance.

In any case, the reports revealed the dilemma in which the PIDE agents found themselves, as they collected, from the different outposts and agents, contradictory information concerning the Tokoists' posture vis-à-vis the conflict in gestation, and met increasing difficulty at the moment of deciding the correct strategies to fight the movement off, bearing in mind the progressive militarization of Angola. Simão

Toko's appeal for the return of the refugees that had fled to Leopold-ville is an illustrative example. With this strategy, the Portuguese authorities' intention was to restore 'normality' after the first military incursions by the UPA in northern Angola against the Portuguese, the *colonos* (settlers in the agricultural ventures) and the Angolan collaborationists. But Toko's appeal not only brought many Tokoists back to Angola but also created new territorialities and loci for the movement's expansion.

One such novelty was the creation, on August 1962, of the Povo Taia (Ntaia Nova) village, decided by the prophet, apparently in agreement with the authorities as a 'compensation' for his work. This took place in his homeland in the Uíge, in a process of repopulation that included the Tokoists that had fled (some them from the Vale do Loge *colonato*) to the Congo, as well as Tokoists from neighbouring communes.[23] This village, named in honour of the commune where the prophet was born,[24] experienced an extraordinary growth and in 1965 housed approximately 1600 inhabitants (PIDE report, 6 October 1965). Located in a cross-cut off the road that connected Maquela do Zombo, São Salvador and Kimbata, the compound was remote and of difficult access, and therefore allowed for a certain autonomy and protection concerning the Portuguese authorities and the military confrontations. Thus, literally a 'Tokoist village' was built from scratch, and became known for its self-organization and urbanistic design. In 1964, one of the inhabitants of Taia Nova described it to Simão Toko:

> The Regedoria ... is composed of nine streets that depart in semi-circle, extending towards the extremities of the settlement, and on the corners of each of these streets, in front of the semi-circle, the more definitive buildings such as the house of the Regedor (village ruler); the Civic Centre; the school, which incorporates two rooms attended so far by 240 students of both sexes; the school monitors' residences; and more recently the commercial house built on the corner of the main street leaving from the village towards Maquela. (Letter from António Domingos Pereira to Simão Toko, 26 October 1964)

The Povo Taia, existing to this day, would in the subsequent years house Tokoist members from other regions, and would eventually play an important role in the territorial allegiances and political processes observed in the church many years later – as we will see in the description of Toko's 'remote leadership' in this chapter and in his disputed legacy, described in chapter 4.

In any case, this situation where the prophet appeared simultaneously as a 'leader of the blacks' and someone who supported the colonial project also produced a necessary amount of ambiguity that, ultimately, condemned the Portuguese initiative to failure and simultaneously fostered an increasing resentment on behalf of the leaders of the liberation movements, who saw him mainly as an instrument in the hands of the Portuguese (*Courrier d'Afrique*, 26 July 1962).[25] A PIDE report written on 24 September 1962 describes how Johnny Eduardo Pinnock (FNLA military fighting on the border between Angola and the Congo) 'does not want to listen to what Simão Toko says' and has ordered that the prophet be arrested and brought unto him. Another confession from a man from Ambrizete connected to the UPA describes the movement's disappointment upon hearing the Tokoist leader declare, in a religious service performed on 30 September of that year, being against the war and willing to go 'with one hundred armed men to fight Portugal's enemies, fight against the UPA and bring back the populations that have been led astray' (PIDE information, 20 October 1962), and they reminded him that this attitude would probably have him killed by the troops of Holden Roberto in his trips to the *mato* (ibid.).

This distancing from the militarized liberation movements was probably due to the pacifist doctrine he conveyed, which led him closer to movements that defended a pacific transition towards independence, such as the MDIA (Movimento de Defesa dos Interesses de Angola, or Movement for the Defence of the Interests of Angola) or the NTOBAKO, for instance. In fact, one of the first precepts instituted by Simão Toko, while still in Leopoldville, was precisely the principle of non-participation in any political or military organization (see Grenfell 1998: 220–221). In any case, the Tokoists would eventually pay a heavy toll for living up to this principle. For instance, most of the *colonos* who lived in the Vale do Loge fled to the Congo after being persecuted by both the Portuguese authorities and the UPA, who apparently sought, sequestered and tortured many of their members (report by Simão Toko on his trip to Northern Angola, 2 August 1962; Agostinho n.d.: 142).

From this perspective, Toko's libertarian project, although interpreted as 'political' in the ideological sense, was not, in reality, partisan. The leader of NTOBAKO, Angelino Alberto, who visited the UN on a diplomatic mission, wrote to Toko (5 December 1962) and explained how certain diplomats in New York inquired about his relationship with the MDIA (Movimento de Defesa dos Interesses de Angola), and how he was unable to respond assertively. The MDIA, in fact, had lobbied for Toko's liberation from the detention in the Baía dos Tigres, and also publicly intervened against his being used as an 'instrument of the Portuguese propaganda' in the policy of returning Angolan expatriates (*Le Progrès*, 8 September 1962). However, Toko never publicly assumed an approximation or identification with the movement.

Today, however, this ambiguity plays differently in the memories of many Tokoists, living in postcolonial and post-war Angola. For many, the church did in fact play a pivotal role in Angola's political liberation (Agostinho n.d.: 142), and what seemed to be contradictory at the time eventually developed into a stabilizing remembrance:

> Concerning the church's contribution to the country's liberation, our contribution, well, as we said, our church is spiritual. Therefore, our struggle was also spiritual, to open man's consciousness, that his goal is to be free. It is from this perspective that the church contributed. And surely it was for this same reason that the governments, both Belgian and Portuguese, understood that we were political. Although our politics is not one of weapons; rather, we contributed spiritually to open the consciousness of the Angolan, but also the African man's consciousness, so they know that man must not remain in darkness and obscurantism.... Even the politicians will testify that we did not fight with weapons, but nevertheless we participated. Our participation was not with guns, but spiritually, against the Portuguese and Belgian governments.
>
> Lamentations by Jeremiah, number 5. We start at verse 1: 'Remember, Lord, what has happened to us; look, and see our disgrace. Our inheritance has been turned over to strangers, our homes to foreigners. We have become fatherless, our mothers are widows. We must buy the water we drink; our wood can be had only at a price. Those who pursue us are at our heels; we are weary and find no rest.' These are some of the prayers that were made at the time, summoning for spiritual liberation. (Interview Doze Mais Velhos, 19 October 2008)

Thus, despite the difficulties and misunderstandings, we observe, through the strategies of resistance, the ad hoc reflection of a process of intellectual identification between emancipatory projects that nevertheless drastically diverged in terms of form and method. From this perspective, the role of the Tokoists in the formation of Angolan nationalism was one of 'epistemological rupture', proposing an alternative vision of Africa and Angola that aligned, as Georges Balandier would portrait for the case of Kimbanguism a decade earlier, with the libertarian consciousness in formation in the 1950s and 1960s.

Azores, 1963–1974: A Remote Leadership

After the partially failed attempt to use Simão Toko to peacefully demobilize the 'natives' in their natal region, the Portuguese authorities,

doubting the sincerity of Toko's interventions and progressively convinced of the destabilizing potential of his figure in Angola,[26] decide for
a more radical strategy: in 1963, they send the leader to a new period
of forced exile, this time to an even more remote and symbolically distant place: a lighthouse in the Ferraria de Ginetes, on the westernmost
point of the Island of São Miguel in the Azores archipelago, in the
North Atlantic, several thousand kilometres away from Angola. At 1:30
PM of Thursday, 18 July 1963, Toko embarked at the Luanda airport,
on an airplane of the FAP (Portuguese Air Force), in the company of
his wife, his two daughters and nephew João, and a young *nacional
mestiça* (Angolan mestizo) girl called Maria de Fátima Cruz, fostered
by Toko. After a brief sojourn in Lisbon, Toko is fixated on the Ginetes
lighthouse, where once again he would work as assistant.

Apart from a strategic motivation,[27] there is in this decision led by
the PIDE an implicit 'phenomenology of remoteness', based on the
expectation that the distance, determined by the Atlantic space, and
which intermediated between the leader and his followers, would be
in some way insurmountable. There was also, on behalf of the Tokoists
themselves, an associated phenomenology, connected to the fact that
their leader was taken to the 'heart of darkness', i.e. the centre of the
oppressive metropolis. Not that the dialectics did not exist previously:

Illustration 8. The lighthouse in Ferraria de Ginetes, Azores, December 2012.
Photo: Simão Vemba.

as he headed towards Portugal, Toko affirmed that he would go 'see what António Salazar wanted. He was a *macaco velho* [an "old monkey"] and would not let himself be fooled' (PIDE information, 27 July 1963). But another rumour also marked the perception of these moments: it is told that, when Toko was flown in the airplane in Portugal, the agents intended to make him disappear in a 'death flight':

> In fact, a special team had been prepared to command the plane that, leaving from Lisbon, would pretend to head towards the island of the Azores – when in fact the intentions were other. And so it was that, when the airplane over flew the high sea, the team proceeded to fulfil Salazar's command, and try to through our Dirigente to see from the airplane. Calm and serene, Our Leader looked up towards the sky and prayed to God. Suddenly, and to the amazement of the flight crew, the airplane stood suspended on the air. It would not go forward nor backwards. (Quibeta n.d.: 50)

However, despite the fact that at the time several rumours circulated that the prophet had been murdered (information, Maquela do Zombo outpost, 16 December 1963), this narrative only emerged several years after this date. In those days, most Tokoists were convinced that the prophet's absence would be a matter of months (PIDE information, 1 August 1963). In this particular context, in the months that immediately followed Toko's departure to Portugal, the relationship between the Portuguese authorities and the church appeared, somewhat surprisingly, to be of cordiality and cooperation. In Luanda in particular, several movements of approximation, led by the council of elders that remained as interlocutors,[28] were reported. Namely, negotiations with a cultural association connected to the government, the ANANGOLA (Associação dos Naturais de Angola, or Association of the Angolan-born), as well as the project of the Luanda City Council to build a new neighbourhood just for the Tokoists (PIDE information, 22 April 1964). In a letter written to the prophet, the leaders of the four classes in Luanda sustained that 'the Government is taking good care of us, both young and elders are being well kept' (letter, 2 April 1964). In the end of 1963, a group of approximately 1200 Tokoists participates, with their hymns, in the reception of the president of the Portuguese Republic, Américo Tomás, in his visit to Angola (PIDE information, 25 April 1964).

But once again, simultaneous to this cordiality, the intelligence services did not cease to cultivate suspicion regarding the Tokoists, namely concerning the hypothetical existence of militarized organizations inside the movement (SCCIA confidential report, 5 March 1964).

In the subsequent years, while the military conflict grew in Angola, the measures of the PIDE concerning the movement also increased in intensity and violence, with the radicalization of surveillance and coercion measures, namely the prohibition of collective meetings and public manifestations of the 'sect'. In October 1965, a dispatch signed by the general governor of Angola (Silvino Silvério Marques) is released, by which all 'official' contact with church representatives is forbidden, as well as any public manifestation on behalf of the church; also, measures of prison and residence fixation of the movement's highest-ranking representatives are renewed (PIDE report, 8 May 1966). In reaction to these measures of renewed persecution, the Tokoist movement reorganizes: they start to promote meetings in *sucursais* (branch offices), small groups of under ten believers that would convene in private homes and designate a representative who would maintain the secret contacts with the movement's central apparatus (Agostinho n.d.: 133).

In the meantime, as the exile begins to extend through time, a 'postal leadership' of sorts emerges on behalf of Simão Toko, who begins to exchange letters on a daily basis with his co-religionists. This exchange, as we saw above, had already begun in the Ponta Albina, through the group of believers that were fixated in Porto Alexandre, and to whom Toko sent and received letters through the most diverse methods (see next chapter). However, it would be in the Azores where this postal leadership would gain expression, where the prophet would receive up to twelve letters per day. Working in day and night shifts in the lighthouse, with his wife Rosa bedridden with her illness and their children in boarding schools in the island's capital, Ponta Delgada, Simão would spend his free time reading and attempting to reply to all the letters that arrived. This occurred at great personal and financial cost, given the meagre salary he received as lighthouse assistant, and the expenses in stamps and stationery involved.[29]

Simultaneously, back in the neighbourhoods of Luanda, Benguela, Moçâmedes and other sites of Tokoist meetings in Angola, his epistles were read out loud to the believers, who absorbed and interpreted their content. In these letters, which counted up to the thousands, a wealth of themes and topics can be discerned: from sermons to readings and biblical reflections to management instructions and other, more personal exchanges. As I will describe in the next chapter, this exchange reverberated into a particular style of leadership that affected several dimensions of the church life and experience.

In any case, in those letters, one can observe a growingly explicit discourse that took Portugal as a comparative framework, namely in what concerned Catholicism and the comparisons Toko established with his movement. In several letters, he would comment on the readings he made of Catholic books or diverse news and events, such as the legacy of the apparitions in Fátima (1917) and the prophecies of Sister Lucia (letter, 27 January 1971; 10 March 1971). From this perspective, we can see how, little by little, the Tokoist doctrine was itself reconstructed around a debate that no longer had the 'white missionary church' as its main counterpoint reference, but also, and more so, a European, Catholic Church.

But also, as became evident in a letter written on 21 November 1964 to the leaders in Luanda, Toko was conscious that his letters (or most of them) were intercepted and read by the PIDE. Thus, the letters were the crux of a dialectics of occultation and revelation, where the Tokoists sought to exchange information, knowledgeable that most of the letters were read by a third party (that copied and translated them if necessary), and where the PIDE sought to 'decode' the eventually implicit meanings they contained – especially in what concerned the reference to biblical passages quoted in the letters, which were allegedly of subversive nature. This postal cat-and-mouse game went to such an extent where it was suggested, already in 1956, that the police itself should produce 'Tokoist letters' with misinformation, in order to provoke misunderstanding and dissent among the believers (Moçâmedes governor report, 26 July 1956).

Police repression notwithstanding, this remote leadership would be performed with several difficulties. Besides the personal and familial problems he had to struggle with in the years that followed, Toko also had to deal with dissent, disputes and attempted coups d'états within the movement, where several different groups and sensibilities began to contest his figure and suggest a new leadership based in Luanda, under the pretext that Toko would never return to the country. In the years that immediately followed his departure to the Azores, several complaints began to accumulate in the believers' letters to the Azores, regarding misunderstandings within the *cúpula* or council designated to lead the movement in Angola during the exile. The literature produced in this period revealed recurring problems: accusations of poor financial management, of collaborationism with the colonial regime and, in sum, the recognition of an absence of a strong leadership. The team that remained in Luanda begins to be internally contested. Luvualo David, Lando André and Panzo Filemón are eventually expelled from the church by the elder leaders of the four classes and tabernacles, invoking the 'law of the church' and under the accusation of acting 'diabolically' in the exercise of their jobs (letter from the Church in Luanda to Simão Toko, 12 March 1964; 15 March 1964).

Eventually, in response to such movements, Toko would promote a 'plan for the betterment and reform of the religious service to be introduced in the church', but it does not succeed in calming the environment (letter by Simão Cossi and Sebastião Pedro to Simão Toko, 8 April 1966). In the following year, the problems continue, and many Tokoists from Luanda write to the prophet declaring that they are leaving the movement. Mwanga Pedro, a Tokoist that had also been in Moçâmedes when Toko was exiled in the Ponta Albina and eventually became one of the leaders in Luanda, is also accused, in a meeting held by the main representatives on 3 August 1966, of being a 'snitch' and of trying to negotiate a collaborationist Tokoist leadership with the Portuguese authorities (letter by Dongala David and António Lopes to Simão Toko, 3 August 1966). The meeting where this accusation took place eventually ended up in heated discussions and physical confrontation between the Tokoists, and subsequently with the invasion of the police, who arrested several Tokoists and kept all the 'charity collected at the church's door' (ibid.; PIDE report, 4 August 1966).

The Portuguese authorities, knowledgeable of these fragmentations and taking advantage of the public disorder they caused, decided to radicalize their actions on the Tokoists that eventually led to the governor's dispatch of October 1965: in February, they promulgate the prohibition of public acts in the Tokoist nucleus in Luanda; in August, they proceed to the prison of the 'main ringleaders of the sect' in Benguela; and finally, after the dispatch, the announcement of the prohibition of any form of Tokoist reunion in Luanda (dispatch of the Office of Political Affairs, 11 July 1967).

In reaction to these events, in December 1966 Toko would write a letter to the council of elders in Luanda, with the following statement:

> In 1963, last year of my stay in Luanda, I had registered in my notes seven thousand Tokoists in Luanda alone, and adding those of north and south of the Province of Luanda, that would make forty thousand in total, not counting those who just attended the services. But that number has decreased, many Tokoists have chosen and found their path to eternal life, mocking Tokoism and saying that the Word we teach is not true. Very well, then have a nice trip.... The individual is free, and no one can withdraw his desires. In the meantime, I would like to draw the attention to the brothers who were with me in the former Belgian Congo in 1943–1949, remind them of what happened in that moment of time, because many of them seem to have forgotten the Word of God they received through the power of the Holy Ghost and which the world does not receive because they are not letting the younger Tokoists, who never knew how Tokoism was born, know how it was so. (Letter by Simão Toko to the Leadership in Angola, December 1966)

This letter, transcribed and copied by the PIDE delegation in Angola, was entitled 'Letter of warning for the closure of the Church of Christ led by the Tokoists'. In it, Toko orders that the church stop proselytizing and teaching the Bible, and that they begin to work through 'witness':

> Stop with Tokoism, do not teach it any more!! The stones have cried out.[30] Man is free, the Tokoists who wish to return to their primitive religions may do so, and those who were witches likewise, they may return to their primitive course. Those who do not want to go back, send them these chapters. Start reading, examining and studying them, and it would be best if you could understand them (Letter, December 1966).

Here we implicitly understand that what seems to be at stake is one of the consequences of the church's ethnic and generational transcendence in the previous decade. Several divisions are produced between different generations of Tokoists: those (the Zombos) who had come with the prophet from Leopoldville and installed themselves mostly in the valleys of the Uíge, and the new generations of Tokoists that would adhere in the locations further south. In fact, one of the recurrent issues in the letters of complaint that Toko would receive was related to the fact that the elders of Maquela do Zombo who had been expelled from the Congo were assuming that only they had the authority to lead the church.

At the same time, reports of problems of cohabitation between the different groups of inhabitants of Taia Nova were revealed, namely between older and newer residents (letter by the Church in Luanda to Simão Toko, 7 January 1964), and between those who had lived in the premises and those who had returned to Angola after fleeing from the Vale do Loge (interview Doze Mais Velhos, 7 April 2011). A few months before the previous letter, Toko had already complained about the letters he was receiving:

> If we divided those 1500 or so letters in three parts, only one part contains only good news; the two remaining parts only contain complaints, confusions, separations, envy, etc. Do they think that because they received the word of God in the Congo they are already going to heaven? They are wrong. When I was with you in Luanda, I never rejected anyone, I loved you all, even though I did not visit all your houses, they were too many. All this, my sons, deeply saddens me! (Letter by Simão Toko to various readers, 10 April 1966)

The arrival of the letter of closure to Luanda, where it was profusely copied and publicized within the Tokoist circles, eventually increased

the divisions between the Tokoists of that city. On a report signed by
Subinspector Pottier of the Luanda delegation of the PIDE in 1967, it
was suggested that that same letter may have provoked the division
between those who subordinated to the prophet's command and those
who contested it, moving towards a 'politico-subversive activity' (PIDE
Report, 29 July 1967). Here, we acknowledge how, in this late colonial
'situation' (Balandier 1963 [1955]), there was not one but several 'Toko-
isms' that reacted diversely – with a varying degree of politization – to
the PIDE repression and also to the physical absence of their leader.

However, in another report concerning a research on the 'subversive
activities of the Tokoist sect', it was recognized that

> demonstrating an extraordinarily solidary spirit, all individuals called
> for interrogation ... revealed a concern for withholding the names of the
> people really in charge, and were willing to face any ordeal in order to
> avoid the possibility of finding out the truth, often assuming responsi-
> bilities that were not of their incumbency, with the obvious intention of
> making our investigation more difficult. (PIDE report, 20 July 1967)

From this perspective, despite the notorious internal dissent, the
movements observed do not ultimately provoke the disintegration of
the movement, and Toko remains as leader of the church that is in any
case willing to resist Portuguese oppression. But this does not mean
that suffering did not continue in the heart of the Toko family. Adding
to his wife Rosa Maria's irreversible mental disease, Simão observes
how his children progressively distance themselves from their father.
In letters exchanged with followers in Taia Nova, Toko revealed his sadness with the way his children, educated in Portuguese schools, had
catolicado (Catholicized) and began believing that his church was 'fake'
(letter by Simão Toko to Inês Geraldes, 5 April 1973).[31]

Around this time, Toko's body also began to pay a toll for all the
suffering. One particularly striking episode that is frequently invoked
by the Tokoists takes place at the end of 1973, when Toko fell ill with
a cardiovascular episode and was interned in the hospital of Ponta
Delgada for urgent heart surgery. According to many Tokoists, during
the procedure, the doctors removed Simão Toko's heart from his body,
with the objective of putting an end to his life. However, despite being
heartless, he opened his eyes and demanded that his heart be put back
in his body (Agostinho n.d.: 71; Quibeta n.d.: 52–53; on this see also
Kisela 2004: 191–200).

Several years later, an interview conducted by Kisela with the sur-
geon that operated on Toko provided a medical explanation for the
events (2004: 190–199). However, the rumour persists to this day, of-

ten presented as a fact that is
illustrative of the processes of
bodily suffering and spiritual
resistance that were invested in
Toko's figure. In this regard, the
available images of Toko from
the days of exile became powerful objects of rumour, argumen-
tation and political discourse.
A similar effect happened with
another famous picture, where
Toko appears at the doorstep
of the lighthouse, dressed in
working uniform and flanked
by two other local workers who
appear to be some sort of security officers (Kisela, personal
communication). This was often referred to as an example
of how Toko lived in constant
vigilance and constraint.

Illustration 9. Toko revealing his scar
after suffering heart surgery, 1974.
Source: Melo (2002).

Luanda, 1974–1984: The Return of a Man of Peace

With the evolution of the socio-political events, both in Portugal in
Angola, the situation of the Tokoist church slowly begins to change.
After the deposition of the Estado Novo regime on 25 April of 1974, the
political situation in the Portuguese provinces also suffered a drastic
turn. In Angola, the developments would lead to the declaration of the
territory's independence in November 1975, after the entry in office on
behalf of the last acting general governor of Angola for the period of
transition, Admiral Rosa Coutinho, in substitution of General Silvino
Silvério Marques.[32] In the meantime, the Angolan delegation of the
PIDE, which began a period of 'service extinction', replaces the preventive and proactive activities with one of observation, limiting their
action to the collection of information and producing internal reports
to the central services, before being dissolved and integrated in the
Military Information Police (Mateus 2004: 457).

Thus, persecution to indigenous religious movements like the Tokoist Church fell from the Portuguese authorities' list of priorities.
Toko's movement would finally be recognized in a dispatch signed by

Rosa Coutinho, on behalf of the Portuguese government, who authorizes public services and communicates this decision personally to the
leader (Agostinho n.d.: 74). The diligences to authorize the return of
the *mais velho* (older one) to Luanda begin. A delegation of the MDIA
travels to Lisbon to meet António de Spínola and officially request his
return (*O Comércio*, 24 May 1974; *Diário de Luanda*, 4 June 1974).

Finally, the authorization is granted, and Toko prepares his move
back to Luanda. He leaves the lighthouse and stays at João Sivi's house
in Ponta Delgada, waiting for his daughter Ilda to finish the school
term and finally embark (*Diário de Luanda*, 14 June 1974). At eight
o'clock in the morning of 31 August 1974, a cloudy day, the ship 'In-
fante Dom Henrique' arrives at the Luanda Maritime Station and Toko
steps down to a roaring crowd. The return of 'old Simão' is grand,
involving the whole city of Luanda. The evening newspapers of that
day mention the 'triumphant return', the 'enthusiastic reception to the
religious leader' and the 'spectacular procession' that crossed the city
on this occasion (*Diário de Luanda*, 31 August 1974). The procession
strolls past the *baixa* (downtown) of Luanda and heads to the old São
Paulo neighbourhood. Toko leads the committee on foot and, once arrived at São Paulo, a public religious ceremony is performed in which
he takes the word and summons for peace among all men (ibid.). The
newspaper *Província de Angola* announces his return in the front page,
describing the prophet as 'a man, an idea, an open heart: an example
of solidarity and civic behavior, orderly welcomed within the people' (1
September 1974). In another newspaper, he would be quoted as rejecting violence and armed struggle (*Diário de Luanda*, 2 September 1974).
The fact that he performed the procession on foot, as he would explain
on the occasion, was also a challenge to the rumours that indicated
that, as soon as he arrived to Luanda, 'the white men would kill him'
(ibid.).

Shortly after, Toko would meet Rosa Coutinho, who remembered:

> He was a man whom I welcomed with great pleasure on the very day he
> arrived at Luanda, after eleven years in exile, determined by the fascist
> regime that governed Portugal – who, for some reason, thought that the
> Tokoist Church's activities in Angola were harmful. Hence the abusive
> extradition to the Azores, where he spent a lot of time, in a lighthouse
> whose name I can't remember any more. When he arrived at Luanda,
> once his return was authorized (as was expected with any Angolan citi-
> zen), there were no longer exiled or political prisoners, and therefore I
> was glad to meet him. And he was a person who left a strong impression
> in me, with his idea to contribute to peace in Angola, and mainly because
> he explicitly affirmed that he did not want to be involved in any activities

Illustration 10. Return of Simão Toko to Angola. Província de Angola, 1 September 1974. *Source:* 'Tocoismo' PT/TT/PIDE-DA-C-1-1546/1. Image reproduction authorized by ANTT.

of political nature. It was, so to speak, a peaceful and dignifying presence. (in Vida e Obra de Simão Toco, 1997)

A few days later, Toko would affirm, in a public meeting with his followers, that the church would be open to 'all races and ethnicities that

would want to attend it', and that weapons 'had no room' inside, con-
demning violent acts of any nature (GEI-Luanda confidential report,
13 September 1974). This anti-belligerent and ecumenical posture
would become a trademark in Toko's public interventions thereafter.
Just before leaving Portugal, he would declare: 'As a Christian, I always
follow what the Bible says. So to me, black or white, we are all brothers. There are only brothers in this world. No whites or blacks. That's
how God determined it.... I cannot see people by the colour of their
skin. That would be to deny the word of God' (*Diário de Luanda*, 29
August 1974).

At the same time, and while the attempts between the historical
leaders of the Angolan liberation struggle to achieve the formation of
the first independent Angolan government failed,[33] Toko issued several statements where he appealed to the unity of the Angolans: 'The
difficulties are tremendous. Our Angolan brothers are divided. It so
happens that many have not yet heard the voice of God, who says that
the guns must be deposed, so we can all united built a fraternal Angola' (*Diário de Luanda*, 29 August 1974). By this time, he had already
prophesied to the political leaders: 'if you don't come to terms, there
will be lakes of blood and rivers of tears in the eyes of the sons of this
good and beautiful Angola' (Agostinho n.d.: 79). In remembrance of
this moment, I was told one day at the church in Lisbon that when
Simão Toko returned from the Azores, in a well-remembered reunion,
he grabbed a stick and broke it; then, he picked a handful of sticks and
tried the same, but the sticks did not break. With this, he wanted to
demonstrate that unity was the only path for salvation – both for the
church and for the country.[34]

These statements reveal the progressive politico-partisan consciousness on behalf of the prophet, who despite his anti-partisan ideology
decides to assume a more active and interventive public role – which,
again, reinstated the debate in the Portuguese police regarding his effective involvement in the process of independentization (PIDE report,
26 November 1974). Upon his arrival to Luanda, he had been escorted
by elements of the PCDA (Partido Cristão Democrático de Angola, or
Christian Democratic Party of Angola), who in turn were lobbying for
the restitution of the wealth confiscated by the regime deposed on 25
April.[35] The PIDE correspondence suggests that he may have been
thinking of forming a political party (GEI report, 7 September 1974).
Soon later, a piece is published in the local newspapers with a message from the MPLA leader, Agostinho Neto, for Simão Toko, where
he would state:

Dear compatriot, although I haven't seen you since our school days, I have not ignored your nationalist activity and your sacrifice for our country. Today, I am very happy to know you are back in Angola. In this crucial moment of our national existence, where the fate of our country is played, I hope that your patriotic lucidity will keep directing many of our compatriots to the paths of Freedom, Independence and Progress, paths that we too pursue. (Província de Angola, 19 October 1974)

Simultaneously, the prophet decides to establish a platform of dialogue between the different political parties involved, acting as 'promoter of peace' (Kisela 2004: 220). In November of that same year, Toko holds an interview in Kinshasa with Holden Roberto, who had invited Jonas Savimbi for a reconciliation ceremony. A short time later, he will travel to Luena (Moxico) and meet once again with Savimbi and the UNITA. On that occasion, a crowd waited in the airport, and escorted him to the hotel where the meeting would take place; there, Toko would enhance his plea for a pacific posture, favourable to the Angola interests (Rebello 2009). The leader of the Galo Negro, according to the Tokoists, accepted the challenge (interview Doze Mais Velhos, 19 October 2008). Soon later, the leaders of the three parties convene in Mombasa, Kenya, before signing the Alvor Agreements in January 1965, which would provoke the transition towards independency and also the confirmation of the civil war that would mark the following decades in Angola (Messiant 2008).

Thus, in parallel with the appeals for peace and union among the Angolans, Toko also bore a political consciousness, exemplified in his will to actively participate in the negotiations for the formation of the first independent government in the country. However, Agostinho Neto's reaction to Toko's conciliatory initiative is indicative of what would happen next. According to some Tokoists, when Toko approached Neto, his reply was explicit: 'Each one to his own path. You have your way, and I have mine, so no one should interfere in each other's path' (interview Doze Mais Velhos, 19 October 2008). Despite their common past in 1930s Luanda, a breach opened between both leaders.

But here we also see the persistence of the ambiguity associated to Toko's position vis-à-vis Angolan nationalism. On the one hand, we devise the memory of the apolitical and pacifist posture of the Tokoists, a desire that emerged since the early 1960s. On the other, we observe the initiative to promote peace among the different political sectors of Angolan society. In the years that followed, this ambiguity would play against Toko himself, adding new episodes to his history of suffering. In the first days of July 1975, Toko's house in the Congolenses (see il-

lustration 1) is assaulted in the middle of the night by soldiers associated to the FAPLA (MPLA's military branch), who steal his car, several
documents and threaten to kill him (*Jornal de Angola,* 2 July 1975, in
Kisela 2004: 228–232).

   Despite these events, on 25 July (in the celebration of the twenty-
sixth anniversary of the descent of the Holy Ghost in Leopoldville), the
Tokoists celebrate a multitudinous religious service in the Buco-Zau
Street, block number 6, house number 156 of Luanda's Bairro Popular
number 2. The leader spoke to the approximately fifty thousand believers that followed the service in the streets and balconies of the neighbouring apartments. Representatives of Tokoist churches from north
to south of Angola flocked to the city to witness the event. Throughout the service, some of those present were *actuados* (acted) by spirits
and entered trance states, being escorted to the enclosed tabernacles.[36]
Thus, this was the confirmation of the Tokoist Church as national phenomenon, transversal to Angolan society.

   But this unified conception of the church did not match, so to speak,
the fractioned political environment of 1970s Angola, marked by the
ethnicization of the partisan allegiances in formation at the time.[37] In
other words, one project of peace, union and ethnic transcendence opposed to another of conflict, division and ethnic distinction. In several
sectors, a generalized mistrust regarding Tokoism's motivations and
allegiances, still very much connected from the outside to FNLA's Bakongo circumscription (Grenfell 1998: 222 and ff.), persisted. On 22
June 1976, the church's Central Tabernacle in Luanda was destroyed
by a group of soldiers, presumably connected to the ODP (Organização
de Defesa Popular, or Popular Defense Organization) and who would
once again pillage the prophet's home. Toko is forced to flee and takes
refuge in the Bairro Indígena (Agostinho n.d.: 80). In that same month,
the OMA (Organização das Mulheres Angolanas, or Organization of
Angolan Women) organizes a massive rally, summoning the Angolan
government to arrest and sanction the members of the Tokoist, Kimbanguist and Jehova's Witness churches (Grenfell 1998: 222).[38]

   The mismatch between religious and political projects was highlighted in one of the main points of contention between Toko and
Neto – in the meantime confirmed as first president of Angola – related with the 'loyalty' of the church to the state. After instating the
obligatory military service, the MPLA pressured Toko to 'give men'
to this party's troops. However, Toko declined, arguing that he would
never command 'brothers to fight brothers' (interview Doze Mais Velhos, 19 October 2008). As a result, the leader would spend up to four-
teen months between arrests, clandestinity and refuge. 'So the prisons

began on June 22nd, 1976, and did not end until 1979, on January 31st. They would come for him, take him to prison for one week and then bring him back; fifteen days later, they would come again for the same thing, and so on … until 1979' (interview Doze Mais Velhos, 19 October 2008).

On 20 July 1976, Toko would perform his last public service in the Bairro Popular, before 'disappearing' from public sight during one and a half years – taking refuge in a place graphically known as *o buraco* (the hole), somewhere in the Terra Nova neighbourhood, although its exact location remains a secret to this day for many Tokoists (interview Doze Mais Velhos, 19 October 2008; Agostinho n.d.). After reappearing, and until September 1979, when Agostinho Neto passes away and the Angolan government is handed to José Eduardo dos Santos, Toko's life will be punctuated by constant visits to the local police quarters. For months, in a period known among the Tokoists as the 'second prisons' of the prophet, Toko entered and left jail up to seventeen times. In 1979, when he leaves his last imprisonment, he made a public appeal that never again would a Tokoist be arrested on accounts of his religious beliefs (interview Doze Mais Velhos, 12 April 2011). Although no one was aware of that at the time, this was the beginning of a farewell.

(De)conjugating Anticolonialisms and Nationalisms

Toko's trajectory in the process of decolonization and liberation was, as we have seen, composed of ambiguities and suffering, determined by two concomitant processes of clandestine institutional growth and ethnic transcendences. This represented simultaneously a move away from an initial territorial circumscription (Bakongo) and an entry into a lusophone, Atlantic landscape where ideologies of empire and nation were being disputed amidst the Angolan liberation war.

One could affirm that Tokoism was able to see simultaneously both sides of the same coin. The very thing that made the movement attractive for many Angolans in the 1950s and 1960s seems to have been the 'modernity' of their project, which combined the ideologies of liberation, emancipation and (spiritual) growth; this was often seen as a print copy of another 'modernity' – that of Angolan nationalism, urban, educated and of Marxist inspiration (Wheeler and Pelissier 1971: 161–162; Chabal 2002). However, it was also and simultaneously connoted with other, ethno-nationalist (i.e. Bakongo) forms of resistance and struggle (ibid.). But Toko's experience in 1950s and 1960s soon became one of transcendence of this ethno-nationalism.

In this regard, the particularly violent way Toko and the Tokoists were persecuted during the last decades of the colonial period became, somewhat ironically, a fertile soil for the identification between this resistant, 'martyr church' and the grassroots movements that later evolved into politico-military endeavors. Today, as we saw, despite the contradictions that were observed at the time, Tokoism is highlighted for its resistance and is often displayed as a spiritual, intellectual version of the liberation struggle. 'Our struggle was also spiritual, to open man's consciousness, that his goal is to be free.... Although our politics is not one of weapons; rather, we contributed spiritually to open the consciousness of the Angolans', the Doze leaders had told me (19 October 2008).

However, as we saw, despite the coincidence of libertarian ideologies, the paths observed by the different actors were diverse if not contrary. The ambiguity and mixed messages surrounding Toko's public interventions during the colonial strife reveal that his preoccupations were guided by a particular sense of leadership and public intervention that ultimately revealed itself as incompatible with the other expressions of Angolan nationalism. Furthermore, once the prophecy – Angolan independence and African liberation – became present, what surfaced were in fact the differences between both: spiritualism versus atheism, pacifism versus bellicosity, ethno-nationalism versus ethnic ecumenism, etc. Furthermore, one cannot ignore that Tokoism, or partisan independentism, was part of a plural, vibrant political scenery that produced diverse and often confronting utopias and paths for independency (Rocha 2003). In this regard, as Michel Cahen rightly points out regarding the Mozambique case (2006), it is necessary to distinguish between sentiments of 'anticolonialism' and 'nationalism' in the analysis of agencies and motivations in this particular historical period. If these converge in a direct way in the case of associations such as MPLA or FNLA, in the case of Tokoism the conjugation played quite differently, progressively inserted within a temporal, messianic ideology that bound the multi-ethnic Angolan nation with Christian faith in a peaceful society – a message that would not be welcome during the first years of Angolan independence.

From this perspective, Toko's progressive politization also revealed a process of 'prophetization' of Angolan politics, through its insertion into theologies of peaceful resistance and future spiritual unity. Despite the fact that he bore a charismatic, messianic message of African liberation since the first days in Leopoldville – thus adequately responding to what Balandier described as the conjugation of prophetism and political consciousness (1953) – Toko's entry into the

Angolan scene produced a narrative of 'opening-up of history' (Lowy 2005), i.e. the detection of possibilities of societal transformation and the branching of possibilities. Albeit encumbered by the noise of gunfire, Toko proposed a 'future that exceeds the present' by offering an alternative path to Angolan libertarianism. This was for the most part interpreted by certain sectors as an abdication in favour of the colonialist endeavour (often quite explicitly, as in his statements to the Portuguese media), but actually revealed two major concerns: an argument against the inevitability of armed confrontation; and a preoccupation regarding his own followers, caught between fires. Despite being pushed by the historical circumstances into a dichotomy and dialectics of repression and resistance between colonialists and anticolonialists, Toko and his followers persevered in an alternative path of 'peaceful resistance' (Grenfell 1998). In this regard, the idea of resistance itself became politically agent (Scott 1985, 1990), an autonomist expression of refusal of exogenously imposed government and demographic 'management' and an assumption of other possibilities of societal organization. A 'society against the state' (Clastres 1974), as it were.

Obviously, the outcome of events confirmed, somewhat tragically, the failure of his messianic political project, but also and consequently the confirmation of his most painful apocalyptic prophecies: the river of blood that would inundate Angola after independence. The post-1975 experience took on a tragic tone of prophetic confirmation and accumulated suffering, during the 'second prisons' and the renewed extension of state repression, now on behalf of those with whom he had shared a libertarian ideology. At this point, it became clear that the different nationalisms became incompatible: if Toko's was inclusive and ecumenical, partisan nationalism was ethnic and exclusive. From this particular perspective, Angolan repression became, in many ways, more painful for the Tokoists than Portuguese repression, as it was performed by 'brothers and sisters', and not by 'foreign' colonialists. On the other hand, it also fed into an ethos of martyrdom and providence, which would be determinant in subsequent expressions of political temporalities within the church (see chapter 4).

Notes

1. Attendu que les indigènes originaires de l'Angola, dont les noms suivent, pratiquent et manifestent le désir de continuer à pratiquer les rites d'une doctrine mystico-religieuse hiérarchisée prêchant la venue d'un ordre

nouveau qui sous le règne d'un nouveau Christ, renverserait les autorités et puissances actuelles, pour prendre leur place et faire règner la justice.

2. The PIDE would only be formally constituted in Angola in 1954, in a process that would still need a few years before it became 'effective' (Mateus 2004). Prior to this moment, the security and order was promoted by the PSP (Public Security Police), in collaboration with the Postos de Administração Local (Local Administration Posts), outposts set in each major region and urban conglomeration.

3. This meant that they were not allowed to leave the territories to which they were destined without official authorization. The goal behind this was also to distance each of these detainees from their lands of origin, deterritorializing them.

4. In 1961, when the first military actions of the liberation campaigns took place in this region, the *colonato* was virtually abandoned by the Tokoists, who fled to the *matas* and the Congo in search of refuge.

5. This is currently one of the most contentious moments in Simão Toko's biography, the focus of intense debate within the Tokoist movement. Many versions place this event as taking place in 1935 (Agostinho n.d.: 42–43; Quibeta n.d.: 60–61), despite the fact that reports such as Cunha's (1959) omit any reference to it. I choose to place it in 1950 following the epistles Toko wrote on 31 October and 8 November 1971.

6. Around this time, his first daughter Ilda was born, in the fields of the Huíla region (personal communication, 2011). His second daughter, Esperança, would arrive during his sojourn in the Ponta Albina (Agostinho n.d.: 88). Rosa Maria would also become pregnant of a third child, a boy, who died at birth.

7. Shortly after, on December 1954, Rosa would suffer a mental illness, of which she would never recover until her passing in 2004.

8. Nevertheless, Tokoists also recall that several of their brothers were objects of torture and assassination during this period (Agostinho n.d.: 203, Quibeta n.d.: 53). Here I am referring to the posterior recognition by the PIDE that the measures adopted against the Tokoists had not been effective (PIDE report, 8 May 1965) – which provoked the subsequent adoption more repressive and violent measures against them.

9. Despite these misunderstandings, a few years later Mancoca would return to the Tokoist church.

10. The construction of the Bairro Indígena neighbourhood in the 1950s was part of the colonial government's urban planning strategy to organize the capital's impending growth (see Amaral 1968; Fonte 2007). The group of Tokoists was placed in the neighbouring *cacimba* (lagoon) until the construction was finalized. Today it is still inhabited by the survivors and descendants of this group.

11. In a letter written in 1956 to the pastors in the church, Toko recommended that 'all the children born from now on should use a Portuguese name', and that it was necessary 'that the Portuguese language be well studied' (letter by Simão Toko, 11 August 1956). Although written originally in Kikongo, the letter performs this recommendation in an effort to safeguard a linguistic unity within the movement.

12. Ferreira (2012: 42) suggests that the organizational model according to classes was inspired in the Methodist Episcopal mission in Luanda where Toko had sojourned in the 1930s.

13. Deus visita África / Suas trevas dissipa / Más acções destruirá / Jeová andará / Feitiçaria Elimina / Comércio humano abolirá / Enlace ilícito invalida / Jeová andará.

14. One could say, at a first glance, that Tokoism, as a particular version of a charismatic movement, promoted here a 'complete break with the past' (Meyer 1998). However, as I will describe in subsequent chapters, what was at stake for the Tokoists was an idea of a 'restored' temporality and of a 're-dignified Africa'. Also, as we will see, these accusations of witchcraft would become inherent to Tokoism itself.

15. 'Pela pátria cantaremos, temos nação feliz / Cantaremos o seu louvor / Do valente país / Desfraldando a bandeira / Contra os adversários lutar / Viva, viva a nossa pátria / A vitória marchar' (For the homeland we will sing, we have a happy nation / We will sing its praise / Of the courageous country / Unfurling the flag / Against the adversaries we will fight / Hurray, hurray for our homeland / To victory we march) (interview Doze Mais Velhos, 19 October 2008).

16. The Tokoist symbol would be object of an anthropological study of its symbolic meanings, ordered by the PIDE to André Gonçalves Vieira in 1957 (report, 10 January 1957).

17. At the time, several foreign politicians and journalists denounced this attempt to instrumentalize Toko on behalf of the Portuguese Government (PIDE bulletin of foreign press, 21 September 1962). But Toko was not the only local leader summoned to pacify the region: Angelino Alberto, founder the NTOBAKO (Association of Angolan Bakongo), was also called to collaborate, in May of that same year.

18. Public statements quoted in the newspaper *A Voz* of Moçâmedes, 26 March 1960. This piece was published as a response to a report published a few months earlier in *The Times*, where it was stated that 'an indigenous religious leader had been arrested by the Portuguese authorities in a prisoner camp near the Bié' (*A Voz*, 24 March 1960).

19. Around this time, according to Grenfell, the Luanda media reported that Toko had converted to Catholicism, presenting him as the 'great Catholic mystic' (1998: 220; see also Rego 1970).

20. In the same report, there is also a suspicion that Tokoists and Kimbanguists could be uniting to 'fight the whites'. However, in a posterior internal addendum to the report there is a comment noting the exaggeration behind such suspicions, apparently provoked by the statements of an Italian Catholic priest who was in bad terms with Simão Toko (report Maquela do Zombo Outpost, 7 September 1962).

21. A reaction also described in other colonial contexts (cf. Comaroff 1985; Comaroff and Comaroff 1989, 1991; Kirsch 2008).

22. Here I am referring specifically to the *vaticinios* (predictions) produced by the Tokoists within their spiritual experiences of charisma (see chapter 3).

23. Such events suggest that the 'reservations' with which Toko presented himself publicly were concomitant to private negotiations he held with the

authorities in order to work for the well-being of his followers. From this perspective, the inauguration of the Povo Taia may be seen as a reward for Toko's efforts in calling the Angolans back from the *matas*.

24. There was originally some disagreement concerning the name of the future Tokoist village. Considering that most of the Tokoists who were called to live in the compound were sojourning in the neighbourhing village of Ntaia (which gave name to the commune), it was decided that they would call it Taia or Ntaia Nova ('new Ntaia').

25. Grenfell explores this ambiguity, noting that, during these campaigns, several people observed 'secret signs' on behalf of Toko, denouncing that he was not acting as a 'free agent' (1998: 221).

26. Grenfell reports that Toko used the sudden freedom of movements granted with his trip to the north of Angola and sojourn in Luanda to evangelize and reconnect with his believers, strengthening the following in these regions (1998: 221).

27. 'The purpose of his exit from Angola has as main goal to separate him from his sect and allow us to undertake the repressive actions decided upon, that is to arrest the main leaders and representatives of Tokoism, which should be done very soon' (PIDE information, 16 July 1963).

28. The Council was composed by Luvualo David, Lando André, Mwanga Pedro and Panzo Filemon.

29. In his letters, Toko's complaints regarding this fact were frequent, as well as the constant requests for his followers' understanding, given his incapacity to respond to all of their demands: 'In the last letter I sent to the brothers in Luanda, I informed that, apart from the letters that have been burnt, I have in my drawers around 1500 letters. I have kept them with me, hoping that I will be able to reply someday, but it's a shame, we are poor, needy creatures in this world' (letter by Simão Toko, 25 April 1966).

30. Reference to Luke 19:40.

31. 'In conclusion, the Catholics in their religion they dance, drink, smoke and have all the fun in the world. We the Tokoists, considered liars, do not do what they do. They do that because that's the Church Christ left in their hands' (letter by Simão Toko to Inês Geraldes, 5 April 1973).

32. In what would become a polemic governance for many Angolans and Portuguese, who accused him of association with the Portuguese Communist Party interest in the process of Angolan independentization, Rosa Coutinho would remain in Angola until the signing of the Alvor Agreements (January 1975) between the Portuguese government and the three main liberation movements – FNLA, UNITA and MPLA. He would also be accused of having directed the political transition in favour of the MPLA agenda, which would subsequently evolve into the civil war that lasted until 2002.

33. The months that preceded the effective political independence of Angola (in November 1975) were marked by a growing tension, with the dispute between the three main parties involved in the liberation struggle against the Portuguese regime – and, immediately after their retreat, against the South African armies who attempted an invasion (Messiant 2008).

34. Despite the appeals, not all Tokoists accepted to be part of that strategy. One group, associated with the Taia Nova compound, abandons the church, claiming that the movement should be based on Bakongo tradition (matriarchy, lineage, etc.). This movement would be known as Mboma (see chapter 4).

35. The PCDA had also contributed to the negotiations with the Portuguese government, lobbying for Toko's return to Angola. In July of that year, they had met with General Costa Gomes and António de Spínola (*Diário de Luanda*, 1 August 1974).

36. In *Simão Toco, O Senhor da Paz*, directed by Francisco Rebello (2009).

37. On the problem of Angolan ethno-politics in late colonial and postcolonial Angola, and its convergence into the civil war, see Marcum (1969, 1978), Heywood (1989), Messiant (1994, 1995, 2008), Pereira (1994), Vines (1995), Bittencourt (1999), Brinkman (2003, 2004), Comerford (2003), Melo (2005), Malaquias (2006), Reis (2010), Schubert (2010), and in particular Angolan writer Pepetela's novel *Mayombe* (1980).

38. Evidently, these movements contesting religion were influenced by the prevailing ideological regime in newly independent Angola, self-characterized as Marxist-Leninist, and thus overtly mistrustful of any kind of religious manifestation, understood as a troublesome element in the society. This posture, however, would progressively inflect during dos Santos's governance in the 1980s.

PART II

HERITAGES

CHAPTER 3

Transmission
Word, Action and Mediation

The way in which Simão Toko's life and deeds are reflected in the lives and experiences of the Tokoists does not end in the mere act of remembrance. It is instead an example of abundant history (Orsi 2008), of materialization and substantiation of multiple consciousnesses, memories and historicities through acts of transmission into identifiable stances and practices. One could say, as does Michael Lambek, that the Tokoists carry the weight of the past (2002) on their backs. Not necessarily as a burden, but rather as a testimony of a religious option they have performed. Dressing in white, wearing an eight-pointed star in your lapel, cutting your hair short – everything connects with the biography and memory of the prophet, and is established as a sort of anamnesis (Palmié 2002: 6), a way of turning it 'present' through the invocation of his visions, his affirmations, his authorships. In consequence, one could affirm that for the Tokoists, to learn Tokoism is, in a way, to learn history, to read past events according to Toko's prophetic biography. Thus, a process of mediation is produced where particular practices and technologies are invoked in order to turn both the prophet and the divine 'present', immediate (Eisenlohr 2009; Palmié 2011) in their lives. Or, as Stephan Palmié would say, a 'sacramental technology of transmission' (2011) that temporalizes and 'presentifies', and therefore produces resonances and convergences (Sarró 2008a: 144–145) that make them intelligible today.

This presence becomes all the more necessary when we realize that, throughout the movement's ecclesiastical history, the leader actually spent more time absent than present in the lives of many of his followers. The moments of prison, escape, hiding, exile and finally passing, as well as the historical limitations of both the leader and his followers'

mobility, made the prophet involuntarily remote, distant for many believers throughout time. From this perspective, the invocations we find
today in the church respond to an historical construction of a semiotics that deals with this absence – a response to the 'problem' it poses
in terms of self-conception (Engelke 2007). This turning the prophet
present in their quotidian makes his ideas, words and vital experiences
transcend the past and materialize in the present, rejecting its 'mythi-
fying' potential (Sahlins 1981) by turning it significant and operative in
the here and now. But, as we will see, this will also provoke an invocation of the future through specific conceptualizations of presence and
temporality, configuring 'methods of hope' (Miyazaki 2006).

From this perspective, the letters invoked in the previous chapter
often acted – and still act to this day – as mechanisms of vital approximation between the leader and his followers, especially in the
periods of more extreme absence, in Ponta Albina and the Azores. As I
mentioned, the postal exchange during his sojourn in the Portuguese
islands reached such an extent that it became multitudinous: Toko
would receive dozens of letters per day and, after abdicating hours of
sleep in his attempt to reply to no matter how small a portion of them,
he would walk, almost on a daily basis, to the nearest postal office
– or, during his residence at Ponta Albina, he would deliver them to a
pombo (pidgeon, i.e. courier) for distribution. Frequently, the same envelope, destined to one person owning a PO Box in Luanda, Maquela
do Zombo, Moçâmedes, etc., included letters for several different people, to be delivered by hand. On other occasions, letters were buried in
previously established strategic locations, and later unearthed, copied
several times and manually distributed throughout the colony. In the
opposite direction, believers would often collect money and mail it so
the prophet could buy stamps and stationery.

Many of these letters – perhaps the most of them – referred to Toko
and his followers' private lives. Ordinarily, they would begin with news
concerning the health and well- (or ill-) being of the author and his or
her family. Many believers would share with the prophet their personal,
familial and marital problems – from wedding proposals to family
members or church members going astray, accusations of witchcraft,
etc. – asking the *Pai* (father) for advice concerning how to deal with
them:

> Dear daughter.... Your father sends you a kiss. The world does not want
> to be loved. The Gospel has been preached in the whole world. Christ will
> return like a thief, to fetch the people who really believed in him and to
> give to each what belongs to him. So how are things with your fiancée?

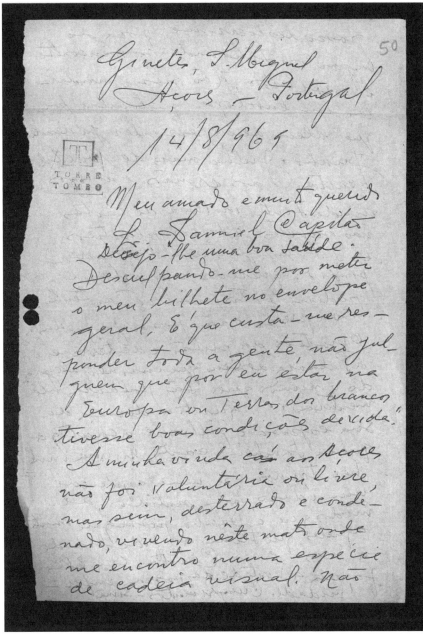

Illustration 11. Fragment of a letter by Simão Toko. *Source:* 'Processo Individual GAB de Simão Toco' PT/TT/PIDE-DA-54009. Image reproduction authorized by ANTT.

> Beware! Be careful with this world! You know what the goshawk does when he wants to catch the dickie bird.... Don't forget that you have the spirit in you. (Letter by Simão Toko, 25 January 1965)

The annexation of photographs to these letters also seemed compulsory.

> My unforgotten brother.... Due to my lack of time, I am not able to share more news with you. I have written a letter to all of you. I send you a small photographic portrait of my own as a souvenir. You can see the other photographs at your brother's house.... These pictures are for all the brothers, so they can remember our faces that disappeared such a long time ago. (Letter by Simão Toko, 18 August 1964)

This concern with the visual aspect of the relationship between leader and followers was, apparently, an initiative of the prophet, who insisted on 'seeing' his flock, knowing and recognizing the faces of the adepts, 'reading their states of mind'.[1] There was, therefore, an intimate, physicalized relationship, which would even end in resentment when one of the interlocutors did not reply to the other.

> If the brothers in Luanda had the patience to transmit my regards to the brothers that live in other lands, they would eventually stop complaining for not receiving my correspondence. However, those in Luanda also have a point, because if they did so they would spend large amounts of money; so I do not know how I can get rid of these complaints. If they understood that I am one person only, perhaps they would rethink their points of view, and would instead complain about not receiving letters from Luanda. (Letter by Simão Toko, 25 April 1966)

In this relationship, Toko would in a way assume a role of progenitor and counsellor, pedagogically offering personal opinions and reflections, and would frame them within the ideology envisaged by his movement. But many of these letters were also collective, redacted for a wider audience, to be read by the whole church in Angola: sermons, biblical lessons, administrative decisions and implementations, and also reprehensions, misunderstandings and attempts to regroup the movement, as we saw in the previous chapter. Therefore, the letters combined public and private transcripts, and fed simultaneously into the readers' and authors' expectations: 'The Tokoists speak about the letters they receive from their leader Simão Toko, letters that are sacred for them, and where he asks them to have faith in the future, relating with biblical events and assuring them he will be back some day!' (PIDE report, 6 October 1966).

In this particular context, this method of approximation – which ultimately developed as an ad hoc reaction to an imposed and uncertain distance – also became a movement of sedimentation and accumulation that progressively fed into the church's structuration and bureaucratization as a religious entity, a process of crystallization through writing, of a spiritually originated wisdom. As Thomas Kirsch notes, the 'spiritual' and 'written' dimensions of religious experience have been often presented as dichotomized (2008); observing from a Weberian perspective, it could be said that the process of religious writing presupposed a form of routinization and bureaucratization that transforms spiritual movements, based on the immediacy of the experience of the divine (Engelke 2004) into collective, complex, formalized entities (see Fabian 1969). But such a categorical distinction does not seem to apply to what we see in the Tokoist church, which was effectively inaugurated in 1949 through the profusion of charisma, but where the writing and postal exchange reveals, apart from the evident institutional complexification, a theology in the making, where there was a constant effort to make sense of the different spiritual experiences.

> Father, the letter you have sent through the church, I have received your comforting words. Father, it is true, as you say in one of the last letters you sent, that everything that is written in the Bible will be fulfilled. Just like in your preachings when you were here with us, what you predicted is being fulfilled. Especially in the chapter you left us just as you were embarking. Acts of the Apostles 20:28.[2] (Letter from João da Costa to Simão Toko, 14 June 1965)

> Father, I know we have never met personally, but through the Spirit we know each other much better than by sight, despite the fact that I am a sinner. Forgive me. (Letter from Afonso Quiala to Simão Toko, 8 April 1973)

We see here a double dimension of writing and action versus expectation that reveals the interplay between the print dimension (the Bible, the document) and the experiential dimension (the interpretation and 'living out' of such documents), which in turn construed a 'semiotic ideology' (Engelke 2004, 2007: 38; Keane 2003, 2007) that became determinative of what it is 'to be a Tokoist' within Christian faith. One example of such a construction was the preparation, directed through several letters written by Toko throughout the years of 1972 and 1973, of a Bible School (called 'Emaús') for the spiritual and theological formation of the younger generations, which provoked the writing of several letters of rejoicing and theological debate. 'I have received the correspondence with ... the Bible study lessons and the book Verbo de

Deus.… I have already finished the exercises, but I'm not sure if the answers are correct. I pleaded, in the love of the Father, Son and Holy Ghost, for help in order to complete these courses. For now, I will wait for the corrections and results' (letter from Virgílio António to Simão Toko, c.1973).

Therefore, much of what is read in these letters is a process of inter-pretation, pedagogy and disciplination led by the *dirigente,* who sought to frame the religious experience within an intellectual, theological binding (see, on this respect, Kirsch 2008). One interesting example of this dynamic happened at the end of 1964, when a group of leaders in Luanda wrote a letter to Toko, asking about prescriptions regarding the consumption of alcoholic beverages. The leader replied:

> I have already sent a letter to the Tokoists that live in Lisbon regarding several questions that many brothers have asked, concerning drinking; because many brothers say that the Bible does not forbid drinking, that people drink in all the other churches, and that I as a leader forbade them. In what concerns religion, you know very well that I have never given an answer without consulting the Bible. (Letter by Simão Toko, 21 November 1964)

> Following the previous letter, I send you this new one so you can copy and distribute.… If by any chance there are brothers and sisters who are not interested in this topic, either because they are not fully understand-ing it, or because they are hypocrites, as far as I'm concerned it is a prob-lem of the utmost importance. The Bible that the Protestant missionaries brought to the natives of Africa, teaching it everywhere, is still studied by many people to this day.… The Tokoists that studied the Bible, and those who are studying it right now, if they understand the importance of this point and want freedom of thought, they are not subject to the law that condemns alcoholic beverages. As founder of Tokoism, I say that, from the moment they receive this letter, Tokoists are free to choose to get rid of all the laws and prescriptions that they feel are harsh and strong.… Choose if you want to remain just or unjust.… We, the sons of this time, must separate things, the ways of living, and must justify our wisdom; we don't go around like atheists. Matthew 11:18–19. (Letter by Simão Toko, 7 December 1964)

This example is revelatory of the pedagogical tone that marked the postal interaction. It is also illustrative of the process of negotiation through which the church experienced a 'self-institution' through stances of discussion, debate and enlightenment – a 'road to clarity', as it were (Keller 2005). This process was, as we see, negotiated through a 'disciplination of experience' that produced the necessary conviction in the believers that followed Toko at a distance, defining its limits and transgressions. Or, in other words, producing orthodoxy (Asad 1993) and delimiting centralities and margins (Cabral 2001). The attempts of secession described in the previous chapter, and the prophet's reaction to them, ultimately revealed this process of distinction between paths of orthodoxy and heterodoxy.

In any case, we can also say that it was through these letters – their writing and public lecture – that the leader's presence 'materialized' before his followers, most of whom had never seen their prophet live. In 1960s and 1970s Luanda, where the biggest Tokoist following was to be found, the religious activities were for the most based on the reading and interpretation of the letters, as well as the collective elaboration of their response. 'Read this letter of mine out loud very slowly; as you listen to it, each one of you will understand that this or that phrase or line is my individual answer to you. Because if I was to write to all of you individually, I would have to do so for three or four days non-stop. Thus, this letter is my reply to all of you' (letter by Simão Toko, 4 January 1964).

Thus, the letters also became a way of preaching – they became sermons. This process of 'becoming' was performed both through the content and the act of reading itself that was incorporated into the liturgy as a modality of sermon, offering multiple locutions (Austin 1963; Tambiah 1985; Keane 2004; Kirsch 2007), both at a verbal and corporal dimension. The written word, therefore, 'materialized' (Engelke 2009) in recognizable acts for the Tokoists, both through speech acts (Harding 2000) and 'listening acts'. Conditioned by the public persecution, Tokoist liturgy was mostly performed clandestinely, in the night and in discrete settings, if not in silent self-communion during the periods of heightened repression. From this perspective, the collective reading of the letters, and their 'ethical listening' (Hirschkind 2006), became a central setting in the way particular ideas and practices were transmitted to the followers. In other words, apart from preaching, the letter also became a habit, a part of the Tokoists' daily life. Today, the letters and photographs, as objects kept and cherished by the believers who still possess them, have acquired a testimonial character, and are invoked as 'proofs' in the different disputes currently observed within the movement. This fact in itself is indicative of the doctrinal weight that this epistolary correspondence acquired through time.

Toko's epistles had (and have) a central role in the church's historical, ideological and existential constitution; they also became a central part of wider mechanisms of diachronic production of experience and religious knowledge for the Tokoists. The whole process of 'institution' and organizational design of the church was, as all processes of bureaucratization, negotiated. That negotiation – and immediatization, shaped into procedures, rules and routines – also becomes explicit in the Tokoist quotidian when we hear about entities and institutions such as the Elders, the Classes, the Tribes, the Sucursais, the Corpo Vate, the Vices, the Cúpula, the Elders and Counselors, the Youth Council, etc. These different entities correspond to the translation of ideologies and directives, expressed through the epistolary exchange and materialized in ecclesiastical bodies, categories, and functions. If, for instance, as we saw before, the Doze Mais Velhos were a product of a nomination by the leader in the first months of the movement's existence in Leopoldville, the appearance of classes and tribes responded to posterior administrative ideologies and needs, dealing with the complexified internal plurality of its demographics after its implantation in Angola, reaching the number of 18 Classes and 16 Tribes (see Agostinho n.d.: 214 and ff.). Other entities would be revealed: the 40 Mancebos (40 Youths, the first group of young Tokoists that was prepared to become preachers with the frequency of the Bible Study course in the 1970s), the 12 Vices (a prayer group created in the same decade), the Anciãos e Conselheiros (Elders and Counselors, an entity resulted from the recognition of such a category of believers, and who had been invested with representation duties when Toko was in the *buraco*), the Direcção Central (Central Directorship) or the '120' (collegial administrative body), the Cúpula (Summit, protocol commission in charge of expedient issues), etc. After Simão Toko passed away in 1984, other consulting or executive entities would emerge from the already complex system of Tokoist organization, action and representation, namely the institution of bishopric (see the next chapter).

In this chapter, I will explore three paradigmatic cases of religious transmission, materialization, construction and disciplination: the calendar, the hymns and the tabernacle. All three constitute the fundamental mainstay, both in terms of liturgical expression and of configuration of a historically informed 'Tokoist way of being' that persists to this day and is socially recognized as distinctive, particular. They also imply a particular form of conceptualizing time (Koselleck 2002) that simultaneously connects the ideology, discourse, experience and expression that are characteristic of Tokoism. They reveal an identification of the past and a conviction regarding the righteousness of the Tokoist path.

However, with this invocation of transmission I am not just referring to the transference of a set of information from one place to the other (Berliner and Sarró 2008), where the 'new Tokoists' would refer to any given manual to assimilate and reproduce a canon. Rather, I am thinking of a dynamic confluence of ideologies and practices, teachings and apprenticeships that contribute (unevenly, if necessary), to the formation of a 'Tokoist posture', imbued with historical consciousness. These apprenticeships are visible, for instance, in the codes of conduct shared within the movement, which involve ways of dressing, eating, behaving, etc., that in a way reflect particular 'persistence cults' (Berliner 2010), i.e. the Tokoists' explicit interest in 'keeping' (by reproducing it) the heritage of their leader's religious trajectory. The transmission therefore occurs in multiple directions and within multiple temporalities, and is also producer of tensions and models in friction (Halloy 2010) – a suggestion that will become more explicit in the next chapter. In any case, it reveals an agency (Lave and Wenger 1991) or consciousness, motivation and capacity processed through agents, mediators and receptors (in the Latourian sense – see Berliner 2010), and especially a mediation, a technology that approximates, immediatizes the relationship between the believer and the divine (Eisenlohr 2009; Palmié 2011).

I am therefore arguing for an historicized 'embodied knowledge' (Scheper-Hughes 1994) where thinking, knowing, feeling and practicing in Tokoist liturgy converge through specific authorizing processes (Asad 1993) negotiated through time and producing recognizable indexicalities and iconicities (Keane 2003; Naumescu 2011). I specifically follow Webb Keane in his proposal of historicizing the materiality of transmission processes through identifiable semiotics and economies of representation (2003, 2007, 2008) and Vlad Naumescu in his argument of considering how particular conceptions of time inform models of religious transmission and respective intentionalities (2011). In the Tokoist case, stances such as commemorating, singing and praying, as expressions of 'embodying temporalities' (Klaver and van de Kamp 2011), are simultaneously the pretext and agent, device and technology of historical knowledge. They are taught and transmitted in the process of 'doing', performing – which is in itself the locus of materialization; they thus configure a 'cognition in practice' (Lave 1988), where the prospective (converted or youth) Tokoist encounters and learns specific temporalities through indexicalities that are presented unto him in the hymnals, calendars and tabernacles.[3]

This encounter and presentation usually takes place in the church liturgical settings, be it in the services or other ritual moments or in specific pedagogical moments such as Sunday school, rehearsals, practices, etc. The familial context also plays a central role, inasmuch as historically it has been through these networks that Tokoism grew and multiplied (Blanes 2011b). But it is also present in acts of commemoration and creativity. One illustration observed in the Tokoist Church is how the Tokoist youths are frequently involved in the creation and performance of poetry or theatre, invariably constructed as a mnemonics of the leader's prophetic biography. I was able to observe many of these moments in specific occasions such as the twenty-fifth of July celebrations, the celebrations of the *Dia da Juventude* (Youth Day) and other important dates.

Organizing Time

On 25 July 2009, I arrived at the municipal pavilion of Odivelas, a suburb north of Lisbon, with a considerable delay to my appointment. A health issue with my partner, at the time pregnant with our second son, led us to an unexpected visit to the hospital. When things calmed down, I ran to the pavilion, where a big celebration was taking place: the sixtieth anniversary of the descent of the Holy Ghost over Simão Gonçalves Toko in Leopoldville. The official ceremony had already finished, but no one seemed to have any plans of leaving the premises. Outside, under the scorching sun, one could smell the improvised roasts out in the back. Once inside, the temperature cooled down, and I saw how the place that minutes before had served as scenery for the liturgical act had been transformed into a giant, improvised refectory, with dozens of plastic tables and chairs spread around the room and where hundreds of people ate, talked and laughed. Near the stage, a group composed by the church representatives and some guests (among which my colleagues Ramon Sarró and Joana Santos, whom I had invited to come along) were chatting away. But the 'real' action was in fact taking place in a side room, where the food (*funge, muamba, kissaka, matete, mufete,* roast meat and other titbits) was being heated and served, with drinks such as sodas and *kisangua* (drink made of fermented corn flower). At the end of the room, a giant anniversary cake green and white birthday cake, populated with candles.

As I walked into the room, I apologized, to those who I encountered and joined the conversation, for my lateness. But they seemed more concerned about my partner's health, and told me that they had prayed for my family and me, wishing us a quick recovery. In any case, we agreed jokingly that at least I had arrived for the 'most important part' – precisely, the food, the drinks and the birthday cake. And in fact, in the months prior to the event I had been keeping up with the complex organization that involved the whole Tokoist community of

Lisbon: the preparatory meetings where tasks were assigned, delays criticized and pragmatic consensus were reached. Closer to the event, the women in the church would cook the delicious dishes that would later be devoured, while the men alternated between more physical and administrative chores. Finally, everything went into place and was carried out according to what was predicted or imagined.

But speaking of food, this wasn't the only time when such delicacies were produced and shared within the community. In fact, there is barely one month of the year that does not include a pretext for a good Tokoist celebration, with guests from the Angolan and Christian communities in Lisbon: from the twenty-fourth of February that celebrates Toko's birth to the Christmas supper celebrated in December and the memory of the 'physical passing' of the prophet on New Year's Eve. From this perspective, the Tokoists' quotidian is intensely and rhythmically punctuated by 'extraordinary', memorial events that provoke pretexts for remembrance and reaffirmation.

> The seventeenth day of April 1935 encloses a very important act in the evangelization of the African continent, the mission of transmitting the message of God according to the Creator's wisdom and will, received by His Holiness the Prophet Simão Gonçalves Toko, and thus contributing towards the awakening of the Africans' consciousness, in particular by teaching them the essence of the Gospel of Christ. If our mission were just a mere adventure, we would not have been able to impose ourselves in the Angolan religious context and elsewhere, and be side by side with the major religions that came from Europe and America. (Speech celebrating the seventy-fourth anniversary of the encounter between Simão Toko and God in Catete; Lisbon, 10 April 2009)[4]

This concern with time and its organization culminates especially in the way the Tokoists structure their dominical services, always following a predefined script that is performed without deviations. One can perceive this in the notorious expressions of discomfort in people's faces when for some reason the established liturgical protocol is breached. When that doesn't happen, the *secretário de serviço* (appointed secretary) announces, at the beginning of every service, the different points in the program:

1. Singing of the opening hymn *Rei do Céu Andará* ('The King of Heaven Shall Walk')
2. Prayer of Our Father
3. Reading of praises in Psalms of David
4. Announcement of the constitution of the Corpo de Mesa (officiating body)

   5. Reception and Farewell to visitors
      5.1. Presentation of visitors
      5.2. Singing of the welcoming hymn
      5.3. Acknowledgement by a representative of the Corpo de Mesa
   6. Offerings
   7. Notices and communications
   8. Choir singing
      8.1. Acknowledgement of the hymns
   9. Sermon performed by the appointed evangelist
  10. Closing of service
      10.1 Singing of the closing hymn *Voluntários de Cristo em Fileira*
          ('Christ's Voluntaries in Rank')
      10.2. Final prayer
(Sunday service, Tokoist Church of Lisbon; see Agostinho n.d.: 211)

The Sunday service, however, is not the only moment that summons the Tokoists for participation: there is a weekly rhythm that occupies the schedules of the believers with administrative meetings, choir rehearsals, counselling and especially other spiritual practice moments, such as the 'intercession' services, the nightly services or tabernacles, or the prayer and fasting meetings.

This structuring reveals a process of temporal disciplination – and of its bodily experience – through the incorporation of a particular Tokoist practical rhythm. But this behavioural regulation also and simultaneously attributes a moral dimension to the idea of discipline (Asad 1993: 62–65), where the individual choice or 'inner motive' (ibid.: 63) implies a conscious and voluntary submission to a prescription and a sense of 'rule' where the management of time appears as pivotal axis. From this perspective, the *protocolo* (protocol, or team of ushers), as an abstract concept and simultaneously a physical entity, is a determinant agent for the establishment and vigilance of conducts, in particular in the liturgical contexts. This concept becomes explicit when one goes through the experience of being a 'visitor' in a Tokoist church, and is compelled to apprehend and understand certain postures, movements and behaviours: how to circulate, where to sit, when you should rise, when to intervene or to be silent, etc.

At this point, one can also perceive the historical process of 'institution' (understood here as a substantive and a verb), the trajectory of transformation from a disperse movement of the spiritual following into an ecclesiastical entity subject to organizations, procedures and bureaucracies, where (individual and collective) time and its organization were linchpin. At least, that seemed to be a central aspect since day one for Toko and his most immediate followers. For instance, a report from 1955 noted that the movement already had an equally intense weekly distribution, ordered by Toko:

Monday: learn doctrine
Tuesday: choir singing, from 8 PM to 9:30 PM
Wednesday: service
Thursday: meeting for the baptized
Friday: idem.
Saturday: service
Sunday: service, two to three times a day
(PIDE report, 5 April 1955)

This calendar intensity was thus imagined by the leader from the very start of his religious trajectory. From very early on (early 1950s) we hear about the existence of a book written by the prophet called *Crepúsculo* (Crepuscule) that circulated among some believers and was perceived as some sort of 'Tokoist Koran' (PIDE report, 5 April 1955), kept away from the public gaze and reserved only for the movement's 'professors' (PIDE report on interrogation of Pululo Joseph, 15 May 1957). In 1956, for instance, Toko made new recommendations where he explained to the pastors 'how we should live', determining dressing and appearance codes (hair, ornaments, etc.), modalities of prayer (standing up, with no need for recourse to candles) and especially defining the weekly liturgical calendar to be followed by each church (letter by Simão Toko, 11 August 1956). In another example, in 1957, when Luvualo David returns to Luanda after a stay at Baía dos Tigres (where he coincided with the prophet), he writes a letter that determined a profound restructuration of the movement. This letter was entitled 'New laws for the good orientation and service of the Lord', and reminded that 'it is our obligation to attend the services at the appointed time; as we see, some only join us at nine o'clock when the scheduled hour is eight o'clock'. Likewise, he would establish a calendar of work meetings and prayer groups within each Tokoist community (report from the Congo Administrative Region, 13 November 1957).

Therefore, the preoccupation with time and its organization was already very present from the start – in such a way that, as is described in many reports of the time, the services were performed with a clock on the presiding table, in order to control and organize the minutes with rigueur (PSP information, 20 March 1957). Or merely to publicly display this concern. Within this organizing framework, prayer seemed to be the central conductor, returning each follower into a particular

Illustration 12. Tokoist ceremony marked by clocks, 957. *Source:* 'Processo Individual de Simão Gonçalves Toco' PT/TT/PIDE-DA-C-731-1. Image reproduction authorized by ANTT.

spiritual disposition several times a day. In 1973, for instance, Toko reminded his readers of the importance and role of prayer:

> [Regarding the] confusion concerning prayer, please listen carefully. The Tokoists used to perform four prayers, but now it is resumed to one: Our Father. The time for prayer is in the morning after we wake up, at noon, afternoon and night. Psalms 55:17. Why do the different religions multiply their prayers? The Church of Christ was not a religion, so we follow his teachings. Let us summarize. When a Tokoist wakes up he rises from his bed and kneels down and prays Our Father. Those who do not need to go to work may pray Our Father at home at noon; if you are at a brother's house, you can pray with him, or in groups of three, four or five people. If you are working or travelling, if you are walking you pray while you walk, if you are many you may kneel down and pray.... At night, you begin with Our Father at around 20h30, and then during the meeting you pray again and you finalize with Our Father again. Three times, but the same prayer.... Understood? (Letter by Simão Toko, 23 March 1973)

Prayer was therefore pervasive, and pushed the individual adherents into a constant adaptation of their quotidian lives into the spiritual realm.

This posture (shown in illustration 13), taught by the prophet to his pupils in the aftermath of the pentecostal experience of 1949, is com-

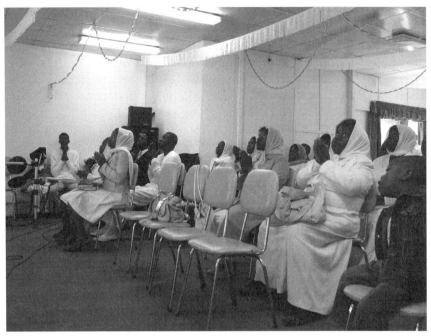

Illustration 13. Tokoists praying, 2008. Photo: Ruy Llera Blanes.

monly understood within Tokoism as a manifestation of faith; but it also denotes a subsequent philosophy: the idea of prayer as perform-ing a direct communication (conversation) with the divine and not a mere submission (as could be inferred from the kneeling posture – see Sarró 2008b), and also as a possibility of intercommunication, of bridg-ing (through spiritual mediation) the 'divine absence' (Engelke 2007). From this perspective, Tokoists often refer to their own prayer as an 'offering of their wishes' to God through a humble interpellation.

Historically conformed by a defining event, prayer is today a dis-tinctive sign of Tokoist praxis, and is shared in the collective space of the Tokoist Church as an inevitability, an act to be repeated as much as possible in order to become pervasive. This is what happens, for instance, in the Sunday service, but also in the fasting sessions, in the *sucursal* and the prayer vigils performed daily in the tabernacles. How-ever, as we saw in Toko's explanation above, prayer is not confined to the liturgical moments, but rather becomes pervasive, recurrent in the followers' lives: 'Christians must pray at all times and ceaselessly', it can be read in the Fundamental Principles of Doctrine that circulate in certain churches, 'because it is in prayer that we will find the as-sistance and protection from God against the traps of Satan. The Holy

Scriptures recommend that we pray a lot and recurrently: in the morning, in the afternoon, at night when we arrive home, and again when
we leave, awake, go to sleep, travel, etc.'. It is also recommended to
pray before the meals, and 'publicly in the house of God, in the retreat
of our families and particularly in our residences', according to the
church's catechism. This catechism and precept denotes an obligation,
a duty, but also a correspondence between the physical and mental
act of believing (Salazar 2008). It is therefore a posture and an act of
'de-centring' of the person in favour of an ideal and expectation (Westphal 2005), and also an apprehended act, a product of a process of apprenticeship (Luhrman 2007) that explains why the Tokoists perform
their prayers with their eyes wide open and inclined heads, seeking the
spiritual mediation and divine presence.

Collectively speaking, the years that followed would see consecutive
attempts of adaptation of this ecclesiastical project to the condition-
ings externally imposed by the socio-political moment Angola was experiencing. In other words, the persecution the Tokoists faced made
them work in clandestinity and anonymity. For instance, in 1971, in
the height of the repressive acts against the movement (which, we recall, was forbidden of any kind of public and collective manifestation),
Toko would recommend the following reorganization, which would
evolve into the creation of the *sucursais* or prayer groups within the
church:

> Brothers, I have a new task for you. Call those brothers, if you know their
> whereabouts, talk to them personally, and if you do not know where they
> live, go to their PO boxes and tell them to come to your houses. Don't call
> them all at once, bring them little by little, and ask them if they are ready
> to work for the salvation of others until the year 2000. Don't go around
> preaching, just pray and explain to them what to do, and visit those Su-
> cursais every one, two or three months. Groups of three people, if pos-
> sible. … Prepare 24 × 3 = 72 × 8 = 576. Sucursais for prayers in Luanda
> and each sucursal of eight people divided into two prayer houses, each
> group is composed of four people. Do you understand? (Letter by Simão
> Toko, 6 March 1971)

So, just as the Tokoist emblem was, as we saw in the previous chapter,
an object of diverse configurations and appropriations, likewise other
aspects of Tokoist liturgy and experience suffered mutation within
their 'webs of significance' (Geertz 1966), historical consciousness and
political action. The result today, apart from the liturgical, administrative and experiential dimensions described above, is the existence of
a list of prescriptions, regulations, statutes and ordinances that de-

fine, delimit, structure and calendarize the Tokoist experience. These prescriptions affect intersected areas of the Tokoist's life, from his or her functions and responsibilities within the structure to the sacred commandments and disciplinary codes, to the sacramental acts that punctuate and diachronically define their participation: baptism, dedication of children, engagement, marriage and funerals. The temporal prescriptions, written down into several documents that circulate within different sectors of the church, reveal a quite distinctive sense of embodied temporality that is ultimately an attempt to grasp a sense of ideological identification and belonging that comes out of their individual acceptance. In this regard, Pedro Agostinho (n.d.: 209) draws an interesting distinction between 'types of Tokoists': the 'adherent' (who are self-recognized adepts of the movement, but are not active members), the 'followers' (who follow the liturgical prescriptions in church, but not necessarily so in their private lives), and the 'genuine' (who follow integrally the law, commandments and prescriptions of the church). Thus, a link is established between temporal, moral and participative dimensions.

Singing Time

In places like Lisbon or Luanda, there are certain melodies and lyrics that are 'emblematic', recognizable at a distance, automatically attributive of a specific meaning and instigative of certain reminiscences. I am referring, for instance, to the hymn I am able to hear every Sunday morning as I approach the Tokoist Church in Lisbon: the strumming of guitar chords, the bass lines and the electronic drum kit that back the voices of over a hundred people. After I greet the controller in charge, I peek inside the church and see everyone standing up, with their bodies in tension, their arms glued to their torsos, following the choir master as they sing:

> The King of heaven will walk
> The whole earth he will move
> The nations accumulate
> Jehovah will walk
>
> Chorus:
> Glory, glory hallelujah
> Glory, glory hallelujah
> Glory, glory hallelujah
> Jesus arrives in victory

God visits Africa
Its darkness He dissipates
Evil actions He will destroy
Jehovah will walk

The divine book is announced
It is victorious before all evil
Increasing our satisfaction
Jehovah will walk

The chosen ones he will congregate
Elders and the young He will enlist
Satanic adepts will flee
Jehovah will walk[5]

It is with this hymn that the ceremony – in Lisbon as in Luanda, Mbanza Kongo, Vale do Loge, London or Rotterdam – of the Sunday service begins. If, as we saw in the previous section, the Tokoist liturgy is scrupulously performed according to the same program, within this organization the hymns act as punctuation, opening, dividing and closing the ritual, as a musical score that determines rhythms, spaces and silences.

Historically speaking, this omnipresence is not surprising, inasmuch as it was through the formation of hymns and choirs that Toko's religious service, his evangelization campaign began. Namely, with the creation of the Coro de Kibokolo in Leopoldville: 'it was from that choir that the Church of Christ was reborn. Period' (Agostinho n.d.: 49). After his arrival to the city in 1942, when he was sojourning at António Ngungu's house in the Malungo neighbourhood, Toko was approached by a group of *mais velhos*, who, having heard of his leading skills, challenged him to form a choir with young boys originated from his homeland. He then decides to move to the house of another friend, Daniel Nsuamani, where he begins rehearsals with a group of twelve children.[6] This group quickly grew and multiplied, reaching eighty-six members, and later reaching the hundreds and thousands (according to Agostinho n.d.: 53). The first hymns taught by Toko to the choir are still remembered and sung in the churches. Namely, the numbers 163 and 249 of the Baptist Mission hymnal (BIEMS), translated to Kikongo by the prophet himself. I myself was able to hear them in one particular service that took place, in April 2011, in the Palanca musseque in Luanda, which celebrated the sixty-eigth anniversary of the formation of the choir – a moment when, according to the secretary in charge that day, 'the church of the future began to be drawn'[7] (10 April 2011). With the deportation to Angola in 1950, the choir would be dissolved and its members dispersed throughout the Angolan territory. However, its legacy and memory persisted through the permanence and circulation of the hymns sung in that period, and also through the maintenance of the Coro de Kibokolo as an 'institution' – the name given to the central choir in many Tokoist parishes.

Therefore, many of the hymns that are sung today in Tokoist churches throughout the world were originated precisely in Toko's youth and in particular in the time the prophet spent in Leopoldville. Some of them, as mentioned above, translated from the Baptist Mission's hymnal[8]; others, composed by Toko himself; and others yet, by his students and followers throughout the following decades. One of the hymns that emerged from this period – known within the church as 'historical hymns' – is one called '*Ngunga nguelé muna nsi za wonsono*' ('The bell tolls in all the world's nations'; Agostinho n.d.: 49), which inaugurated an iconic imagery within the posterior Tokoist ideology: that of the bell as Africa's awakening and spiritual liberation (Quibeta n.d.: 179).[9]

Nguelé, nguelé bell, in all nations
Nguelé, nguelé, nguelé bell

The book of God that we read
Was taught to us by the missionaries

We greet all the mothers
Greetings, greetings

We greet everyone
Greetings, greetings
(Agostinho n.d.: 149)[10]

Regarding this same hymn, Agostinho stated: 'It is one of the most important hymns in the history of the Tokoist Church's existence, because every time it is sung it makes us remember the historical past of the church, the first days of its remembrance' (n.d.: 148). From this perspective, the hymns intellectually 'teach history' to those who learn and sing them in and outside the religious services, articulating consciousness and visions of the past with future projects of victory. They also materialize, as we see, into specific iconocities. The existence of 'historical hymns' that teach not only through their content but also because of their mere existence as such, as mementos or objects of memory, 'conceptual values' (Sahlins 1981: 70) that circulate in the everyday and are remembered, taught and apprehended in the choir rehearsals, youth meetings, dominical services, etc. The hymns verbalize, re-present and performatize historical episodes (and the value and sentiment publicly attached to them within the church), but also represent testimonies of a practical diacronicity. Pastor Pedro Lukau, one of the first members of the Coro de Kibokolo and original translator of many of the hymns sung today in the church, stated in a sermon in the Palanca:

> The Tokoists have as priority in their lives to sing.... The church began with the hymns.... Those who sing convert people to the church.... Because we began by singing.... Simão Toko was not a preacher, but a hymn teacher. From that moment, he began sharing biblical teaching to some of us who remain in this church. He taught us the basics of music and instructed musical masters.... Let us walk in a straight line, and not deviate to the left or to the right. Simão Toko used to say that, since he knew the truth, he preached the gospel ('if I didn't know the way, I wouldn't have entered in your lives', he said).... The path that Simão Toko taught us is steady. Young boys and girls, safeguard this work as much as you can; I was about your age when I started. Stay beside the elders in order to know the truth of the church.... We can say that all the choirs that sing hymns in the Church of Our Lord Jesus Christ on Earth have their centre in the Coro de Kibokolo. (10 April 2011)

But perhaps, instead of talking about historical hymns, we could describe them as 'temporalizing hymns', inasmuch as they are not just mere mementos, memories that bring history into the mundane, but also the collectivization of expectations:

> When terrene life ends
> Jesus will wave at us
>
> Chorus:
> Believe in God and in Jesus
> Put nonsense behind you
> Jesus Christ is our is our king
>
> We will fight for Christ until the end
> We will win, we will win
>
> In Christ we trust until the end
> We will live in his country
>
> When the trumpet sounds
> There will be resurrection
>
> When the promise arrives
> Christ will bring us together

The atheists will be separated
Like straw from wheat

(Hymn Quando a Vida Terral Findará 'When Terrene Life Ends'; cf.
Agostinho n.d.: 153; Quibeta n.d.: 186)[11]

This hymn, frequently invoked in the closing ceremonies of the Sunday
services, is also illustrative of the 'politics of self-knowledge' (Miyazaki
2006) that are simultaneously inherited and shared among the Tokoist
believers, introducing, from within a millenarian eschatological ideology, a stance (posture) of conviction and faith (hope) in those who
chant the hymns out loud. There is, therefore, a proclamatory character imbued into the hymns and the act of singing, textualized in the
verbal times in which they are sung, denoting the Tokoists' particular
posture, who, when they sing, 'look onwards'. It reflects, as we will see
below, an 'orientation towards the future'.

From this perspective, this teaching is not just intellectual, it is also
corporealized in the postures of the singers, who organize themselves
into different choir groups and combine melodic regimes under the
guidance of the choir leaders. Father Albert Dandu, an Angolan-born
Capuchin priest from the Catholic Mission of Kimpangu who came
across the movement right after its expulsion from the Belgian Congo,
described what he saw in his visit to a Tokoist gathering in the frontier
with Angola, not far from his Catholic mission:

> Two sisters, standing close to the movement's leaders, cheered the crowd
> singing with great enthusiasm and no reservations, making signs with
> their head. ... 'Why are they so satisfied?' I whispered to Pedro, who knew
> them for a long time now. 'First they sing to welcome us. And then they
> think that such personalities that come and participate in their ceremo-
> nies are surely future adepts of their sect. Furthermore, listen to what
> they are singing:
>
> We thank you for your visit
> God, send us your Spirit the Saviour
> We are very satisfied
> Because you brought good things for us
> It is not long before we are rescued
> The Africa we were looking for we already found
> Glory to our Father Simão
>
> (Report by F. Albert Ndandu, 7 June 1951)

Another report concerning Tokoism in the Uíge province in 1957 described a situation that is not very different from what we find today:

> In general, the ceremonies always begin with chanting, often with the hymn number 445 (The King of Heaven will Walk), in Kikongo, from the hymnal used in the Protestant religion; after that, they pray by the Bible, alternating with new hymns, namely numbers 171–228 and 384. The choir groups are formed, like orpheons, with the following suits: altos, tenors, sopranos and bass. It so happens that, sometimes, the men are separated from the women, but their mixing has also been observed, although each always belonging to its suit. They sing with great enthusiasm, discipline and with their eyes wide open looking at the sky. The songs are also well rehearsed and blindly follow the master – who, at the beginning of each song starts with the intonation of a small 'la-mi-ré'(A-E-D). During the chants, sometimes we hear a few 'solos' performed by the altos, when there are voices capable of such a thing. (PIDE report 'Changes Observed in the Tokoist Sect', c.1957)

These two reports denounce the process of institution of the hymns' centrality within Tokoist praxis; but they also reveal the way they become vitally omnipresent in the movement's communicational dynamics, affecting the praxis of singing, performing and listening in such a way that it not only invites the participant into a specific 'spiritual intent' (Jules-Rosette 1975: 151), but also conducts specific corporal interactions and ethical dispositions (Hirschkind 2006). I had a particular insight of this feeling in my first attendances to church services, when the naturally tense initial moments of ritual participation were relieved at point five of the programme ('Reception and Welcoming of Visitors'). After the solemnity of the collective prayer, biblical reading and initial announcements, the church usually breaks into a more relaxed and festive mood while everyone claps and sings an uptempo song – 'In the name of God, be welcome, be welcome, be welcome!' – while the church leaders leave their seats and welcome you with a strong handshake or a hug, and remind you that you are 'at home'.

The hymns also and explicitly insert the believer/participant into an interaction that continues outside the liturgical sphere and into the church organization. Today, apart from the Coro de Kibokolo, every Tokoist centre incorporates in its internal organization several choir groups that work mainly in the dominical services: the Central Choir (present in all parishes), the Tabernacle Choir, the Youth Choir, etc. These choral groups, in places like Lisbon, for instance, incorporate members from the almost entire church. But in places like Luanda, they instead reproduce the administrative structure by classes or other expressions of internal organization (Choir of Mother Sara, Choir of the SAPU class, etc.).

Illustration 14. Tokoist choir preparing to sing, Luanda, 2011. Photo: Ruy Llera Blanes.

But this corporealization, as we were saying, incorporates a history. This becomes particularly evident in the way the Tokoists sing and dance the *kembo,* usually in the moments after the official closure of the dominical service. *Kembo,* in Kikongo, stands for 'rejoicing' and refers to the 'grace' felt through the power of the Holy Spirit. The dance, characterized by the accelerated and 'disconcerting' way of moving the body, clapping and stomping your feet on the ground, reflects the idea of rejoicing and liberation in communion with the spirit.

However, the *kembo,* as a corporal expression of a sentiment of faith, is also the result of a process of transmission and disciplination of practices. In September 1972, Simão Toko wrote a letter to several churches in Angola, in response to a misunderstanding between two centres in the south of Angola (São Nicolau and Moçâmedes), who argued over their different perceptions on the role the *kembo* should play inside the church, and questioned if the Tokoist believer should 'dance the world' or not:

> Are all dancers and all Tokoists spiritual dancers? I already explained to you that spiritual dancing is no sin, if danced correctly. This chapter you

are sending me in all your letters, and particularly Psalms 47:1–7, what does verse seven say? … I never told the Tokoists to go and dance in the parties of the world.… To sing the religious hymns and to dance where the people of the world dance are two very different things. We used to dance after the service in our backyard, where we prayed; that's where we used to dance.… So that there are no more rivalries, dancing among the Tokoists is simply over. If someone invites you, just sing the praise hymns, there shall be no more dancing in the congregations.… Whoever is not willing to obey this order may leave Tokoism. (Letter by Simão Toko, 2 September 1972)

However, as we see, *kembo* continued in the church, albeit confined to specific spatialities and temporalities. Despite the menacing tone in the letter, Toko eventually agreed on the importance of such corporal manifestations within the sphere of the congregation. Hence, the negotiational aspects of this pedagogy were ultimately processual, in the making, multi-directional.

Tabernacles, Remembrance and Prophetic Revelation

Dear brothers, sisters, nephews and nieces, I wasn't lucky enough to leave to New Jerusalem. But it is clear that God was, after all, saving us for a big event. What was that? To deliver ourselves to his Word, which he had previously given to prophets and disciples. (Letter by Simão Toko to Faria Prata and others, 7 April 1973)

In my first visit to a Tokoist church in 2007, in Lisbon, I couldn't help noticing a small door in one of the sides of the room where the service was taking place. I observed how certain members of the church would come in and out through that door, not without removing their shoes first. Among those members were the body that would preside over the liturgical service I was about to attend – the secretary, the designated pastor, the evangelists and other representatives – and a small group of people in charge of fiscal and spiritual duties. From the outside, despite the noise of electric guitar tuning, talking, singing and laughing, I could distinguish some clapping and what seemed to be praying out loud, collectively. A short time later, the instrumentalists began to play a song and, as everybody prepared to sing a hymn, the door opened and through it the church officiators exited. After the service, the same people would enter through that door once again and close it behind them.

I quickly learned that that door gave access to the 'tabernacle', a sacred space destined for the performance of certain religious activities, both in the context of the Sunday service and outside it. This place is withdrawn from the common visitors' view, but nevertheless occupies a central place in the Tokoist liturgical practice: it is inside it that the Tokoists 'work', not only in the moments of ritual, but also during the week, in the 'days of tabernacle' or whenever it becomes necessary. It is therefore a hallowed ground where, adequately anointed (with perfume and purifying cream), its frequenters are inspired by the Holy Spirit and where 'a diversity of gifts, as revealed by the Holy Scriptures, 1 Cor 12:1–11, operate', as is stated in the church's Fundamental Principles of Doctrine.

As far as I could understand, the access to the tabernacle is not entirely denied, but instead it is restrictive and differentiator – not everyone has access, only the 'servants' and 'helpers', 'as long as their Christian conduct earns the approval and assent from the church's elders and counsellors', as I was told later on. This conduct implies, among other things, an adequate dress code and a particular mental predisposition. As a Tokoist *mamã* (mother, elder woman) told me once in Luanda:

> The tabernacle is a holy place, in the essence of its word it's a holy place, where things that are not allowed cannot enter. For instance, we the Tokoists have as rule: when we go to the tabernacle, we dress in white, we don't bring any money, no watches, no dark clothes – if they are white, crème or a light colour, better yet…. I'm talking about things that are forbidden in the access to the tabernacle. (4 December 2007)

In this same conversation, Bishop Afonso Nunes, current leader of the church's Universal Directorship, furthered the explanation:

> Regarding the tabernacle, we must go to the Bible in order to specify why one cannot just enter the tabernacle like that. If someone wants to go inside, he must first meditate in his heart, if he is ready or not. In the past – see Hebrews chapter 9, verse 4 – only the high priest could enter the tabernacle, and only once per year. But now, in the era of Christ, after Christ paid such a precious price, these things were abolished…. Thus, to enter the house of God we must first meditate and find if there is something in our past. If you enter without meditating first, the spirit of God will attack you and tell you, 'You did this, you did that, you cannot come here, or else you will be punished automatically.' Therefore, you must enter with your right foot, that is you must meditate during the day and be sure you have done nothing, it's okay, I prepare myself with white clothes in order to enter the holy house because inside I will hear the voice of God. It is the most holy place in the church. As I said, after we begin the first actions, no one else can enter, only those who are chosen, and in the right moment, to worship God. And that place is not just for

us to receive messages and be consoled, but also to be warned of future events. (4 December 2007)

This explanation reveals the sense of doctrinal prescription and spatial separation produced by the tabernacle. One can apprehend that, as a space for 'pure prayer', it is not only interdicted to the occasional ethnographer, who will only imagine what it looks like inside, but also to a significant portion of the Tokoist community, and acts as measure for the level of commitment of the believer. From this perspective, the fact that there is a dress prescription associated to a behavioural dimension, mediating the possibility of entering the tabernacle, is significant, exemplifying the confluence between instruction, obedience and free will, as was suggested by Talal Asad regarding the regimes of discipline and power in religion (1993). To enter the tabernacle implies, in principle, a coherent behavioural pattern – or at least the self-reflection on behalf of the candidate who expects to cross the door – connecting statute and power through an ideology of righteousness displayed in the ritual process (Bloch 1989), or to be more specific, in the pre- and post-ritual moments. It is, therefore, an axis of spatialization and measurement of Tokoist Christian spirituality and faith.

After the initial moment of curiosity, I quickly understood that, just like with the ritual liturgy, prayer and hymns, there was imbued in the tabernacle an historical and ideological substance that bore its existence. I noted that what seemed to be at stake was a concomitant process of recognition of a physical space and a history of spiritual institution that converged in the tabernacle (see also Blanes 2009d), directly connected to the genesis of the Tokoist movement.

As we saw, the events of 1949 were foundational for Tokoism as an ecclesiastical entity, enclosing a 'prophetic circle' initiated years before and through which its historiography flew. But what happened on that night of July also assumed a more transcendent role that not only determined a specific type of historical knowledge but also a prophetic-charismatic production of religious knowledge mediated by specific notions of temporality and spatialization. Remembering that night, Simão Toko wrote:

On July 25th, 1949, I congregated a group of 3 × 12 = 36 people at night in my house in Leopoldville, in order to ask God if he did or not hear the prayer we directed to Him in 1946, requesting the Holy Ghost. At midnight, we heard a big noise and saw a light. Many of us began to shake, others spoke in tongues. Many things happened that night. I did not shake, but began to acquire a knowledge concerning certain chapters of the Bible that I was previously unaware of. One strange and admirable event was that some could see mysterious things that others couldn't. Our brother Feto Dominique would grab hot, burning metal, glowing ember, but would not get burned. My deceased cousin Tumissungo Cardoso and myself, we saw things the other brothers couldn't see. Many people attacked by the spirit ran to their houses and brought a variety of spells and other magical things that dominated other people by selling them to other lands or killed them by mysterious means to become rich, etc., etc. I can't tell you everything that happened in those days in the former Belgian Congo, many secrets were disclosed by the Spirit. There were wonders that had never been seen in Angola. We had, in the houses of the good Christians, spiritual phones – in other words telegraphs with no wire, with which we called people that lived in distant homes, 3, 4, 10 kilometres away. Each telephonist had a spiritual telephonist (medium) that could be a young boy or girl. That telephonist would open a hole in the wall even in walls built with stone, metal and cement, with their bare fingers, opening cracks in a matter of seconds, and through those cracks we could hear the voice of other telephonists that were many kilometres away. One time we needed an urgent that required the services of João Mancoca (today estranged from us), and since his house was far away we wouldn't have time to send someone over. But since there were two mediums in my house, the deceased Tumissungo Cardoso and also Vouga the choirmaster, I ordered that he should be called urgently. Well, Mancoca was not a medium, but he was warned in his own house that he was needed at mine. Not even five minutes passed from the spiritual phone call and João Mancoca was already in my house.... Many other things happened that are not worth describing. Live snakes caught, their tongues ripped out and left to leave on their own. (Letter by Simão Toko to his followers, December 1966)

'We saw things the other brothers couldn't see.... I can't tell you everything that happened in those days in the former Belgian Congo, many secrets were disclosed by the Spirit' – with this description, Simão Toko reminded his followers in Angola about the charismatic power they had been given on that night of July 1949. The shaking, the speaking in tongues, the vision, the mediumship, the 'deep knowledge' of the Bible, the miracles they witnessed. According to someone who was in Leopoldville at the time, the house where Simão Toko sojourned 'became a tabernacle' to where many Angolans and Congolese, upon hearing the news, flocked, looking for blessing and miracle; many were equally 'attacked by the Spirit' and began to speak in tongues and prophesy (interview Doze Mais Velhos, 19 October 2008).

But, as Simão Toko also explained, there were certain secret things that could not be revealed. This secret, that surely inspired more than one conspiracy theory in the PIDE offices in Luanda (see chapter 2), became in any case a structuring axis in the Tokoists' prophetic ideology. This was firstly because, as Bishop Afonso Nunes, one of the current leaders of the Tokoist church in Luanda, announced in a visit to the church in Lisbon (December 2010), 'I have much more to say to you, more than you can now bear' (as in John 16:12). This sermonized reference to the gospel of John, is, as you may recall, in many ways reminiscent of what happened with velho Simão in Catete when he encountered God: 'I will put something inside you, that will not know or understand.' This 'postponement of understanding' translated, together with the events of July 1949, into an anticipation of the future, a declaration of an expectation. In other words, through the grace of the Holy Spirit, the Tokoists were able to know 'things of the future', namely in what concerned the fulfilment of the millennium of Christ, but also concerning the events 'of the world'. In sum, they received the gift of prophecy that would allow them to produce a specific sense of certainty pertaining their own actions and visions of the world. Edgar, a Tokoist friend and one of the founders of the church in Lisbon, once told me: 'The Tokoist has come to reveal the greatness of the kingdom, that which is concealed from the sight of the human being.'

This sense of certainty has been revealed throughout history with the prophecies that the Tokoists have disclosed and 'advanced' concerning the 'upcoming events' – as for instance the existence of electric cars in the year 2000, or satellites inhabited by humans, among other things (letter by Simão Toko, 26 October 1970). It was also this certainty that mediated the development of the history of suffering and resistance, both internally (within a sacrificial temporal theology) and externally, inasmuch as many Tokoist *anúncios* (announcements) were interpreted as conspiracies against the Portuguese government: 'The elders make believe that they divine the future and know the date when Salazar will give Angola to the black natives. The leader of the Sambizanga (Luanda) nucleus is also a prophet and claims to know when Salazar will give Angola its independence' (PIDE report, 25 April 1966). Some contemporary commentators, like pastor William Grenfell from the Baptist Mission of Kibokolo, related (c.1957) that 'future-oriented' theology in Toko with his progressive interest in the material he compiled from the Watch Tower, namely a brochure called *The Kingdom, the Hope, the World* (edited in 1931), which Toko had translated to Kikongo. The leader himself would admit, in an interview with colonial administrators, that the great divergence that separated him from the Baptist missionaries was the issue of 'explaining the Bible' and the interest he cultivated regarding 'Jehovahs's Kingdom' and the chapters of the scriptures that dealt with the future life (PIDE report, 2 August 1957).

This eschatological and pneumatological orientation is also reflected in the Tokoist movement in the particular modality of prayer that, as we described above, is performed within the church: with the palms of their hands enclosed or facing up, their heads inclined backwards and their open eyes fixed upwards, looking in the direction of the sky.

But the fact that the descent of the Holy Spirit and consequent dispensation of gifts was collective, and not necessarily confined in the founder, also provoked a 'distribution of charisma' (Shils 1965), a collectivization of power that allowed for the knowledge to not be 'detained' and individual, but rather public and creative – a 'democharisma', to use Asmarom Legesse's (1994) words. From this perspective, just as the leader spoke in his letter of 'mediums' in those first days in Leopoldville, the church would progressively establish an internal body of *vaticinadores* – also known as *vates* (that is, foreseers) – people touched by the spirit and that offer their gift for the service of the church. In a report delivered in 1956 to the PIDE, 'according to an eye witness' the following description appeared in a Tokoist ceremony in Sadi-Kiloango, not far from the prophet's place of birth:

> When they read the Bible, especially at night, one can frequently observe cases of inspiration, they say they receive the inspiration from above. Those who are inspired start acting, through gestures and shaking, which increases. The inspired one is then strongly agitated and indicates to the Bible readers the chapter that has just been given to him through the inspiration. The readers read the selected chapter, the assistants surround the illuminated and incite him to communicate his inspiring ideas, and he is then acclaimed and taken by the assistants in honour and veneration. It is frequent to witness two to three cases of people shaken-inspired by the Mpeve Muvuluzi. (PIDE report, 'Movements of Indigenous Sects of Religious Character in Angola', 1956)

This image of 'shaken-inspired' people reproduces what is recognized in the church as the process of 'inhabitation' by spirits that *vates* are subject to and through which they produce information for the church. The *vates* are touched by spirits of diverse character, and through different mechanisms: dream, vision, illumination, corporal possession, etc. (Agostinho n.d.: 113).[12] Their messages constitute prophecies in a broad understanding of the term: announcements, visions and knowledge of the church and the world in times past, present and future. These messages are received by the church, which writes and archives the information handed by the *vates*/spirits/prophets in order to analyse and then decide upon its pertinence and opportunity for the church and the world.[13] There is, therefore, a production and management (sanctioning) of knowledge that is directly connected to the problems of secrecy and certainty mentioned above, and which we now know are based in the process of spiritual mediation.

This spiritualist modality, complementary but not equal to that of the Pentecostal moment of July 1949, seems to have begun in 1950 in the Vale do Loge, after a summoning performed by Simão Toko that the spirits of the ancient prophets would help him in his endeavour of remembering the ancient church of Christ. Upon the plea performed by Toko to the spirits, and before he was deported to the south, he instructed one of his followers in the *colonato*, the elder Simão Vuvu, to install a 'tabernacle' in order to 'communicate with the saints'. The answer to that invocation provoked the conclusion of the temporal cycle initiated after Christ's resurrection, when the prophets became spirits – as is described in Matthew 27:52–55[14] – as well as the institution of a specific, spiritualized temporality. 'But when we arrived at the 1950s, it was on that moment that we asked the prophets to help us. We asked for the Spirit of the prophets after praying and fasting. That's when the prophets descend. The prophets Daniel, Isaiah, Zackary, Abraham, all of them. ... And that's how the Spirit begins to work in the vates' (Pedro 2008: 16).

Thus, it is through the process of inhabitation and spiritual prophetic operation in the bodies of the *vates* that the connection with the 'original times', the remembrance and the proclamation of a time of messianic confirmation, is established. This remembrance, as I mentioned in the introduction, is theologically grounded on an idea of a 'continuation' of the apostolic work of Jesus Christ (the *pedra angular*, or angular stone) and his immediate followers. The descent of the Holy Spirit in 1949, as a consequence of the previous summon of 1946,[15] configured the act by which the original, true church was 'remembered' after its disappearance 'after the Pentecost'. But the posterior performance of the prophetic trajectory implied a *revisão de toda obra divina* (revision of the divine work), from the patriarchs, judges and prophets to Jesus Christ and the Apostles, transforming it, as a Tokoist explained to me (personal communication, 7 October 2011), into a direct, live, transparent path to understand the word of God in current times: 'Through Simão Toko, we retraced the biblical events, including those of Jesus Christ: what he did on earth is what is being done in the Remembered Church in Africa.' From this perspective, a task of *actualização* (updating) is performed through the work of the *vates* and the spiritual messages they convey. Therefore, it is not so much the act of remembering per se, but rather the acknowledgement of a temporality that connects past events with the 'here and now', according to the operation of a particular eschatology, what is really at stake.

In any case, the tabernacle and the work of the *vates* are, for many Tokoists, *the* factor of differentiation between theirs and all other religious movements: 'There is no difference between Protestantism and Tokoism. The difference between Protestantism and Tokoism is that we have vates. Vates look like prophets, but they are not prophets: it is someone who is inspired by God, and when he is inspired he begins to explain the Bible' (interview by Simão Toko to RTP, c.1973). The *vates* are today an officially recognized ecclesiastical entity within the church (the *corpo vate*), to where believers who manifest a particular vocation or charisma (in the Weberian sense) are directed. It is through them that the prophetic-charismatic tradition inaugurated in 1949 and 1950 is fulfilled, inasmuch as despite the fact that they do not carry out any political role within the church organization, they often act as mediators between the political, experiential and spiritual dimensions of the movement. Through their prayer in the tabernacle, they produce knowledge and assume healing capacities, and are sought by believers in moments of affliction in the *sucursais* or parishes where they work. They are, according to this configuration, 'clean bodies' (Pedro 2008: 17) through which a mediation is produced between the spiritual and the quotidian needs.

Likewise, the fact the descent of the Holy Spirit occurred in a circumscribed space to a specific group of people also produced other doctrinal and liturgical implications. Namely, the instalment of the tabernacles, spaces of prayer and spiritual work.[16] As I argued above and elsewhere, this seclusion is significant, as it acts as a form of restriction and sanctioning of the contact between the believer and the divine (Blanes 2009d).

However, historically speaking, it is known that the process of public inhabitation was also recurrent. Silva Cunha described how 'almost always, during these ceremonies, there are moments of hysteria, where the believers fall in the ground, tremble compulsively and hallucinate. … During these moments the believers have visions, some of those we interrogated said they saw the Holy Spirit and the angels' (1959: 57). Carlos Estermann will also compile a similar description in the centre of Angola (1965: 336). Likewise, in a documentary produced by Fernando Rebello, a close friend of Simão Toko, one can appreciate the images of a celebratory service held on the twenty-sixth anniversary of the twenty-fifth of July in Luanda's Bairro Popular in 1975, where some believers are 'attacked' and 'escorted' to the tabernacle (Rebello 2009). Thus, the places of worship seemed to be public and with unrestricted access. Silva Cunha describes how in Maquela do Zombo, before the increase of state repression on the movement, the public

services were held in 'temples built by the faithful that almost always
followed the same model – a house made of wood staffs or adobe with
a meeting room. ... For those who officiate there is a table that acts as
altar, covered with a cloth and upon which a Bible, the book of Protestant hymns, jars with flowers and almost always an alarm clock are
placed' (1959: 58–59). From this perspective an historical process of seclusion of the spiritual work seems to have taken place. But already in
1965 Estermann mentioned the existence of *casas santas* (holy houses)
in the places of worship, to where believers 'taken by the spirit' were
brought (1965: 339). It could also be that this seclusion was a product of the friction between their liturgical expectations and the para-
noid vigilance of the Portuguese authorities. For instance, there are
countless references in the PIDE material of the 1950s pertaining to
the alleged existence of 'secret meetings' performed by the Tokoists, of
different nature than the more public celebrations. In Father Dando's
1951 report, the following description can be read:

> During the Ntongosa, a ceremony that I will describe as diabolic takes
> place: the shaving of the hairs in the armpit and pubic area, both in men
> and women. It seems that in these occasions they are all naked. Men sleep
> with women. Each one chooses the women that pleases him the most, de-
> spite the presence of her real husband. A man can also choose one of the
> so-called Sisters of the sect. (Report by Alberto Dando, 7 June 1951)

This description by Dando echoed in the images that the Portuguese
authorities built concerning the Tokoists. We find 'copies' of this description in subsequent PIDE reports and also in Silva Cunha (1959:
61) and José Gonçalves (1967: 685). Many Tokoists are knowledgeable
of this description, seen from within as a fascist incredulity (Agostinho
n.d.: 239–240). In any case, it was the outcome of a process of occultation and suspicion built from within and without the church. Today,
however, it is not very frequent to observe moments of 'attack by the
Holy Spirit' or other spirits. Normally and normatively, the inhabited
vate is escorted by the spirit into the tabernacle, where it will find an
elder and an *escrevente*, responsible for the reception and annotation
of its messages, that thus become part of the church's historiography.

Prophetic Memories and Heritages, Part I

Calendars, hymns, tabernacles: these three materializations illustrate
what I have suggested to be a process of immediatization and updating
of a particular heritage, that of the prophet Simão Toko's biography

and its implications. Tokoist history is permanently and inarguably seen as one of 'suffering' (Blanes 2009a) due to the hardships experienced by the leader and his followers throughout the ordeal of the church's institutional development. This suffering is composed by the different narratives of imprisonment and captivity such as those I described in the previous chapters: the 'first' and 'second' prisons, the displacements, exiles, detentions, tortures, interrogations, etc. This association with episodes of repression, trauma and violence (see Sarró 2007; Sánchez-Carretero 2011; Blanes 2012b) invokes particular modalities of memory and anxiety that equally affect theological, ritual and experiential dimensions of Tokoist spirituality. In this process, the prophet's martyrdom and resilience simultaneously motivated that anxiety and offered a template for a providential reading of the past.

From this perspective, these processes of transmission and temporalization, no matter how negotiated and contested throughout the history of church institution, are perceived within contemporary Tokoism as stances of stabilization, a response to the anxieties and absences produced by the history of suffering. They are therefore mediated by ideologies of certitude and righteousness fed by the recognition of logics of memory, martyrdom, sacrifice and expectation. Learning Tokoist orthodoxy, performed through church and familial contexts of transmission, implies an understanding of a particular historical (biographical) trajectory. This understanding is simultaneously intellectual, but also corporeal and material, translating into specific convictions and dispositions.

What these contexts of transmission also reveal is a process of 'personal heritagization' – the transformation of a prophetic biography into particular organizations, sites and practices that permanently invoke it within a multiplicity of indexicalities that become present (Ballesteros and Sánchez-Carretero 2011). In this regard, if for an external observer Tokoist liturgical practice may appear from the outside as unusual, different, complex or complicated, for any conscious participant it is imbued with a complex set of meanings and significations that are, to the detail, connected to a particular personal history. This is processed through the observation of ideologies and directives stemmed by the leader's individual volition, but also through the ad hoc, postmortem acts of remembering, celebrating and updating his biography (Blanes 2011a), performed as Tokoists preach, pray, sing and prophesy. From this perspective, this personal heritagization is necessarily hagiographic, heroic (Mary 2005; Khalili 2007).

These mechanisms of transmission and heritagization are, in the way I described them, ultimately internal and inherent to a particular religious and social tradition. From this perspective, there are also other stances of heritagization involved that do not necessarily belong to the church's internal sphere. Namely, wider processes of generational transitions, cultural flows and heritage politics occurring in Angola during the post-1975 period (Gonçalves 2003), which surround the church's development. In this regard, problems of public leadership and personal charisma become paramount. Toko's figure, as a part of Angolan late colonial and postcolonial history, is not only present in the church realm, but also in the Angolan public sphere; likewise, as I will describe in the next chapter, many Tokoists have themselves engaged in non-religious logics and discourses of heritagization, entangling church and political history.

In any case, for the Tokoists this heritagization is not a mere act of nostalgic memory, of recognition of things past, but instead its anamnesis, its transformation into something present through its meaningfulness. It is also not a mere fabric of a survival against an idea of irreversibility (Berliner 2012; Berliner and Bortolotto 2012), nor a performative act of mourning and remembrance against a history of suffering (Margry and Sánchez-Carretero 2011), but rather a poetic act of making history present, its realization through what Michael Lambek tongue-twistedly described as a 'characteristic historicity or historical consciousness' (1998: 106). There is in fact a compositional dimension to Tokoist heritagization, affected by remembrance, but also by mediumship and historical acknowledgement, producing characteristic chronotopes that are identifiable in their spaces of practice and interaction. But as I argued in the introduction, this stabilizing act also works as a response to the trepidation provoked by internal events that occurred during the process of generational transition, which render Tokoist memory as utterly heteroglossic. There is therefore a constant sense (or necessity) of 'claiming' associated to Tokoist memory and heritage; as we will see in the following chapter, these claims invoke problems of temporality through the entanglements of generation, innovation and adaptation. The memory of the prophet, despite the acts of stabilization, provoked differentiated notions of heritagization, patrimonialization and authority.

Notes

1. Joaquim Albino Kisela, personal communication (April 2011).
2. Acts 20:28; 'Keep watch over yourselves and all the flock of which the Holy Spirit has made you overseers. Be shepherds of the church of God, which he bought with his own blood' (New International Version).

3. From this perspective, there is somewhat of a continuity between religious and ethnographic apprenticeship, where we learn to decode and historically place the practices and materialities that we observe and participate in.

4. On this particular episode, see chapter 2.

5. Rei do céu andará / Toda a terra moverá / As nações acumulam / Jeová andará / Glória, glória aleluia / Glória, glória aleluia / Glória, glória aleluia / Vencendo vem Jesus / Deus visita África / Suas trevas dissipa / Más acções destruirá / Jeová andará / O livro divino é anunciado / Está vencendo todo o mal / Aumentando a satisfação / Jeová andará / Os escolhidos ajuntará / Velhos e crianças alistará / Adeptos satânicos fugirão / Jeová andará. In the BMS hymnal, choir number 445, in Kikongo. Translated by Simão Gonçalves Toko.

6. Initially, the choir was formed by the following boys, ages twelve to fifteen: Miguel Massukinini, Dodão Paulo Pedro, Emanuel Kinzica, António Kiala, Fernando Kiesse, André Kiaku, Sebastião Tussamba, Simão Lázaro, Domingos Manuel, Ambrósio Massamba, Carlos Agostinho Kadi and Mancondo Leão.

7. The original Portuguese word used was *desenhada*, which can mean both 'drawn' or 'designed'.

8. This BIEMS hymnal can still be found circulating in the Tokoist churches, in a bilingual (Portuguese–Kikongo) edition.

9. In the statutes of the church's Universal Directorship, the bell is stated as an 'official symbol', with the 'spiritual significance of liberation of man from the slavery of sin and awakening of man's heart in the assumption of the responsibilities attached to the Word of God' (Article 10°).

10. Ngunga nguelé, nguelé muna nsi za wonsono / Ngunga nguelé, nguna nguelé / Onkanda Nzambi tu tanganga / A missionale batu longa wo / Kia mbote kieno yeno aki mama / Kia mbote, kia mbote / Kia mbote kieno o yeno awonsono / Kia mbote, kia mbote

11. Quando a vida terreal findará / Jesus vai nos acenar / Credes em Deus e em Jesus / Deixai a insensatez / Jesus Cristo é o nosso rei / Lutaremos por Cristo até ao fim / Venceremos, venceremos / Em Cristo confiamos até ao final / Viveremos no Seu país / Quando a trombeta soará / Haverá ressurreição / Quando a promessa chegar / Cristo vai nos ajuntar / Os ateus serão separados / Como palha do trigo.

12. There is a distinction within Tokoist spiritual ideology between 'true' and 'false' spirits (Agostinho n.d.: 117). This explains why it is compulsory that the spirits who inhabit the *vates* identify themselves in the tabernacles before the *escreventes* (writers), so that their message be considered valid. Here, the process of writing becomes even more fundamental (Kirsch 2007: 155 and ff.).

13. Not all the messages delivered pertain to the 'things of the church'. They may even refer to quite mundane issues (interview Doze Mais Velhos, 7 April 2011).

14. Matthew 27: '(50) And Jesus cried out again with a loud voice and yielded up his spirit. (51) And behold, the curtain of the temple was torn in two, from top to bottom. And the earth shook, and the rocks were split. (52)

The tombs also were opened. And many bodies of the saints who had fallen asleep were raised, (53) and coming out of the tombs after his resurrection they went into the holy city and appeared to many.'

15. These two moments are seen as the culmination of several 'acts of remembrance' that took place before the creation of the church, such as Virgin Mary's apparition in Fátima in 1917, or spiritual events that took place in Zulumongo, the prophet's place of birth (Nzila 2006).

16. In the first moments after the descent of the Holy Spirit, in Leopoldville, Toko would talk about 'mediums' and 'outposts' as places of spiritual manifestation and mediation (interview Doze Mais Velhos, April 2011). The terms *vate* and *tabernacle,* in reference to this spiritual work would only appear later on in Angola.

CHAPTER 4

Trepidation

Spirits, Memories and Disputed Heritages

In the passage of 1983 to 1984, Simão Gonçalves Toko, the Mayamona, passed away at his residence in the Congolenses-Terra Nova neighbourhood in Luanda, after a cardiovascular episode (Quibeta n.d.: 56).[1] The funeral ceremonies lasted ten days, and involved several important Angolan and Portuguese figures. On 7 January, the casket is transported in a committee of twenty-six vehicles from Luanda to Ntaia, the prophet's place of birth, for an eternal rest. In a multitudinous ceremony officiated by Pastor Lopes Martins Panzo, Toko is buried there on 10 January 1984.

These were times of great sadness for the Tokoists. The church found itself, after the prophet's 'second prisons', still in a situation of clandestinity and precariousness, and the deterioration of his health increased the tension in its structures. In his last days, Toko was often seen crying, as if guessing that in his upcoming absence 'the wolves would enter his pen' (Agostinho n.d.: 82). In his last public intervention, on 25 December 1982 in the Congolenses neighbourhood, he stated: 'The farmer, when he is farming, doesn't cultivate the same land without end. He always establishes a limit or a moment where he should stop cultivating. Is this true or not, my brothers? … The same thing happens in the word of God, my brothers! Everything in the world has its limit. Now, brothers, let us wait for the future' (Agostinho n.d.: 83). These foresights and metaphors were somewhat justified. According to Kisela, the prophet's tears fell because he intimately recognized that his followers were, spiritually speaking, insufficiently united, and anticipated the crisis to come (2004: 245). The prophet himself performed this anticipation with an interesting parable he used to invoke – that the church was like a dying elephant in the forest: after its death, the vul-

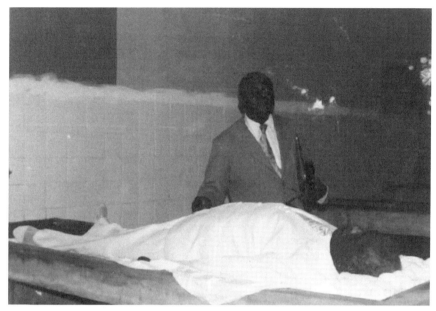

Illustration 15. Simão Toko, deceased. January 1984. *Source:* Ruy Llera Blanes's personal archive.

tures would come to peck their piece of the carcass (ibid.) – since the leadership problems he struggled with during his exile in the Azores, partially appeased after his return to Luanda, began to re-emerge. As we saw in chapter 2, the PIDE archives revealed cases of dissidence and attempts of upheaval against Toko on behalf of some of his followers throughout the history of the movement. Such was the case in 1955 in his sojourn in the South; in the 1960s, in the Azores; and finally in the 1980s, with the Mboma group (as I explain in the pages below). In 1984, however, the dissidence became an open conflict and, ultimately, disaggregation.

In fact, this became a crossroads moment in the life of thousands of Tokoists, since not only did they bear the pain of losing a beloved and adored figure, but were also forced to deal with a problem of political succession. In prophetic churches structured around the centralizing figure of its founding leader,[2] the problem hyperbolizes – the examples of such movements that end up dissolving after the disappearance of the founder are countless. From a political point of view, it was in fact a classic problem of religious leadership succession, as has been studied by several Africanist anthropologists, for instance (Balandier 1963 [1955]; Fernandez 1970, 1973; MacGaffey 1983; Sarró 2008a). However, apart from the transference of cabinet, the case of Toko's succession also unearthed problems of charisma, leadership and authority from a very Weberian perspective. Throughout the history of Tokoism, despite the distribution of charisma described in the previous chapter, it was in the *dirigente*'s figure that multiple charismatic agencies converged: political (as cause and consequence of a leadership process and a collective project), theological (as expression of gifts and mediations on a spiritual plane), experiential (through the history of mission, sacrifice and martyrdom), psychological (revealing personal traits of leadership and conviction) and aesthetic (inaugurating a specific style of leadership with repercussions in ritual and liturgical dimensions). From this perspective, charisma is presented here as a relationship, a multifaceted mediation (see Feuchtwang 2008; Blanes 2010), the result of projections and expectations (Lindholm 1990; Feuchtwang and Wang 2001) and the construction of inter-subjectivities between person and spirit (Csordas 2009). Upon his disappearance, despite the fact that there was an existing leadership structure to supposedly govern its affairs, the church could not find a substitute with a similar charismatic impact.

Thus, as a prophetic movement, and despite its history of remote leadership, Tokoism nevertheless 'depended' on the figure and charisma of its leader; his physical disappearance not only posed a pragmatic problem, but also inaugurated an agonistic memory regime that, among other things, culminated in the prophetic biography described in the first two chapters of this book, and on the processes of transmission depicted in chapter 3 – where the issue of time is once again exacerbated – and finally on the memory disputes described in this chapter. Especially because it questions the problem of providence and sacrifice, i.e. of messianism and prophetic agency, where those intervening seek to understand and justify (amidst the on-going conflicts) the *reason* for Simão Toko's mission, and what it represents as legacy and vital project for thousands of believers.

As we will see in the following pages, the memory disputes produced within the church in the post-1984 period reveal attempts to transcend the trepidation provoked by the prophet's disappearance. In other words, attempts to 'survive the prophecy' initiated by the leader and supported by his charisma and the subsequent memory exercises – although simultaneously challenged by the problem of generation and ideologies of transcendence and/or conservation. We are therefore faced with a problem of 'continuity' (Weber 2006: 88; Engelke 2007) and 'rupture', or eventually iconoclasm (Meyer 1998; Engelke 2004; Sarró 2008a) mediated by memory and its updating for the Tokoists who 'survived' the prophet's passing.

Succession, Transition and Conflict

Officially speaking, the process of transition in the Tokoist Church began on the fall of 1983. Simão Toko's final anxieties, together with the sudden deterioration of his health, prevented him from resolving, through an explicit pronunciation, pending internal conflicts within the church. In fact, during his last year of life he remained virtually unseen in public, secluded in his house in the Terra Nova. One episode that seems to have triggered the posterior separation was an unresolved conflict that took place in the financial management of the church. The situation of clandestinity experienced by the movement in those years – still subject to control measures on behalf of the MPLA regime and in the middle of the on-going civil war in the country – made the administrative management of such an entity, which congregated dozens of thousands of believers in Luanda alone, painstaking and subject to administrative complications. After an internal campaign to raise funds to buy musical instruments for the church, a good portion of the money collected disappeared without explanation, and provoked harsh discussions between different members of the leadership. The same would happen after an excursion Toko planned to visit his followers in the north of Angola in 1983. The leader had organized an expedition of approximately four hundred people to visit the church of Ntaia; however, the Angolan government only authorizes a committee of twenty people, a decision that forces Toko into cancelling the mission (Agostinho n.d.: 77); in the meantime, a considerable amount of money raised for the occasion disappears. Finding himself physically feeble, the *dirigente* appoints a committee with the incumbency of investigating the events and proposing a solution, to be finally decided by him. But unfortunately, the prophet passes away without announcing a verdict. The problem remains unresolved because those involved refuse to accept a determination that is not explicitly sanctioned by him (interview Doze Mais Velhos, 7 October 2008).

> So it was under these circumstances that the conflicts began to increase, and people saw that well, 'the leader is gone', and they began to divide the church. It wasn't just verbal discussion; it also culminated in violence and some trying to annihilate the others in order to see who was able to withhold the church direction. Because the church direction was closer to those who came from the Congo and are from the North, others thought that that wasn't possible, 'we have to do something to recover the church leadership', and also something else: the comprehension of understanding what was the church after all. (Interview Bishop Nunes, 12 December 2007)

Thus, it was not just about a financial or bureaucratic problem. In many ways, the prophet's passing paved the way so that personal and collective dissensions between members of different Tokoist groups played out in an increasingly open and extreme manner. Without a centralizing, present prophetic leadership, the different allegiances progressively distanced themselves and began regrouping in autonomous groups, each of which claimed the authority and legitimacy of the 'Tokoist project'. From this perspective, the financial problem was but a fuse that deflagrated the latent division. In my visits to Luanda, I rehearsed a sort of 'ethnography of conflict' in a field (luckily not literally) 'under fire' (Nordstrom and Robben 1995), and could distinguish several levels of explanation for this process of dismemberment that, today and ultimately, is revealed in the poli-ontologies (Scott 2007; McIntosh 2009) and ways of being and believing within Tokoism.

A first set of explanations can be rehearsed through the process of mobility and ethnic, territorial and generational transcendence that marked the history of Tokoism to this day, evolving from a Bakongo, Zombo movement to a multi-ethnic national Angolan project.[3] One of the tensions displayed reflected precisely the crossing of ethnic and territorial belongings with a generational trend, between Bakongo Tokoists of the Uíge region (Vale do Loge or Ntaia) and those of Luanda and other places. As I described in chapter 2, many of the leadership problems with which Toko struggled were related to both dimensions, and the historical creation of 'tribes' and 'classes' within the movement was, from this perspective, an attempt to anticipate and resolve these problems. Even shortly before his return from his exile in the Azores, Toko called this problem to mind:

> Well, there is a great rivalry inside the church because of the weddings. Those from the Ambrizete [Zaire region] want their daughters to marry the boys from Ambrizete. Those from Santo António do Zaire [likewise], same thing. Those from the Zombo [Uíge], same thing.... Well, I ask you: what does Christian Unity mean? Since the moment the prophets received the word of God, they died all united.... Now, we are the only ones carrying his Church, and we don't want to unite. (Letter by Simão Toko, 11 February 1974)

In 1982, a gathering takes place in Simão Toko's residence in the Congolenses. A meeting including the leader, the church elders and several Tokoists living in Ntaia Nova, with the objective of resolving the divergences between the residents in the compound, divided into two groups: those who were originally from the Bembe and Vale do Loge region (and had fled in 1961 to the *matas*, returning to inaugurate the Povo Taia)[4] and those who were originally from the neighbouring towns and villages, fellow countrymen of the prophet. The deterioration of their relationships, which had been motivated by both theological and 'cultural' divergences (*costume*; interview Doze Mais Velhos, 7 April 2011), provoked a literal division of the compound in half, without any attempt of relationship between each side. In a first moment, the leader had adopted a salomonic decision, dividing the offices and representations equally between both sides. However, the situation of 'rivalry' became unsustainable, and the leadership in Luanda began to receive different accounts of internal clashes in the village. This motivated a reunion at the Congolenses house with representatives of both groups, including, as representative of the 'locals', the *regedor* (*soba,* or customary authority) João Gino.

That day, as a Tokoist in Luanda recalled to me, 'there were bad spirits in the house'. The council meeting takes place and a decision is reached: the group represented by the *regedor* was to be expelled from the church. One of the elders present, however, upon hearing the decision, invokes an old Kikongo proverb that, in a literal translation, says that 'the snake [*jibóia,* or boa constrictor] is furled in the eggs', meaning that not all those included in the expelled group were worthy of the punishment. Toko intervenes and confirms that *soba* João Gino is, in fact, the snake (*mboma* in Kikongo). The accused reacts, claiming, 'If you think I'm mboma, well mboma is what I will be.' From this moment, the first official excision within the church takes place, with the creation of the Mboma group, associated with Ntaia Nova and years later led by Temo António, a direct nephew of Simão Toko.

Some time later, the financial issues take place, which remain unresolved. But the prophet's passing, or the followers' reaction to it, also provokes additional dissent. Namely, in what concerned the ritual mourning of his death. After the obsequies, the church declares sixty days of official mourning, during which there was to be no official act and a withdrawal from public affairs would be promoted. However, during this period, a young boy called Pedro Sangumbe arrives at Luanda from Huambo, escorted by a group of local elders. Sangumbe claimed that he had been *inspirado* and visited by the spirit of Simão Toko, who had given him the message that the sixty days of mourning that had been decreed were 'a joke' and should be raised to ninety days (interview Doze Mais Velhos, April 2011). As soon as the news of Sangumbe's arrival and message begins to circulate, a big discussion is installed within the different tribes and classes. The committee of the Doze Mais Velhos assembles and decides that it is the Anciãos e Conselheiros who should make the final decision. This group chooses to adopt an intermediate decision: bearing in mind that the previous committee had already proclaimed the sixty days of mourning, which would be respected, an extra thirty days of prayer and restricted activity would follow on behalf of the leadership. However, not everyone accepts this decision, and an internal scission occurs. When the sixty days are completed, a 'restoration service' (*culto de restauração*) is convoked, but a group led by Samuel Mambo Domingos and Manuel Lelo António decides not to participate, and officially declares a division within the Tokoist Church. As this group was associated with that administrative entity, it would be later known as Cúpula[5] or Direcção Central (Central Directorship).

But the process of internal scission does not end here. The council of 18 Classes 16 Tribos, which had remained together with the Doze Mais Velhos, begins to progressively contest their authority and requesting changes, introducing political elements that the Doze reject. Thus, in 1986, just two years after the prophet's death, we find four different 'Tokoist groups': the Doze Mais Velhos, the Cúpula, the 18 Classes 16 Tribos and finally the Mboma group. It is, therefore, a fragmented Tokoism, dispersed through several different alliances and affinities associated to different political entities, and building opposed argumentations and justifications to the sequence of events that occur after January 1984. The oppositions grow into several episodes of violence and mutual accusations, and members of each sector are forbidden from attending gatherings or even contacting members of the other groups. In this line, many Tokoist families are divided: mothers and fathers in one sector, sons and daughters in another. Many Tokoists thus begin to carry *testificações* (attestations), in order to be able to identify themselves before members of the same allegiance. One remarkable but tragic moment for the movement took place in Kalumboloka (near Catete, Bengo) on 15 February 1987. A group of believers of the 18 Classes 16 Tribos, attempting to release from jail a second group that had been imprisoned a few months before due to 'illegal public manifestation', clashed with the Angolan security forces. The authorities react and attack the Tokoists in Catete and also in Terra Nova in Luanda. In the aftermath, thirty to forty Tokoists are killed and many others remain imprisoned (Paxe 2009). But, deaths and prisons notwithstanding, the effects of this event would prove once again tragic for the Tokoist movement. In the first place, the state declares a full prohibition of any kind of public manifestation on behalf of the Tokoists, including collective services. Simultaneously, the 18 Classes 16 Tribos group itself would suffer a new internal scission, and new Tokoist churches emerge: a Direcção Mundial (World Directorship) and a Gabinete de Jesus Cristo (Jesus Christ Office), led by Mateus Rogério.

But concomitantly, despite the active prohibition, the group of Anciãos e Conselheiros of the Direcção Central does not interrupt their religious services and is somehow able to pursue their work. This, according to the Doze Mais Velhos, explains the growth of this group throughout the subsequent years and its development in the current hegemonic situation (interview, 7 April 2011). In the meantime, one sector of the 18 Classes 16 Tribos joins the Direcção, which in turn will suffer its own dissidences with the formation of two new autonomous groups: the Direcção Profética Mundial (World Prophetic Directorship) and the Tabernáculo.[6] Thus, in the late 1980s, we are no longer looking at a church divided into four groups, but rather an interminable set of leaderships – which, eventually, reached the existence of nine simultaneous and co-existing Tokoist churches (interview Doze Mais Velhos, October 2008).

This succession of events is remembered today as one of the most difficult moments in Tokoist history, and is illustrative of the accumulated difficulties experienced within Simão Toko's movement: the internal divisions, the decrease in church attendance motivated by the conflicts and also to Angolan emigration (see chapter 5) and finally the state repression, where the MPLA rehearsed a final deconstruction of Tokoism as an Angolan project (Paxe 2009).

From this particular perspective, however, the following years would witness an inflection in the state policy, where the relationships between the government and the church leaderships somewhat stabilized. This was partially due to the slow opening, on behalf of the MPLA cabinet of José Eduardo dos Santos, to the recognition of religious affairs in Angola (Viegas 1997, 2007, 2008), progressively withdrawing from the initial stances defended by Agostinho Neto, who had 'prophesied' the end of religions in this country (Viegas 2007: 12). In 1987, a first round of legalization of religious entities takes place in Angola, where the Catholic Church – who regains its status and sees its assets and patrimony returned – plus eleven Protestant denominations are officially recognized.[7] By this time, a Direcção Nacional de Assuntos Religiosos (National Directorate of Religious Affairs, or DNAR) is created, later becoming the Instituto Nacional de Assuntos Religiosos (National Institute of Religious Affairs, or INAR).

These governmental movements clearly denounce a turn in the MPLA policy regarding churches such as the Tokoist Church. But this movement would not be able to take advantage of such a turn, in terms of promoting its internal unity. In 1992, the government promotes a second campaign for the official recognition of religious entities. But given the absence of a centralizing hierarchy within Tokoism, there is no control over the process of submission, and finally three different Tokoist churches are officially recognized: the Direcção Central, the Doze Mais Velhos and the 18 Classes 16 Tribos – precisely the churches that were able to deliver the required documentation on time (Viegas 2007). Thus, this was the confirmation of the final dissolution of Simão Toko's church as a unitary project. Or so it appeared.

The Agency of Spirits

By the mid-1990s, however, things started to change (also see chapter 5). Several rumours and reports begin to circulate within the different leaderships in Luanda, concerning the apparition of Simão Toko's spirit to several different believers. One such case was Fernando Tchiwale, who would later become known as O Mensageiro (The Messenger). Coming from the region of Capelongo (Huíla), Tchiwale arrived in Luanda on 1996, with the following claim: 'Our Father Mayamona was with me, Luke 24:36–45. This is no inspiration or dream. In truth, father Mayamona, Simão Toko, manifested himself four times in the church of Capelongo and in my house. My wife, when she saw him, was struck and bed-ridden for three days' (Quibeta n.d.: 162). The message from Simão Toko that Tchiwale brought for the elders in Luanda was the following:

> I wanted to manifest myself in Luanda on July 25th, 1996. But where was I supposed to go, when the church members are completely divided? The church must foremost and urgently unite. Have the elders forgotten so quickly about all the suffering I had. Was the work I developed a joke? 1 Corinthians 4:18. This chapter you must take to the brothers of the 18 Classes 16 Tribos. Likewise, you must take 1 Corinthians 12:12 to the brothers of the Doze Mais Velhos. It is most important that the church reunites. Reconvene and then go to the government to cancel or remove the three recognitions in favour of one single church. I see this division within the church with great sadness and pain, because you have deviated from my teachings! (Quibeta n.d.: 162–193)

Tchiwale then met successively with the leaders of the different groups, but was not able to convince them regarding a reunification, a possibility only considered by the Direcção Central and the 18 Classes. The Doze Mais Velhos refuse to take his word, arguing that Tchiwale should have only transmitted his message and not attempt to order or influence the paths to be taken by the church (interview, 19 October 2008).

Despite the partial failure of his endeavour, Tchiwale decides to stay in Luanda and continue his attempts to push his message through.

As I mentioned above, the apparition of Simão Toko's spirit to Tchiwale was not the only one to be reported within the movement. Other cases of apparition or re-apparition are commented among the Tokoists, some of which occurred very recently. Another example is that of the *vate* Afonso Makiesse (from Kivelo, in Maquela do Zombo), who claimed to have met, in 1982 (thus when the *dirigente* was still alive) with a man claiming to be Simão Toko and who ordered him to fulfil a mission in the Béu region, where he would later build the Erasto Tesoureiro da Cidade (Erastus Treasurer of the City) movement,[8] which eventually gathered some following among the Tokoists of the Northern Tribe (Pedro 2008: 14).

In another case, it is reported that the prophet returned from the dead soon after his passing in 1984, and is hiding in the Cassequel neighbourhood, communicating exclusively with Mateus Rogério, leader of the so-called Gabinete de Jesus, a group that eventually separated from the Direcção Mundial. There are also reports of the incorporation of Simão Toko's spirit in several different believers, such as Augusto Bernardo (from Kibokolo in the Maquela do Zombo) and João Miguel Joana (in Luanda). Such reports continue to be delivered to the leaderships in Luanda to this day.

These different episodes of apparition, resuscitation and incorporation conform, as a Tokoist friend in Luanda told me, a 'spiritual warfare', with disputed agencies and mediations. Thus, the discussions, debates and confrontations observed to this day reflect the recognition (or lack thereof) of these episodes on behalf of the different sectors of the Tokoist movement. The novel spiritual agency, inspired by the church's prophetic tradition, nevertheless challenged it and shattered its theological foundations, revealing a problem of orthodoxy, sanctioning and authority. Politically speaking, this war could be interpreted within the framework of the 'surviving prophecy' attempts, responding to the necessary anxieties of the moment and presenting solutions to bridge the problem of the leader's absence, by making him once again present within the church. On the other hand, they are also revelatory of a particular ontology that invokes the mediation and power that constitute the church's tradition. In other words, they invoke – diverse and contrastingly – the mediating charisma of the grace of the Holy Spirit, cultivated within the church since its inception, and through which diverse phenomena of contact between material and immaterial dimensions take place. Here, once again we perceive the complexities behind the notion of charisma within this context, which invokes different understandings and levels of agency.

In the first place, if in the previous chapter we described the impact of charisma essentially through the manifestation of the Holy Spirit, in the attribution of the gifts of vision, knowledge and healing, here we acknowledge a different modality of spiritual agency and mediation: the 'spiritist' agency of an individual volition – reverberated in the prophets and angels that manifest themselves in the *vates* and believers – that is not necessarily connected to the Pentecostal experience of 1949. At a first glance, this expression of spiritual agency (understood within Tokoism as 'spiritualism') would appear to break a previous orthodox boundary work (see Espirito Santo 2010) within the church, which in this case would refer to the rejection of spiritism (such as cults of the dead and kimbanda), as an 'expression of Satan's iniquitous and evil work' (Agostinho n.d.: 122–123). But the conflict generated in this period reveals that the 'bad spirits' were also present in Tokoism's heart. This thesis reinforces the idea of a 'spiritual warfare', inasmuch as it was through the manifestation of spirits and its political application that many of the church's cleavages heightened. This explains why, for many Tokoists, the *vates* are a central piece in the puzzle of the trepidation experienced in the church since the prophet's physical disappearance. The conflict is thus taken up by an 'agency of spirits' (Espirito Santo and Tassi 2012; Espirito Santo and Blanes 2013) and a notion of charisma as power and mentality – as the spiritual power was invoked in order to serve specific political purposes, such as leaderships and attempts to transcend internal trepidation.

But this spiritual war is also revelatory of another vicissitude: the absence of a sanction, i.e. of a process of ideological and doctrinal stabilization that would allow for an edifice of authority and unquestionability around Toko's religious project.[9] From this perspective, one could say that the war of the *vates* began at the precise moment when individual interpretations concerning Tokoist spiritualism prevailed, and these internal disputes would then translate as discussions concerning Toko's spiritual legacies and its distinctiveness. Tokoist spirits, invoking João Vasconcelos's expression, became 'homeless' (2008), orphan.[10] Their agency becomes increasingly impacting, as they escape the process of sanctioning – given the absence of a consensually legitimate person, entity or rule, producer of a 'contested authority' (Lambek 1990) – and creatively impose their own discipline. Dreams and apparitions thus become part of the political landscape (see Mittermaier 2011), and authority becomes an object of dispute between persons and spirits. And so do texts, through the movement of ad hoc interpretation of the prophet's epistles, in an attempt to rescue stances and processes of theological sanction. Here, an 'archive fever' (Derrida 1995) developed, where many Tokoists investigated Toko's previous announcements, in order to locate the veracity and confirmation of current events (see, for instance, chapter 3 concerning Catete).

It is in this particular context that the appearance of Tchiwale from Capelongo becomes central in the Tokoist historiography and contemporary situation.

Personification and Biographical Extension

At the turn of the century, when Tchiwale was persisting in his mission in Luanda, a few hundred kilometres up north in a small Tokoist nucleus in the Damba commune (Negage, Uíge region), a young man begins to reveal preoccupying physical and mental sings: 'Young Afonso Nunes was seized, to the point that people said he was crazy, after he fell ill for a week, and didn't speak or eat or anything; one day he rose and requested that a prayer be performed. After that he had some broth. And then he announced a message concerning what he experienced' (*O País*, 10 November 2009). A few days later, Nunes experiences another crisis, and his family, thinking he was psychologically disturbed, took him to the psychiatric hospital in Luanda, where, apart from a very high body temperature, nothing was detected. They thought of interning him for insanity, but the people who followed the case quickly realized that everything he announced would eventually come true the following day. The young man prophesied (ibid.).

After performing some rituals in the church, Afonso Nunes stabilized, and 'the Holy Spirit entered' (ibid.). Very soon he would be acknowledged as a *vate* and sheltered by the church in Negage. But later he is visited in dreams by Simão Toko, who warns him that he intends to 'work in him': 'In you I will talk, go to Luanda' (ibid.). After some hesitation, the elders and *vates* from the Negage church, against his family's will, bring him to Luanda, where he meets with the different Tokoist leaderships. In December 2007, in a conversation with Bishop Nunes, he explained how the process of 'personification' occurred:

> Sixteen years passed, in 2000, after all those confusions the church experienced – when a great leader leaves, there is most certainly a struggle for the succession, and the Tokoists could not avoid that fight. The church fragmented, but God our Father knew better, what happened is that I appeared in Negage in the year 2000, and told Bishop Afonso Nunes that I

would talk through him to reunite the church and raise the truth of what had fallen. This happened at 6h20, this vision, this encounter. But as you know, man sometimes resists the will of God, and that summon, the spiritual church, the spiritual messages were not accepted, but afterwards it was seen that he had to accept, but it took time. I think it was from April to July that the mission was accepted, it took time to accept because in the beginning no one knew what they were supposed to do. But the spirit said they should go [to Luanda] because if you don't the church will remain, so to speak, hidden under the sea for a thousand years. This was the only message. So you will have to accept and go to Luanda, so that I talk through you. This vision occurred, and then again and again, and with the strength of the Holy Spirit in the other bodies you will also see that they were prophesying in the name of God that brother Afonso Nunes must accept this mission. So it was that, on July 15th of the year 2000, the commission to go to Luanda to spread the message of church unification and the rebuilding of the church, of the biblical tabernacle that had fallen, was accepted. So from then on, Afonso Nunes, as in Galatians chapter 2, verse 20 – you can do the reading of what the apostle said: 'It is no longer Afonso who lives, but Simão who lives through him.' (Interview Afonso Nunes, 3 December 2007)

Thus, in an operation of 'personification' – believers also frequently refer to *revestimento espiritual,* or 'spiritual coating' – a biographical extension was performed through which the prophet Simão Gonçalves Toko, after being born in 1918 and physically disappearing in 1984, returned from heaven in the year 2000 in order to proceed with his vital trajectory. In other words, a process of conversation between body and spirit took place, through a simultaneous production of a personal sacrifice (on behalf of Nunes) and a continued individuality (on behalf of Toko), made present, 'familiar' (Lambek 2006) through the process of coating. Likewise, it also produced a new form of mediation and immediacy (Eisenlohr 2009; Palmié 2011) that accumulated the previous 'non-cerimonialized' or liturgical manifestations (Hess 1990) of Toko's spirit, while simultaneously sanctioning its charismatic profusion through the operation on a *vate* apprentice's body.

In this return, Toko brought a message divided into three idealizations: the church's reunification; its redesign into a 'universal' project; and the construction of a Universal Temple in Luanda (Quibeta n.d.: 165–166). Nevertheless, this ontologically challenging proposal still required political legitimation. In July of that same year, upon Nunes's arrival to Luanda, a private meeting takes place between him and Tchiwale, and after its conclusion it is announced that the spirit that visited the Mensageiro in Capelongo in 1996 was the same one that occupied Nunes in Negage: the spirit of Simão Toko. In a matter of months, Nunes conducted countless meetings with the different tribes, councils and *sucursais* of the church, and finally assumed the leadership of the Direcção Central when the then leader Luzaísso Lutango decided to step down in his favour. In the months that followed, several groups that had fallen out, among them most of the members of the Direcção Profética Mundial, the Mboma group and the 18 Classes 16 Tribos, decided to return to the Direcção Central.

The transformation observed after this transition eventually affected most sectors within the Tokoist Church. Of the several changes, three became paramount: the instauration of a bishopric in the church, in the meantime restructured into a Direcção Universal (Universal Directorship); the initiation of the construction of the Universal Temple in the Golfe neighbourhood (southeast Luanda); and especially the proclamation of the inauguration of a new 'Millennium of Christ', after the 'restoration of the tabernacle' that had fallen after the prophet's physical passing (Quibeta n.d.: 165). This declaration wasn't just political, but bore ontological implications, as it simultaneously fulfilled a prophetic declaration and inaugurated a 'new era' within Tokoism. In several of his epistles, Toko had prophesied:

> Therefore we, the spiritually and materially poor, must prepare ourselves for prayer until the year 2000. But how do we know that the year 2000 will be the year of true events? … There are still 29 to go, if the days don't cut short we will remove certain Tokoist laws and increase others, because in the world of today the religious man is doing reforms, and so we must do one of our own in our Church of Christ. (Letter by Simão Toko, 6 March 1971)

> From the creation of the world and Adam until the deluge with Noah, two days equal 2000 years passed, and from Noah to the birth of Christ two more days equal 2000 years passed, counting in total 4000 years; and since the birth of Christ until today its 1973 years; adding to the 4000 years that makes 5973 years. Thus, in order to complete 6 days of creation or 6000 years, there are still 6000 minus 5973 equals 27 years. Can you handle the 27 to come? After 2000 years it will then be the kingdom of 1000 years of Christ and his faithful resting in the hands of God. (Letter by Simão Toko, 21 September 1973)

Thus, according to the *dirigente*'s 'spiritual math' (letter by Simão Toko, 27 February 1974), the year 2000 would be highly meaningful for the Tokoists, the year of the millennium. The appearance of Afonso Nunes in Luanda would therefore inaugurate, for those who decided to follow him, a new spiritual calendar, and simultaneously confirm its reformist spirit.[11] This initiative became effective in the official instauration of the new era in the Direcção Universal,[12] marked by an ideology of reformation and renovation that would affect several stances of To-koist experience and action. And effectively, after the change of cabinet and declaration of the New Millennium, the Direcção Universal experienced dramatic changes.

The message brought by Afonso Nunes had a great impact in the church, to the point of radically transforming its situation transversally in just a few years. After reading and hearing from the beginning of my fieldwork about the pains and suffering of a church that had been historically persecuted, when I arrived in 2007 to Luanda to visit the Tokoist church for the first time, I was taken aback with the sharp contrast I observed: I attended services and spoke before dozens of thousands of people; I visited the construction work at several points of the city of Tokoist temples and schools; I read, heard and watched public interventions by its leaders in the national newspapers, radio stations and television channels (see also Hansen 2006), etc. I also learnt about their future projects envisaging the creation of 'Tokoist media' and social networking, Tokoist universities, museums, etc. I visited the secondary school built by the Direcção Universal in their compound on the Golfe (ibid.), and witnessed the construction work going on there. These first interactions with the leadership often became excursions where I would be presented with an *obra*, the work of a church experiencing a dramatic growth. In December of that year, together with Ramon Sarró and Fátima Viegas, I visited the construction site of the new Universal Temple and was overwhelmed with the scale of the project, involving so many believers (who contributed financially in the services for the construction, but also physically, aiding in backup activities).[13] One specific interview we conducted around this time with Bishop Nunes at his provisional office located at the construction site, I recall, was constantly interrupted by the sound of a jackhammer on the floor above.

In these encounters with Bishop Nunes, Luzaísso Lutango, and other members of this allegiance, apart from the generosity and warmth they offered to me, I appreciated their confident, assertive and proactive postures, commenting and intervening in different sectors of the Angolan society and promoting their particular, Christ-centric vision of the country and the world. I would later meet them in their subsequent visits to Lisbon (see chapter 5). I also progressively acknowledged how, in the Angolan public space and particularly in the media of this country, the 'Tokoist Church' was, in fact, none other than the Direcção Universal led by Nunes, leaving little room for the public visibility and manifestation of other groups or following of the prophet Simão Toko. For example, in a recent interview to the Televisão Pública de Angola

Illustration 16. Tokoist Universal Temple, January 2013. Photo: Ruy Llera Blanes.

(TPA, Angolan National Television), Nunes summarized the church's activities for the year 2010:

> At the internal level of the country, we, as a national church, can consider this a positive year. The church was able to be part of the great activities, making itself present in many moments. Especially, the organization of the CAN[14] in our country. It was in fact an event like no other, in a country that, after ending the war, was able to congregate several African and world nations and witness this great event. And at another level, as we have been able to see, we are witnessing the country's reconstruction in terms of transportation infrastructures, as well as the edification of new cities. All this makes us believe that struggling for peace was worthwhile, and it is still worthwhile to keep preserving that peace in all aspects, both spiritual or religiously. On the other hand, as attentive counsellors in the development of the country's political life, we will keep playing our role and exerting our influence, so that peace effectively remains, because it will facilitate the national reconstruction and the country's stability, as well as the church's. (Interview TPA, 30 December 2010)

From such statements we infer a new realignment concerning the movement's ecclesiastical memory vis-à-vis Angolan political history.

Nunes's interventions in the national media became, after his ascent, progressively pervasive and produced a religiously based commentary to events taking place in Angolan society and politics. One such initiative was the public stance assumed by Nunes against the on-going civil war that prolonged in the country since its independence. In one of his first appearances in the Angolan media, Nunes stated: 'If you want war, you will witness a bigger disaster than what you have seen up to date; I had already warned in 1975, if this is what you want, what will become is even worse, the war you have seen until now was a joke' (2 January 2001). In May of that same year, he publicly announced his 'Plan for Peace in Angola' entitled *Deus Volta a Falar aos Angolanos* (God Speaks Once Again to the Angolans), which was delivered in hand to the deputies of the National Assembly, and contained thirty proposals for the resolution of the armed conflict (*Alfa & Omega,* June 2001): 'Sons of Angola, if you listen to my advice, now that I talk to you in spirit, God will be with you. Your sons and grandsons will live safely in this land, without being driven away, rains of blessing will fall over the land and you will eat abundant bread, in conformity with what is stated in the book of Leviticus 26:3–6' (Bishop Nunes, Deus Volta a Falar aos Angolanos). This announcement would receive confirmation a year later, with the end of the armistice that followed Jonas Savimbi's death on 22 February. In the meantime, a progressive rapprochement between the church and the state and parliamentary forces was observed, as for instance in MPLA secretary Bento Bento's request for a 'blessing for the Tokoist Church' (*Angonotícias,* 7 July 2004), or UNITA President Isaías Samakuva's participation in the church's celebration of the eighty-eight years after Toko's birthday (*Angonotícias,* 1 March 2006), or Nunes's consideration that Angolan independence was, thirty-three years later, positive for the expansion of the Holy Scriptures (*Angola Acontece,* 12 November 2008) or finally in José Eduardo dos Santos's official statement congratulating the church for the sixtieth anniversary of its inauguration (*Jornal de Angola,* 27 July 2009). Such examples are mere corroborations of the Direcção Universal's new approach to Angolan politics and partisanship, also illustrated in the fact that there is almost no Sunday service in the Golfe compound that doesn't welcome the visit of an official representative of the government, parliament or other intermediary structures of authority and representation. Today, the notion of 'partnership' is often invoked to describe this relationship (*Jornal de Angola,* 27 December 2011).

In the subsequent years, Nunes's office has among other things publicly announced its availability to collaborate with the Angolan government towards a more peaceful society (*Jornal de Angola,* 22 December

2009), debated recurrent problems in Angolan society (*Jornal de Angola,* 25 July 2009), organized a public march against drug abuse (*Jornal de Angola,* 27 June 2010) and renewed vows for the consolidation of the newfound peace, appealing for the importance of cultivating tolerance for a better conviviality between formerly estranged brothers (*Jornal de Angola,* 7 April 2011).[15] They have also promoted several aiding campaigns, donating goods, food and money to combat social tragedies.[16] But these pacifying and nation-building speeches and actions could also be read as a double-ended message, directed outside towards Angolan society and politics in general, but also inwards, for a Tokoist public. From this perspective, the reunification discourse frequently observed in these interventions and statements converged within a religious and political plane. In a 2008 interview, Nunes explicitly aligned political and religious history, associating the end of the civil war with the inauguration of a new moment of Tokoist evangelical expansion (*Angola Acontece,* 12 November 2008). He also spoke in a second interview about 'healing the wounds caused by the divisions that separated whole families' – a phrasing that could be applied equally to Tokoists and Angolans (*Angola Press,* 25 July 2009).

Concomitant to this political realignment and public re-institution, a process of public heritagization of Toko's figure and memory begins to take place, echoing through the media and public sphere. During a lecture given in preparation of the sixtieth anniversary of the church's foundation, Nunes invoked the prophet's role in the 'awakening of the Africans' consciousness', highlighted his precursory libertarian ideas, and pleaded for an official recognition of Simão Toko as a national figure by the state authorities (*Rádio Nacional de Angola,* 8 June 2009). Luís Nguimbi, member of the Conselho de Igrejas Cristãs de Angola (CICA, Angolan Council of Christian Churches) would later describe the Tokoist Church as 'national heritage', noting its 'genuinely Angolan and African character' (*Angola Press,* 8 April 2010). Likewise, in August 2010, the Direcção held a ceremony in tribute to the Tokoists who had been deported to concentration camps in Angola and abroad during the colonial period (*O País,* 31 August 2010). A similar intention was to be found behind the recent initiative to build a memorial site in Negage to remember the Tokoist adepts of that region that were murdered by the colonial regime and buried in mass graves (*Jornal de Angola,* 3 March 2011).

These interventions, still taking place now, clearly insert the Tokoist trajectory within public registers of national memory and imagination, installing and monumentalizing visible landmarks in the Angolan scenery. But they also speak to internal processes of stabilization and destabilization, precisely originated by the disputes described above. In chapter 3 I described the encounter Toko had with the 'Good God' in Catete in 1950, also noting that this date was the subject of contention between the different factions, some of which placed the event as having taken place in 1935. When I visited the site in early 2011, I noticed how a Chinese construction company was building a *jango*[17] around the famous tree, in order to safeguard and facilitate the site's monumentalization (see *O País*, 26 April 2011). This denoted a continued preoccupation vis-à-vis the officialization and publicization of a particular version of Toko's prophetic trajectory. This preoccupation translated into such processes of heritagization, which were in fact novel in what concerned Tokoist interest for historiography. For instance, many Tokoists in Luanda and Catete with whom I talked to about this episode reminded me that this interest in the Catete landmark was quite recent and sudden, and re-emerged after Nunes's appearance and first visit to the site – as the Simão Toko personified – on 25 September 2000 (see Quibeta n.d.: 172). Before that, it was just one of several landscapes from the prophet's spiritual and vital trajectory.

In sum, despite Toko's permanently multitudinous biography, the Tokoist experience after his death had become secluded, clandestine, withdrawn. With Nunes's appearance, it became once again a public phenomenon. In what concerned the Direcção Universal, there was little left of the history of suffering and persecution I had heard about.

Who Owns Tokoism? Leadership and Temporal Disputes

If Nunes's efforts for Tokoist reunification were notable and quite successful from many points of view, it is also true that not all Tokoists light-heartedly accepted his proposals for renovation. Despite the fact that a superficial or media-filtered impression of Tokoism in Angola gives the impression of a hegemonic Direcção Universal that is working towards the final reunification, once we begin strolling down certain musseques in Luanda, or in certain areas outside the capital, the reality appears before us in a somewhat different light, revealing further complexities and dissent. One first group that did not accept Nunes's reunification strategy appeared after an internal scission in the Direcção, led by Osório Marcos (former programming secretary in this allegiance), from the so-called Sulana (southern) tribe (Caconda), who refused to follow Nunes and eventually created a new group, also structured around a bishopric. Today, they constitute an important nucleus in the Benguela region.

Another group who rejected the reunification was precisely that of the Doze Mais Velhos, who are today probably the most visible (although not exclusive) face of opposition to the *cúpula* led by Nunes. The group is based today in the house that served as Simão Toko's last residence before his passing, in the Congolenses-Terra Nova neighbourhood, and their central temple is being rebuilt in the Palanca musseque, where a school is also to be found. Through their internal organizations, namely the Grupo Coral Nova Esperança Tocoista (GC-NET, Choral Group New Tokoist Hope), they have become very active in editorial, media and social support initiatives, through which they promote countless activities of study and reflection concerning the prophet's biography. This is somewhat unsurprising, as it is within this group that most of the elders who worked with Toko are congregated, accumulating material and intellectual memories of those times. It is also, I argue, a reaction to the current state of affairs where they struggle against the Universal hegemony.

The Doze Mais Velhos, as I explained above, stem from the original group designated by Simão Toko while still in Leopoldville. It is therefore not very difficult to imagine that their ethnic background is the same as that of the *dirigente*'s: Bakongo and Zombo. After the deportation to Angola, most of them were sent to Luanda, Porto Alexandre and especially Vale do Loge, where a significant group sojourned together with their spouses and children. The group found today in the Terra Nova and Palanca is mostly composed of their descendants and others who followed the members of this particular leadership during their subsequent sojourns in the Taia Nova and Luanda.[18] As the oldest recognized formal entity within the church, they are usually seen as representing in many ways a 'traditional' branch of Tokoism, associated not so much to a syncretic understanding of the movement, but instead to a conservative stance, directed to Toko's initial reformist proposals in the times when the movement was still circumscribed to the Bakongo ethnicity. They also promote a very spiritualist discourse, cultivating the *vates*' production of knowledge and understanding.

After getting in touch with this group, I progressively established a rapport with the leadership and many of its younger members, with whom I improvised several debates concerning Tokoist history and spiritual activity, and exchanged documentation, written drafts and comments to each other's production. But our first interactions were obviously focused on the crisis and reunification. In October 2008, after a first courtesy visit performed one year before, I returned to Simão Toko's house for one of many long conversations regarding the topic we held from there on.[19] While we sat around a table in the living room and were being served some comfortingly fresh beverages, we asked the main leaders of this branch why they didn't accept Nunes's proposal for a reunion. Having first met the 'other side', we had arrived to the Congolenses somewhat imbued with an idea that reunification was pretty much inevitable, and resistance to it was a matter of time. But their answer incorporated suggestions that contained several philosophical, political and ontological implications. In the first place, they did not recognize Nunes as someone with the sufficient political legitimacy:

> Well, inside the church, even when Simão Toko was alive, we never heard of Afonso Nunes, he was never part of the church's directing apparel. Neither administrative nor ecclesiastical. Even after the death of the *dirigente* Simão Gonçalves Toko and until the year 2000, we had never heard of Afonso Nunes. Even today we don't have a clear idea of him. We don't because for us Afonso Nunes is just someone who appeared in the year 2000. ... He appeared as a messenger, just as Tchiwale had done. But if the first one came as messenger, he came as Toko himself. (Interview Doze Mais Velhos, 19 October 2008)

But eventually, the Doze Mais Velhos accepted to meet with Nunes and hear him out. However, upon hearing him, they decided that they did not 'recognize' Toko in his body and words:

> Yes, we received him, as a messenger who brings a message, coming from the Negage, province of Uíge. Okay, that's fine. After the reception, we gave it some time. And in fact, when he presented himself, he identified himself as Simão Toko: 'I am your *dirigente*, I am Simão Toko, I was among you.' ... During three hours, as the saying goes: he who talks too much doesn't get it right. (ibid.)

This recognition, or lack thereof, is interesting as it is not necessarily based in the rejection of the idea of personification per se as rationally or intellectually absurd, but instead in the specific personalization of this spiritual operation, rendered unidentifiable by the Doze. In any case, it reveals the anxiety and willingness of the Doze to 'meet' Simão Toko again, to make him present once again. Nunes's experience, despite being one such example of 'making present', did not meet their political expectations.

But perhaps the strongest divergence was, in fact, theological, and reverberated in the millennial confirmation operated by Nunes through the restoration of the tabernacle:

I mean, we pointed out the mistakes we noticed in him. He would even
say: 'You must all follow me. If there is a group that doesn't follow me,
that church you are waiting for, that is up in the sky and waiting to come
down, will never do so.' And we asked: 'Mr. Simão Toko, if you are in
fact Simão Toko, what we understood on July 25th, 1949, after the Holy
Spirit descended, the words that followed were that the Church of Christ
descended and was delivered to us. And now that church is up in the
skies and if we don't follow you the church won't descend but will actually climb higher, will it fall in another continent?' No, it's the opposite:
the church descended in 1949. And now the question: between 1949 and
the year 2000, what church have we been in, if the church after all hasn't
descended? (ibid.)

Thus, the divergence was placed through a problem of messianic
providence and on the prophet's place in the church's configuration:
the Doze Mais Velhos wouldn't accept the process of paracletization
and consequent prophetic fulfilment produced by the return of Toko
in Nunes's body. In first place because the act of remembrance and
posterior salvation, which had attributed the gifts and wisdom to the
church, had already occurred in 1949. Secondly, because for them
Toko was an 'envoy from God, to whom was given the task of congregating the sheep and show them the way to God' (interview Doze Mais
Velhos, 19 October 2008). Within this context, the work of sacrifice
and martyrdom had already begun before, and not in the year 2000.
Therefore, another theology and teleology was at stake: the sacrificial
and providential sense attributed to Simão Toko's trajectory, inserted
within a process of temporalization of prophetic knowledge. As Vasco
(from the Doze) told me once: 'I still remember very well his last words
in a public service here in the Bairro Indígena. He said: 'all of these
things I am telling you, you will be able to see them with your own
eyes. And when I'm no longer around, that's when you will remember
that among you was a prophet' (19 October 2008).

This tension reveals the importance that the language of sacrifice
assumes in the way the Tokoists remember their prophet, collapsing
methods of historical knowledge (Cole 2001) and moralities (Strenski
2003) – i.e. memories and expectations, hope. Simão Toko's trajectory
of martyrdom and sacrifice is, from this perspective, a trajectory of
a Christian prophet who paid a price for trying to fulfil his mission
– the typical hagiographic narrative of saintly self-sacrifice in itself, if
it were not for the fact that there is a shared testimoniality between the
prophet and some of the members who are still alive and bearing the
memory of the prophetic trajectory.

This is in fact a Tokoist sacrificial logic embedded in certain ritual
and practical acts such as the commemorations and mnemonics de-

scribed in the previous chapter; however, this prophetic self-sacrifice is also understood as a form of temporal acknowledgement that ultimately and theologically binds remembrance with expectation within a providential time frame. In other words, the shared sense that there was an ulterior reason behind Toko's prophetic trajectory which transcends his own personality and corporeality – for instance, the salvation of Africa and, ultimately, mankind. More than invoking the immediate consequence of the sacrificial act – or, as Marcel Mauss and Henri Hubert had suggested, its 'benefit' (2003 [1899]: 21 and ff.) – this theological insertion of a biographical narrative into a logic of sacrifice unfolds temporal acknowledgments and theories of time, posing problems of 'beginnings' (Lambek 2007) and ends (Agamben 2002). As we will see, the prophetic heritage appeared within the movement deploys these problems within the process of Toko's post-mortem charismatization and consecration. What is at stake is the way lives of leadership such as Toko's become narrativized, collectivized into local or institutional histories and memories – in such ways that martyrdom and memory become entrenched (Castelli 2007) through particular processes of intellectual production and literary transformation (Douglas 1999) into particular ideologies of faith. In other words, the way prophetic lives become 'mythologized' (Middleton 1999) and 'heroicized' (Mary 2005) in collective memory stances, such as stories (Castelli 2007) that may either produce orthodoxy or heterodoxy/innovation. The process of personification performed by Nunes by way of a 'borrowing of charisma' – importing that of Simão Toko into his own – can also be seen as a specific form of heritagization that deploys a temporalized sacrificial logic.

The issue here then seems to be how the same sacrificial logic is interpreted within the different sides of the conflict. For the Doze, for instance, Toko was a scapegoat, a victim who paid a price for his own righteousness and selflessness, for abdicating his life into the 'advancement of a cause'. For Nunes, one could argue, a double sacrifice was performed through the operation of the prophet's biographical extension: that of his own body and pre-personification personality; and that of Simão Toko, forced to return from heaven in order to continue and renew the work of sacrifice he had performed between 1918 and 1984. Such interpretations affect notions of providentiality and agency, as was revealed in the discussion above on whether the church had in fact 'descended from the skies' or not. In this regard, a subtext emerged in this discussion concerning the work of the *vates*, spiritual inhabitation and bodily mediation: What is Toko's spirit's place within the Tokoist orthodox spiritual gallery? What are the mechanisms and dispositions that allow for a recognition of the 'authentic spirit'? In what terms does this respond to the announcements and revelations performed within the tabernacle? What are its theological implications?

To date, I haven't had a chance to observe, in my interviews with Bishop Nunes, his reaction to the Doze's allegations. However, he continues to publicly embark on a discourse of hope, announcing that the reunification will be complete in the near future: 'Today we feel that the reconciliation is much more accelerated than before; there is still a very small group [that hasn't joined], but we are praying the they too, soon enough, may integrate the church' (interview Bishop Nunes, 3 December 2007). In the meantime, the public display of reunification continues. For instance, in mid-February 2011, a public ceremony of reconciliation took place in Negage, where two thousand Tokoists that were *desavindos* (had 'fallen out') re-entered the church (*Jornal de Angola*, 24 February 2011). Presiding over the act, Nunes stated: 'We are working to reconcile the families, because there will be no strong church nor strong country without a united family' (ibid.). This approach surrounds the on-going situation with an aura of inevitability that is nevertheless contested by the other groups.

Prophetic Memories and Heritages, Part 2

One day in June 2008, I was sitting down at Moamba, a famous Angolan restaurant in Lisbon, having a drink with Simão Vemba, then evangelist of the Tokoist church in Lisbon. I had just finished reading one of the two biographies of the prophet that I had borrowed from him (Melo 2002), and was explaining my surprise after reading a portrait of the prophet somewhat unknown to me at the time: an Afro-centric description that in many ways removed Toko from the Angolan socio-political scene and simultaneously inserted his trajectory within a process of revision of standard Christian historiography.

Entitled *Jesus the African*,[20] Pastor Melo's work is a hagiography of Toko, presented as an 'African Christian saint' who represented the confirmation of the 'true third secret of Fátima'[21] – that the paraclete announced by Jesus Christ would be born in Africa, despite the Vatican's disclosure in the year 2000. From this particular perspective, the movement of remembrance provoked by Simão Toko would be in fact and answer to the 'stolen legacy' of Christianity, operated by the white, European civilization (Melo 2002: 75–114). In contrast with the other prophetic biographies circulating within Tokoism, Melo's text performs a deep theological exegesis of Toko's significance, transcending the internal, denominational sphere. Transcending the dimension of political dispute, it elevates Toko's figure into the dimension of Christian archae-ology, historiographical reconstruction and spiritual providence.

But Melo's book also represented a different intellectual and spiri-tual approach to Toko's prophetic trajectory, as it combined an intel-lectual exercise with the de-territorialized public display of revealed knowledge, performed by someone who had never met the prophet in life.[22] As Melo later explained to me, it was 9 March 1983, and he was peacefully sleeping in his apartment in the Épinettes in Paris, when, at around 3:00 AM he felt a sudden 'electric shock' in his navel. Melo rose in disconcertment and saw a ball of fire, as a 'burning bush'. He began to shout with all his strength 'Fire, fire!' but curiously no sound came out of his throat.

Melo then entered a trance and heard a voice inside him saying: 'Take something to write and write!' In a daze, he opened the drawer at his bedside table and pulled out a wad of A4 sheets. He sat down at his desk and, as an irresistible force completely paralyzed his whole body, his right hand began to write automatically, as if he were a re-mote-controlled robot. He produced ten pages without knowing what he was writing, and after ten minutes his hand stopped, the burning ball disappeared and he finally regained control over his body. When he returned to the pages he wrote, he recognized his handwriting, but it looked strangely jerky. When he read what had been 'dictated', he realized it was the revelation of the third Great Secret of Fátima, held captive by the Vatican since 1960. Melo's work ever since, until he com-pleted his publication, was one of research and archaeology, searching for evidence to complement and verify the revelation.[23]

This Afro-centric portrait, feeding off key moments in Toko's bio-graphical trajectory, can also be found in other narrative dispositions, as for instance the metaphorization of his birth into the 'star of dawn' (see chapter 1), the recurrent connection into a 'prophetic chain' with Simon Kimbangu and others (ibid.), or the explicit configuration of Toko as the 'Black Christ', as is conveyed, for instance, by the Direcção Mundial today. It also translates as part of the act of remembrance that re-centres Christian historiography. As Bishop Nunes commented to me once,

The church exists since Christ left, year thirty-three. After Christ, the church remained with the apostles, who led the church until year 90 AD, when the last Apostle, John, dies. After this, the church is conducted by elder presbyters who had followed the work of the apostles, until roughly 312–315, moment when the true doctrine of the church was diverted. As you know, when Constantine adopted the church, many spiritual prin-ciples that Christ had left with us were diverted. The true church, as we Tokoists understand it, was diverted. (Interview, 3 December 2007).

Such intellectual constructions reveal how Toko was, in life and in death, subject to different personal appropriations. His prophetic trajectory became the object of exegesis and public interpretation. However, in addition to these Angolan-based configurations, Melo's book represents a 'global theological critique', perhaps motivated by the fact that it was written not in Angola but in Paris and inserted within a pluralized, Euro-centric Christian setting, representing a novel reading of Toko's life. Likewise, Kisela's book, also written by a diasporic Tokoist (see chapter 5), highly stressed Toko's legacy in the Azores, enhancing his transnational outreach (2004).

Back in the Angolan restaurant in Lisbon, when I questioned Vemba with these thoughts, he replied: 'You see, it's like this glass. It is sitting here on this table, but whoever looks at it will say it is half full or half empty. The same happens with the prophet. Depending on where you stand and which are your motivations, you will see him differently.' This image summarizes an inescapable fact found within this movement: the complexity that conforms the images and memories associated with a charismatic leader. One can detect several modes of appropriation and conjugation of the prophet's memory at play: an updated, presential method, such as the one proposed by Nunes, Mateus Rogério and others; a testimonial method, operated by those who lived and worked with Toko, and who may or may not recognize him in Nunes's body; a hagiographical method, which seeks to contextualize his vital trajectory within an historical, theological and teleological framework; a spiritualist method, which inserts the prophetic memory within the plane of a divine, providential timeline, as proposed through the prophets and spirits working with the *vates*; etc. These approaches build a composite picture of Toko's memory and legacy, which once again becomes 'heritagized' through processes of recognition and political discursification. But if in the previous chapter we observed these processes develop within ritual and experiential settings in the sake of stability and certitude, here they become politically active and significant precisely in the context of an unstable, conflictual situation. We could in fact say that the memory realignments – and in many ways revivals – were promoted and enhanced by the trepidation provoked by the prophet's death. From this perspective, the burgeoning processes of personal heritagization that Toko is experiencing today are part of 'differential demands on memory' (Rowlands 1993: 141) on behalf of the different Tokoist sensibilities.

In any case, if there is something on which all Tokoists agree, it is the importance of reminiscence. For most Tokoists, to perform this heritage is to make Toko 'present', to resolve a particular ontological and political anxiety through stances of materialization and immaterialization (Engelke 2007: 226 and ff.). If, for instance, the Doze relied on the spiritual dimension of Toko's presence, for Nunes and his followers the presence became materialized, corporealized through a process of *actualização* (updating).

The problem here, the conflict, would therefore be one of representation and authority concerning those temporal stances of presentification (ibid.). The different memories, agencies and charismas associated to the leader, provokers of the different images and names attributed to him throughout his life and in his memory, reveal the historical abundance (Orsi 2008) and simultaneous tension (Antze and Lambek 1996) that substantiates in different modes of identification, recognition and allegiance.

But these methods of appropriating memory also reveal the different ontologies produced by the diverse territorialities, affinities and allegiances that populated Tokoist history. On the one hand, as we saw in the previous section, there are multiple and simultaneous political and experiential notions of temporality and providence that have become (or stemmed out of) political disputes originated, among other things, from the spiritual warfare. On the other, both time and its apparent irreversibility are revealing: there are in these conflictual dynamics two distinct processes of political and ontological opposition. In the first place, an opposition between theologically conservative and progressive dynamics within the Tokoist universe, where some (the Doze Mais Velhos) are accused of 'living in the past', of not accepting the innovation and updating reforms of the prophet's teachings because they are 'in the same place where the prophet left them, in 1984' (as a Tokoist friend told me in Luanda), and others (the Direcção Universal) are accused of 'living in another millennium' and forgetting the past, ignoring the material legacy left behind by Simão Toko (his teaching, his words, his documents), as I often heard among the Doze. This double temporality is also, at the end of the day, an expression of the tensions between hetero and orthodoxies, mediated by the inevitable generational transition – typified in the (exaggerated) idea that the 'old folk' are with the Doze, and therefore this allegiance would be doomed to disappear in the near future, while the 'young generation' is all on the side of the Direcção. Despite the fact that the Direcção Universal has indeed attracted a renewed, younger audience, the seniority was not exclusive to the Doze. In fact, a younger generation of followers of this allegiance have recently staged a new contestation concerning the role played by Bishop Nunes, taking place especially on social networks, where different proofs and allegations circulate against his enterprise, often described as a 'falsity' and the 'work of an 'adulator'.

However, this dichotomy, as a product of a conflictive setting, may hide other, more plural understandings of Toko's collective memory. As I mentioned, my fieldwork to this date has focused on the two most representative Tokoist groups, which could create a possibly false sense of a twofold opposition regarding Toko's life and legacy.

Notes

1. There is some controversy regarding the exact date of death of the prophet. Agostinho (n.d.: 83) advances the date of 1 January 1984, while Quibeta (n.d.: 56–57) and Kisela (2004: 245) argue that it took place on 31 December 1983. From this last perspective, considering that Toko had been declared dead many times during his life, the leaders that were closer to him at the time apparently decided to 'wait and see'.

2. One could argue that in the Tokoist case, this centralization came as a response to the leader's almost constant absence throughout the existence of the movement.

3. In the Angolan context, the intersection of the ethnic in the religious field is obviously not exclusive to the Tokoist Church (see, for instance, Henderson 1971; Schubert 1999; Pereira 2004; Messiant 2008; Sarró, Blanes and Viegas 2008).

4. This group, which would eventually establish in Luanda, is often referred to as *ngunga nguele* – literally 'the bell that tolls', but with the connotation of movement and 'spreading the word' (see chapter 3). Most of them, and their descendants, are associated to the Doze Mais Velhos group.

5. The Cúpula had been nominated by Toko as a provisional executive board during his absence in the *buraco*.

6. Other smaller, autonomous groups would eventually appear during this period, such as a Sucursal in Luanda's Bairro Operário, or the so-called Casa da Oração (House of Prayer), a *sucursal* movement created among a younger generation of Tokoists who worked with Simão Toko in the Bairro Indígena after his return from exile in the Azores. This group stayed with the Doze Mais Velhos until they decided to separate and assume as main objective the reunification and pacification of the church. They remain active to this day.

7. These denominations were the following: the Assembly of God, the Angola Baptist Convention, the Evangelical Baptist Church of Angola (IEBA), the Evangelical Congregational Church of Angola (IECA), the Synodal Evangelical Church of Angola, the United Methodist Church, the Evangelical Church in Angola, the Reformed Evangelical Church in Angola, the Church of Jesus Christ on Earth (Kimbanguists), the Pentecostal Assembly of God in Angola, the Adventist Church of the Seventh Day and finally the Union of Evangelical Churches in Angola.

8. Name apparently inspired by the figure of Erastus of Corinth.
9. Abel Paxe, personal communication (April 2011).
10. Many Tokoists also define this moment as one when evil spirits invaded Tokoism.
11. Agostinho had also stated in his book that 'The reformation in the church go as far as the year 2000. And this, brothers, implies that we must adapt the church in light of the development of every era and the prevailing reality in the world, without in any case deviating from the doctrinal principles and ideas defended by our beloved leader Simão Gonçalves Toko' (Agostinho n.d.: 21).
12. In fact, in the Direcção Universal, a new calendar has begun and today we are on the year 0012.
13. The temple would be inaugurated on August 2012.
14. The African Nations' Cup in football, which took place in Angola in January 2010.
15. These public statements are not, obviously, exclusive to the Tokoist Church. It is quite common to read or watch interventions of other Angolan religious leaders in the national media – a consequence of the 'proliferation' observed in this country (Viegas 2007).
16. See for instance Bishop Nunes's interview on *Angola Press*, 25 July 2009; or the donation campaigns in several schools, retirement homes and prisons in Angola and São Tomé and Príncipe (*Angola Press*, 5 January 2010; 12 February 2010) One particularly striking case took place in November 2009, after a diplomatic incident between Angola and the RD Congo which resulted in the expulsion of thousands of Angolan expatriates in the Kinshasa and Lower Congo region. A delegation from the Direcção Universal quickly headed towards the improvised refugee camps established in the border and donated food, medicine and blankets.
17. Structure under which villagers traditionally met to discuss collective issues in rural Angola.
18. Today, the recognized and distributed leadership of this branch includes Dofonso Fernando Manzambi, Vumambo David, Sebastião Vuaituma and Vasco Pedro Nzila, among others.
19. In that first visit, my friends and colleagues Ramon Sarró and Fátima Viegas accompanied me.
20. The original French version was published under the title *Jesus L'Africain, Le Vrai Grand Secret de Fatima* (2002).
21. This is a reference to the apparition of the Virgin Mary in Fátima, Portugal, on 13 May 1917, before three young pastors, to whom she disclosed three secrets. Two of the secrets were disclosed by the Vatican soon after the event, but a third one remained undisclosed until the year 2000. See this book's introduction.
22. In the episode I describe henceforth, and in another event that took place in a tram in Brussels, Melo encountered Toko's spirit and later converted to Tokoism (personal communication).
23. Melo also shares these events on his blog, http://www.123siteweb.fr/Fatima-Le-Secret/70023064.

CHAPTER 5

Transcendence
Tokoist Diasporas

It's August 1992. A group of over ten people is heading towards a notary office at the Correeiros Street in the central Baixa area of Portugal's capital, Lisbon. Among them are António Gomes, Albertina Gomes, Simão Vemba, António Costa Massokolo, Francisco Manuel Filipe, Vítor Santos Pedro, António Garcia Kanga, Mário Quadrante, Filipe Paulo Kombela, Alberto Coxe, Joaquim Albino Kisela, Ndongo Edgar and Agostinho Mundiako Pedro. Apart from the fact that they were all Angolan migrants, they shared another common feature: they belonged to the Angolan Tokoist Church. On that day, this group of people met with the intention of registering the Association of Tokoists of Portugal, an entity that would be used to shelter the Angolan Tokoist Church in this country and finally allow for a juridical, public recognition of their practice. Papers are signed, stamps are placed and hands are shook. The moment is then celebrated with pomp and circumstance: the first 'official Tokoist service' takes place in the Presbyterian Church of Anjos – which, thanks to the kind invitation of its pastor Paulo Salvador and the successful intermediation of the German missionary living in Portugal Michael Knoch, opened to welcome this group for this memorable occasion. A photograph is taken to celebrate and remember the moment.

The expressions of ceremoniality in the Tokoists' faces, mixed with certain doses of nervousness and satisfaction, were justified. It was, after all, a historical moment: it was the first time that the Tokoist movement officially inaugurated a temple outside of their original continent. Apart from the implantation in Angola and DR Congo, and despite the historical self-ascription as a 'church in the world', the Tokoist Church was after all a religious movement restricted to the African space – one

Illustration 17. Celebration of the first 'Tokoist service in Lisbon', Igreja Presbiteriana dos Anjos, 6 September 1992. *Source:* Joaquim Albino Kisela.

of the thousands of independent movements that were springing and being charted in colonial and post-colonial times throughout the continent (Barrett 1968). Through this process of transcontinentalization towards the European continent, the Tokoist Church promoted, along with other movements such as the Kimbanguist Church (Mélice 2006; Sarró 2009a; Sarró and Mélice 2010), a new territorial paradigm that exemplified like no other what many commentators are referring to as the 'southernization' of Christian faith: the progressive acknowledgement that, from a demographic, sociological and also theological point of view, in what concerns the following of Jesus Christ the gravitational axis is no longer situated in places like the Vatican, Fátima or Lourdes, but rather in places like the Congo or Brazil (Jenkins 2002).

One such theorist of Christian southernization was historian Philip Jenkins, who has argued for the need of an understanding of a 'next Christianity' (2002) by looking at its renewed focal points, and to acknowledge that, from a sociological point of view, if one wants to study contemporary Christianity, one must acknowledge the 'epochal change' in course and realize its pluralisms and mutations, to the point that they barely relate to the 'Vatican style', theologically, liturgically and politically speaking (Jenkins 2002, 2006, 2007). Similar points of view and arguments have been conveyed and empirically grounded by Kwame Bediako (1985, 2000), Gerrie ter Haar (1992), Lamin Sanneh and Joel Carpenter (2005) and many others. In these last examples, what is offered is a different directionality in terms of Christian agency, mobility and creativity, revealing new protagonists, idioms and logics of power that are African-based or African-oriented – as in e.g. Archbishop Milingo's ministry and misunderstandings with the Vatican leadership (ter Haar 1992) – which in turn echoes into diverse senses of territoriality and belonging.

The development of a 'Tokoist diaspora' is, in this setting, particularly striking. On the one hand, it invokes and reveals a specific trend of Atlantic history that is complementary to the major narratives of 'Global Christianity' (see Robbins and Engelke 2010): the centuries of Lusophone Christian exchanges in the Southern Atlantic, mediated by a long history of colonialism, commerce and transference (Thornton 1998; Heywood 2002; Birmingham 2006; Thornton and Heywood 2007) but displayed in novel expressions, directionalities and destinies in the postcolonial period (see Sarró and Blanes 2009). For instance, if it was historically possible to map the emergence of an 'Afro'-religious culture through the processes of forced colonial African diasporas from Africa into Brazil (or the Caribbean, for that matter), today, in the post-colony, different appropriations and historical reinterpretations are forged within the Atlantic (see e.g. Matory 2005; Palmié 2007). A similar argument can be made regarding Southern African prophetic Christianity, usually depicted as a local response to Western mission, but appearing today as a new expression of transnational Christian evangelization.

On the other hand, it is representative of a conscious transcendence of the traditional 'localization' associated with prophetic Christianity. In contrast with, say, Christian missionary cultures, which have (unsurprisingly) been perceived in terms of mobility and contact (e.g. Beidelman 1982; Comaroff and Comaroff 1991; Valverde 1997; Pels 1999; Keane 2007; Vilaça 2010); or with current 'transnational charismas' often self-displayed as movements of 'conquest' (e.g. Coleman 2000; Beyer 2003; Robbins 2004; Hunt 2005), prophetic or messianic movements such as the Tokoist Church have been traditionally linked to specific circumscriptions, ethnic or territorial, portrayed as 'local responses' to particular socio-historical exogenous impositions. Such was the case of the 'Bakongo messianisms' debated in the beginning of this book; or, outside the Christian sphere, the Amerindian messianisms (Laternari 1963; Queiroz 1965; Clastres 1993 [1975]) or the Melanesian cargo cults (e.g. Worsley 1957; Scott 2007). Within these frameworks, locality and defiance of external agency seems to play an important role in such movements' processes of self-constitution.

However, the diasporization of prophetic movements of this kind produced a differentiation in these associations, not only in terms of how the academia learns to acknowledge new territorialities and belongings, but also and especially in terms of how such movements experience and define themselves amidst internal debates and movements of change. This poses relevant questions pertaining to belief, belonging and place, and the role played by Christian theology and experience in its self-constitution in terms of globality and locality (see Robbins and Engelke 2010). In what follows I will delve into the specifics of such processes, looking at how the development of a Tokoist diaspora speaks to ideologies of space and belonging in the postcolonial era.

Church in the World, and in Portugal

In the narratives of Simão Toko's visit to Afonso Nunes, the spirit's concern for the church's 'place in the world' was obvious and explicit. In his apparition to Tchiwale from Capelongo, it had explained how he sought a place to return to Earth, but did not know where since the church was divided, the 'centre' had disappeared. Now, with Nunes, he appeared to have found his lander.

Thus, it wasn't a surprise to find that, apart from the process of spiritual coating and the message of institutional unification, the other two agencies of this process of return from heaven were attached to a problem of 'place'. On the one hand, as the prophet had already claimed in his epistles, the church would have to build its 'centre', the central temple: 'and if [the money] arrived until today, we would build the temple in order to worship our God creator; but we know what happened to the old disciples and Christians' (letter by Simão Toko, 20 September 1971). But, on the other, the temple would no longer be 'central', but rather 'universal'. In this respect, it is frequent to hear references to the future temple in many sermons in the Direcção Universal, complemented with quotes from the second book of Chronicles: 'And the house which I build is great: for great is our God above all gods' (2 Chr 2:5).

This universalizing strategy wasn't, therefore, unheard of in the Tokoist circles. As I noted in the previous chapter, throughout the 1980s and 1990s, a movement of dispersion occurred within Tokoism, pro-voked by the crisis of succession and authority provoked by the proph-et's passing; however, another concomitant movement of centripetality also contributed towards a dissemination, enabled by the particular demographic history of Angola.

In this regard, if these decades were particularly difficult for the Tokoists, the same feeling was shared by the vast majority of Ango-lans. The seemingly endless civil war, in particular after the failure of the Bicesse peace agreements in 1992, pushed many Angolans outside their country and to eventually form an 'Angolan diaspora' that was to become progressively recognizable within academic and institutional contexts (see Brinkman 2000; Van Wijk 2005, 2010; Oien 2006, 2008; Grassi 2007; Vidal 2007; Messiant 2008). Much of these movements were initially a direct consequence of the war and displacement, which provoked the development of forced migration and refugee camps in places like the DR Congo, Zambia and Namibia (see e.g. Hansen 1979; Hansen and Tavares 1999; Brinkman 2004; Amassari 2005; Oien 2006). However, following the wider trends of global (and African, in par-ticular; see Akyeampong 2000; de Bruijn, van Dijk and Foeken 2001; Manger and Assal 2006) migration – the extension of Angolan diaspora multiplied and diversified in the subsequent decades.

In the Portuguese case, if African (particularly Agolan) migration towards this country was not necessarily new – as was pointed out by several studies on immigration in Portugal[1] – the last two decades of the century witnessed an important increase in Angolan emigra-tion with Portugal as (transitory or definitive) destiny. This movement quickly produced the recognition of an 'Angolan community' in Portu-gal, one of the largest foreign groups present in the territory,[2] inserted within wider societal and demographic changes observed in Portugal after the political turn of the 1975 Carnation Revolution, especially in what concerns emigration and immigration trends – with a significant increase of, among other groups, African and Brazilian immigration into Portugal (Esteves 1991; Bastos and Bastos 1999; Baganha and Gois 1999). In this particular context, places like Lisbon's Rossio or Martim Moniz central squares, where migrants of African and Asian origin dwell and work, have become emblematic in the recognition of a social (and religious) pluralism in this country (see e.g. Bastos 2001; Mapril 2007, 2009).

The reasons for this increase are many and complex, especially if we take into consideration the heterogeneity of the Angolan presence in Portugal, combining diverse moments, strata, motivations and trajec-tories, and tracing different kinds of social and geographical mobility.

From an Angolan perspective, there are transitions and emergencies (Chabal and Vidal 2007; Messiant 2008) that help us contextualize such motivations and choices: the civil war that devastated the country from the first months of 1976 until 2002, and which 'produced' its victims, refugees and exiled, as well as the flight of several young men who refused to take arms; the labour and living conditions in an Angola mired by problems of stagnation and precariousness in the labour market, while a progressively larger Angolan middle class sought for opportunities for progression, professional reward and cultural consumption outside their country (Lopes 2007; Rodrigues 2007; Ferreira, Lopes and Mortágua 2008); the bilateral diplomatic relationships between Portugal and Angola within the framework of the CPLP,[3] which facilitated opportunities of collaboration and exchange, both in terms of education, health, etc., in the lusophone space; and, since 1986, the construction of a 'Schengen Europe', a complex, appealing space for the African migrant searching for better life conditions and experiences (see e.g. Sayad 2004; Ferguson 2006; Sarró 2009b; Graw and Schielke 2011); and, finally, the reproductive character of the migratory dynamics, constituted through networks that involve family, friends, work and trade opportunities.[4]

These multiple causes begin to explain the heterogeneity of the Angolan presence in Portugal constituted through successive and diversified migratory waves. We could first look at what is described as the return of expatriates from the former colonies (the *retornados*, or returnees; see Pires 1987; Esteves 1991) and then the so-called guest workers (or workers with low professional qualification occupying the lower strata of the labour market) and political refugees (Bastos and Bastos 1999), though more recent studies point to different dynamics. For instance, there was the presence of qualified migrants searching for professional qualification (Grassi 2007, 2008; Ferreira, Lopes and Mortágua 2008), of children under foster care programs (Oien 2006), etc. And finally, outside these accountancies and statistics, there were the thousands of informal migrants with no residence status that nevertheless and obviously are part of this 'Angolan presence' in Portugal (Bastos and Bastos 1999: 51 and ff.; Grassi 2007).[5]

However, the reality of Angolan communities in Portugal transcends in many ways the economic determinisms and sectorial 'national analyses'. For instance, Cecilie Oien rightly describes many cases of mobilities and momentary, temporary transits between Portugal and Angola: work contracts, medical consultations, more or less extended visits to family, etc. (2007: 27). From this perspective, the Angolan migrant experience (much like any other) bears not only the act of migration itself, but also the act of circulation – between countries of origin and destiny, but also between both and other countries of the Schengen space. This, as I describe below, is also an inherent aspect of the 'Tokoist diasporic experience' in Lisbon.

Perhaps it is this heterogeneity and circulation that explain the 'dispersion' that characterizes the Angolan presence in Portugal. On the one hand, available statistical data suggests that the majority of Angolans and Angolan descendants in Portugal lives in the Lisbon Metropolitan Area, namely in the Lisbon and Setúbal districts (Malheiros and Vala 2004; Possidónio 2006). But, in contrast with what happens with other communities such as the Cape Verdeans, it is not easy to associate them to 'other neighbourhoods'[6] in the Lisbon scenery (Possidónio 2006); instead, they populate, inhabit and circulate the city, as 'new (or not so new) Lisboners',[7] in a constant movement between Restauradores and the Vale do Forno, between Martim Moniz and Chelas, between Saldanha and Odivelas, etc.

On the other hand, if the different spaces and historical moments produced different trajectories and profiles of the 'Angolan migrant'– if we propose to discuss migration experiences from a diachronic perspective – we cannot set aside a fundamental dimension: that of the so-called second and third generations of migrants (see Possidónio 2006; Rosales, Jesus and Parra 2009). In fact, looking at the Tokoist group in Portugal, we realize that most of its youngest members are not only born in Portugal, but probably have never stepped on Angolan soil. However, this doesn't necessarily imply the loss of a link with their parents' land of origin. As we will see here, 'Africa' and 'Angola' are always somehow present among this group. In any case, this forces us to distinguish between nationality, place of birth and identity: the feeling of belonging to a country does not always and necessarily imply its pre-defined 'physical' and 'geographical' experience of circumscription. This, in turn, reveals differentiated experiences of 'Angolan identity' that do not necessarily match those produced in the African continent.[8]

Furthermore, the development of an 'Angolan community' in Portugal in the late twentieth century also had necessary implications in the religious scenery. Without recourse to figures on religious frequency per nationality or ethnic origin (see Vilaça 2006), recent research in the Lisbon Metropolitan area reveals that, within the plural and transnational religious and Christian publics that attend churches in Portugal, there is in fact an 'Angolan audience' of sorts, reflected not only in the existence of Angolan-based churches – among which the Tokoist Church, the Assembleia de Deus do Makulusso, the Igreja

Illustration 18. Kimbanguist choir singing in a Tokoist ceremony, Lisbon, July 2011. Photo: Ruy Llera Blanes.

do Bom Deus or, partially, the Kimbanguist Church – but also in the presence of Angolan publics in international churches such as the Universal Church of the Kingdom of God, the Assemblies of God or the Catholic Church (see e.g. Blanes 2008b; Swatowiski 2010). One can perceive such a public in certain festive occasions promoted by some of these churches, who usually invite their 'sister (Angolan) churches' to participate in meaningful dates.

Lisboan Tokoists

It was therefore with no surprise that, before and after the visit to the notary, the idea of 'Lisboan Tokoists' began to circulate within the church.[9] For many, the inauguration of a church in Lisbon became a highly symbolic moment that would irreversibly affect the movement's 'place in the world'. There was also a certain degree of irony and curiosity invoked in this event, since, as we saw in the first part of this book, the historical development of the church became intimately associated with the colonial Lusophone enterprise and its Atlantic

dispositions, through Toko's sojourn in the Azores and the multiple di-
chotomies produced between the metropolis and the colony. From this
perspective, the presence of a Tokoist church in Portuguese territory,
as an outcome of a process of institutional expansion that participates
in wider processes of Christian pluralized reconfigurations, became
a significative element in the redefinition of the Portuguese religious
field by inserting it in the colonial and postcolonial political histories
written throughout the Atlantic space (Sarró and Blanes 2009).

 I doubt, however, that this political agency was the main concern
in the minds of the pioneering group that created the Tokoist Association in Portugal. For them, as Pastor Gomes recalled to me (November
2010), it was very much and pragmatically about being able to congregate together. Simultaneously, the inaugural service at the Anjos
Presbiterian Church not only supposed an 'officializing' celebration of
the movement, but also inaugurated a trajectory of mobility of these
believers around the city of Lisbon, searching for their own place of
worship. Gomes, Vemba, Kisela and the others began by congregating every Sunday in a small pension in the Restauradores (downtown
Lisbon) called Pensão Elegante, a small establishment that acted as a
hub for many Angolan immigrants. 'It was a meeting point for all the
Angolans who professed the same faith; that's when we had the idea
of not wanting to lose our roots, our culture, but also promoting our
unity in faith', explained Simão Vemba (18 October 2007).

 The news of a Tokoist congregation in Lisbon quickly spread within
the Angolan migrant circles, through what Francisco Filipe, one of
the church leaders, once described as *'palavra puxa palavra'* (ear-to-
ear communication). With the progressive growth of the group, which
began to incorporate other Angolans and respective families, it was a
matter of time before they acknowledged the need for a more adequate
space for their activities. After using Pastor Gomes's house in Chelas,
the group decides to seek the help of other 'sister churches' to pursue
their activities. Thus, initially, the Anjos Presbiterian Church becomes
the place. But soon after, they end up by renting the pavilion of the
Liceu Camões, a high school in the city centre, Saldanha. This pavilion
was also used by other migrant Christian groups of African origin (see
Blanes 2007, 2008b), implying that the services had to be scheduled in
order to accommodate every group. This situation lasted roughly until
1995, when a new school board is elected and, following the bad press
that 'foreign evangelical movements' began to have in Portugal in those
times,[10] the Tokoists were forced to look for a new place of worship.

 The place they found was a basement in the Martim Moniz neighbourhood, in Lisbon's historical centre, once again shared with other

groups of Angolan Evangelical Christians. Sebastião, one of the oldest members of the community, told me over laughter, 'We had to count the minutes, at a certain hour we had to finish, because it time for the next church to enter!' By then, this was no longer a small group of believers and their families, but a few dozens of people seeking to perform the Tokoist calendar and liturgy. The group's headquarters was maintained in Campolide, in the house of one of the believers, Mano Santo, where the tabernacle was also to be found.

It wasn't until the year 2000 when, finally, the Tokoists found their current – and so far definitive – temple. Rented to a neighbour in the quarters, and situated above a small cloth factory, the space was restored and redecorated with the believers' physical and monetary contribution. The walls and ceiling were painted white, the floor covered with green carpet and the windows decorated with translucent curtains. White plastic chairs were scattered throughout the room. The musical instruments were set in a corner of the room, and the presiding table was covered with white and green cloth; on top of it, a Bible and a flower jar were placed. In the rectangular room, there are only two independent divisions. One of them is converted into an office, and the other a tabernacle. For the first time, the Lisboan Tokoists inhabit a space they can call their sanctuary.

Illustration 19. Tokoist church in Lisbon, May 2010. Photo: Ruy Llera Blanes.

Since then, this has been the home of the Tokoists in Lisbon. Besides the dominical cult itself, it is there where the tabernacle sessions, the Lord's Supper, the prayers, the celebrations, the choir rehearsals, the instrumentalists' practice, the work meetings of the different committees, the marriage parties, the baptisms, the *dedicações* (presentations of the newborn), the Holy Suppers, etc., take place. It is also there where the Tokoist children, when not summoned to Sunday school or rehearsals, improvise their own games, playing football in the parking lot in front, climbing up and down the stairs, teasing each other, fooling with the instruments, etc., while their parents are busy working or chatting.

In a way, the Tokoist house in the Vale do Forno – a small neighbourhood standing on a hillside stuck between several freeways, at the doorway of the suburb of Odivelas, with not much more than a few houses and apartments, a cafe, a small mall and two other churches (one Catholic and one Pentecostal; see Formenti 2011) – acts as a hub for its believers and visitors. Considering that none of the members actually live in the neighbourhood, the church members spend many hours of travel in different transport means to reach the place. This happens not only at the Sunday service, but almost every day of the week: from Monday to Friday after work hours and on Saturdays for the whole afternoon, there is always a pretext for a meeting, reunion, chores or plain socializing.

Today, the Tokoist Church is composed of approximately one hundred active members, where younger and elder members, coming from Angola or already born in Portugal, cohabitate and interact. It is therefore a heterogeneous group of people in different social conditions and with diverse histories of relationship with their country of origin: from the old believer who arrived from Luanda to be treated for some illness, to the Embassy official, the staffer of an international company, the domestic worker, the construction worker and the university student who intends to return to Luanda after obtaining his degree.

Despite this heterogeneity, it is also true that the community is defined by the (familial and political) ties that simultaneously work for its sedimentation. Fathers, sons, grandparents and uncles of different families – the Vembas, the Gomeses, the Mateuses, the Filipes, etc. – all share and interact in the same space. Other members and families would eventually join and take an active role in the congregation: Sebastião Ma'huno (choir leader), Pedro Segunda (church representative), José António Malanda (same), António Macanda, etc. From this perspective, it is possible to detect two different regimes of participation: a core of families that for the most part come from the original

founding group from twenty years ago, active and consistently participating in the church's activities; and a floating set of people who,
for personal and professional reasons, participates in a more marginal
or sporadic fashion.[11] Thus, there is an operative distinction between
forms of participation, belonging and commitment in the church, also
understood through two complementing acknowledgements: in first
place, the kind of involvement that the church 'demands' from its adepts, a commitment that implies a high physical, mental and moral
availability on behalf of he or she who accepts to be a part of the community – the praxis described in chapter 3, for instance. In second
place, the fact that the church is constituted in a migrant setting, and is
therefore affected by specific dynamics that are not necessarily found
in Angola. Namely, the vicissitudes, needs, obligations and routines of
the African migrant in Europe. 'With kind words everything is easier;
but with them man will be his own lover and the weak will fall from
faith. The brother who began this path must reach the end. These are
the hardships of the last times', claimed Pastor António Gomes in the
first service of 2009, when he reflected in his sermon upon the 'hardships that await us'. These hardships alluded eschatologically to the
'tribulations' of the battle between good and evil. But they also spoke to
the 'dangers' and 'constant struggle' that mark the lives of the expatriate Tokoists, object of diverse solicitations.

I will discuss the moral and political dilemmas of Tokoist migration
in the coming pages; in any case, what seems to be at stake here for
the Tokoists is a question of choice and participation, a self-demand
within the community that pushes them into a constant appraisal and
re-enhancement of their commitment. As I mentioned earlier, not all
Tokoists that pass by the church in the Vale do Forno play the role of
full-time members. Those of us who attend the church on a regular
basis for a given time are able to appreciate 'new faces', people who are
either passing by or visiting, people who do not consider themselves
'ready' from a moral point of view, to belong, or also people who are
simply looking for a space of 'comfort' (Miller 2008). In this case, the
common feature of all these options and personal trajectories is the
fact that their protagonists find themselves, in a sense, 'in transit', either geographic or personally, emotionally.

Religious Trajectories and Mobilities in Lisbon

From the photograph of the first service in Lisbon, only half of the
Angolans portrayed in the picture are still in this city. Kisela returned

to Angola, as well as Massokolo. Kombela is in Spain. Ndongo Edgar lives between Angola and Portugal. This doesn't necessarily mean that some sort of scission occurred in the church. Instead, it means that the vicissitudes in each of their lives led them elsewhere. In fact, since I began visiting the church in Lisbon, I was able to see how some of its members returned momentarily to Angola (like Pastor Segunda), or to another European country (like brother Noé), usually for work reasons.

These dynamics reflect an intrinsic characteristic of migrant churches like the Tokoist: they incorporate an inherent precariousness, which is simultaneously a producer of dynamics and vitality, as an outcome of the trajectories of mobility of their believers, who circulate within transnational and transcontinental circuits between Africa and Europe (see Bilger and Kraler 2005; Maskens 2010). In fact, if we were to perform a systematic listing of the moments of *recepção e despedida* (reception and farewell) in the Sunday services, we would be able to draw a complex map of routes between Angola and Portugal, and between Portugal and other European countries, both in terms of momentary visits and more long-term migration projects. From this particular perspective, the metaphor of the church's vital space as a hub becomes enhanced: if it is part of the quotidian itineraries of this group of believers, it also acts as space for welcoming and bidding farewell to others in transit. Many believers in Lisbon, in fact, have family or friends spread throughout Europe with whom they build diasporic relationships and visit as much as possible.[12]

It was therefore in the intersection of these mobilities that the first Tokoist Church in Europe was born.

> The work began when a handful of young Angolans, many of them Tokoists, without a chance to progress in their own country, was forced to migrate outside in search for better life conditions, considering the war that spread in Angola. Many of them chose Portuguese lands as final destination. In the 1990s, the young Tokoists, several dozens spread throughout the whole country, bringing with them the sentiment of preserving the Tokoist ideal and struggling for the expansion of the Good News, meeting each other in the streets of Greater Lisbon and its surroundings, finally culminated the wish for the traditional congregation of brothers of the same faith. (Francisco Manuel Filipe, in a speech celebrating the sixteenth anniversary of the church in Lisbon, 6 September 2009)

The Tokoist Church in Lisbon is thus a microcosm that illustrates the intersections, mobilities and motivations between Portugal and Angola.[13] There, we find examples of these diverse profiles of migration and descendency. But this also pushes us into questioning: what is the role of 'religiosity' in this migratory process? Apart from being an obvious 'consequence' of these phenomena, to what extent are churches like the Tokoist producers of particular religious experiences? As I will propose here, there is a process of mutual constitution in this formula. Also, as Paul Christopher Johnson suggests (2007), there is an inherent aspect of diasporic cultures that makes it unique and condemns attempts of comparison, or to distinguish 'original' from 'composite', to failure.

One good example of such agencies in migrant territory is how, through the Lisbon group, an 'entity' later known as the Tokoist Communities in the Diaspora developed. If in Portugal the church sprung from the migratory networks between this country and Angola, it was also through those networks and their 'extensions' that further initiatives made the instalment, from the late 1990s, of new Tokoist churches in Europe. The man behind this was the head of the church in Lisbon, Pastor Gomes, who dedicated most of his free time to engaging with networks of Angolan migrants in Spain, France, the Netherlands, the UK and Italy, and finally managed to establish formal nuclei which remain permanently connected. Today, after retiring from being the leader of the church in Lisbon, Gomes spends his time travelling back and forth within different European countries. In one of those nuclei, Paris, a first initiative to create a 'Tokoist TV' – RVTI, Radiovisão Tokoista Internacional – emerged, transmitting audiovisual content through YouTube and other social networking platforms. Similarly, the Lisbon group created an online radio, transmitting essentially Tokoist hymns and other compositions. But during my research with the Tokoist diaspora, I encountered several other contexts where the development of this Tokoist diaspora produced new intersections of mobility, presence and belonging.

A Church in a Suitcase

One Saturday of February 2011, I passed by the Vale do Forno church, hoping to attend an evocative debate on the ninety-third anniversary of Simão Toko's birth, where I was to present some of my own notes on Toko's 'biography of martyrdom' – as I had previously proposed to the church members. However, as I suspected, the event was not going to take place after all. The reason was very pragmatically that the church was undergoing renovation and, contrary to what was intended, things were not yet ready. So I took the opportunity to look at the construction going on, and appreciate the renovations in the church's floor and ceil-

ings, as well as the remodelling of the bottom floor, which would later
become the church's office, kitchen, service area and meeting room.

A few months before, Simão Vemba had told me that they were considering looking for a new space to base the church, and I also helped
in the search for possible new sites. The leadership and the members
were concerned about the church's somewhat marginal location, and
thought about a more central setting. But eventually they changed
their minds and decided to invest in the current location, increasing
its facilities, size and comfort.

This process of renewal and occupation was in a way emblematic,
as it represented an intention of moving away from a sense of tran-
sience and towards a renewed sense of permanence in Lisbon. From
this perspective, it seems to have been a response to a particular history of relationships with the motherland and its leaderships. In 1992,
precisely when the group of Tokoists began to congregate officially in
Lisbon, you may recall that the political situation in Luanda was one
of division and separation: around the same time, the Angolan state
recognized the three different 'Tokoist churches', and members of each
sector were forbidden to contact the others. This posed a pragmatic
problem for this small, diasporic group. Most of its members belonged
to the Direcção Central, in allegiance with then leader Luzaísso Lutango, who had been informed of this small group's intentions and
given his blessing to the initiative. However, there was in fact a minority of members of other groups in the small crowd. Thus, considering
whether such logics applied to Lisbon – 'each Tokoist Church would
have only one or two members' – Gomes and the others decided that
the community in Portugal would adopt an ecumenical approach and
not distinguish between allegiances nor request its members' *testifica-
ção*. The diasporic Tokoists initially welcomed this, but not the Golfe
leadership, who threatened them with expulsion if they did not follow
the established directives.

This threat lingered for some time, but was never acted on. In any
case, it signalled a practical and moral dilemma: if, in contrast with
other 'African churches' in Lisbon which are constituted autonomously
in diasporic terrain (Blanes 2011b), the Tokoists proudly define themselves as a 'branch' stemming from the motherland, it is also true that
its installation and development occurred mainly within migrant networks and resources, in an autonomous direction vis-à-vis its moral,
political and bureaucratic centre. In other words, if in the diaspora the
church was experiencing dissemination, in Luanda it was experiencing disintegration. From this perspective, the church as an entity was
moving in two opposite directions, revealing simultaneously a tension

between centrifugal and centripetal movements (see Sarró and Blanes 2009).

But with Nunes's arrival and posterior inauguration of a universalist policy, things changed dramatically.[14] On 9 November 2008, a Sunday, the church at Vale do Forno was overcrowded: instead of the average one hundred people I usually encountered there, I estimated at least double that. 'No wonder', I remember thinking, the occasion justified it: Bishop Afonso Nunes had come all the way from Angola to visit them.

This visit to Lisbon was, in fact, the bishop's second. His first visit had been two years earlier, in April 2006. At the time, as I was able to observe in video footage of the occasion, Nunes had praised in his sermon the fact that this 'pioneering group', the Tokoists in Lisbon, despite having come to Portugal for their *ganha-pão* (to work and earn money, literally 'to earn their bread'), they 'did not keep the flag of Christ down, but brought it out with them and built a temple in the "metropolis", despite the personal sacrifices involved': 'You took from your own personal and work time, and dedicated it to praising God. That which lies within your hearts, that boils inside, made you look for a place to worship His name.… We have faith that the church in Europe will grow; and with my return, so will you.' Yet this time, on this occasion in 2008, Nunes told his audience that things had to change dramatically if they wanted to remain a part of the 'Tokoist project'.

> We have come to Europe to meet the people that are adding wood to the fireplace, in order to prevent the flame from dying. So we chose Portugal in the first place.… In this world we will suffer, we will have tribulations.… So you must have the courage.… Spiritually speaking, if we are not brave enough to face the evil and obstacles before us, we end up in blasphemy; but if we are brave, we will overcome all obstacles.… But there will be no courage if we don't have hope in our victory and that the word of God will be fulfilled. My Lord won, and so will I.… In this congregation, if we don't have hope, confidence and courage, we will not overcome the difficulties.… Why do you not have determination? Why do you not have courage? Dear church, have you been fulfilling the Lord's word? [No sir!!] It is time to be one, like father and son. If your finger hurts, do you cut it off? What will you do? Heal it.… I have always searched for peace between everyone. I have tried to overcome ethnic, tribal frontiers, racial frontiers and barriers. My father and I are one. When I was here the first time,[15] I warned you: don't be deceived by this pretty Europe. In a hymn we sang before, we said: 'God visits Africa and darkness dissipates.' The darkness was removed from Africa, but returned to Europe. In another time, Portugal was a country of God adorers, of true God adorers, but today … the churches are empty.… Do you want to end up like Sodom and Gomorrah? [No sir!!] We must not

compare ourselves to the world, because we are church, and not from
the world – we must seek to transform it, take the good news to those
who are lost. (9 November 2008)

In the sermon, he did not specify exactly what it was he disagreed
with in the church and what were the things to be changed. In a posterior interview to Angolan media, he hinted that his trip to Europe had
made him realize the hardships the members experienced in their task
of fortifying their faith, and thus needed to stay more time in Portugal
in order to guide them (*Angola Press*, 19 January 2009). Nevertheless,
during the visit I was lucky enough to be granted a hearing with him
the following day. In our interview, which took place in a central Lisbon hotel, he summarized his point of view: 'If you build a church that
you can just drop into a suitcase and go back to Angola, then what's
the point?' This explained his disapproval of the situation regarding
Tokoist churches in the diaspora: he felt they were not truly proselytizing, 'reaching out', but comfortably installed in the Angolan networks.
They were not transcending their migrant, Angolan, African condition
and reaching out to Portugal. They were not growing 'roots' outside
Luanda.

The botanical metaphor invoked by the Bishop was illustrative of
the concepts of presence and agency that were circulating in his vocab-
ulary and strategy regarding the Tokoist diaspora. According to him,
the churches in Europe should become Portuguese, Spanish, Dutch,
British, etc., and abandon the exogenously imposed labels of foreign-
ness and minority. For instance, national churches should be led by
national pastors, services should be held in local languages, etc. Thus,
'belonging' was to be understood and performed as a religious – and
not territorial and identitary – category.

These concepts, although perhaps more resonant with the metaphor of a rhizome than that of an arborescent root, stressed in any
case a centrifugal view of the Tokoists' 'place in the world' that should
become henceforth mediated by multiple and connected notions of autochthony and produce a renewed idea of proselytism.

During the months that followed, I was able to observe the reactions to Nunes's second visit to the Lisbon church. These evolved from
an initial puzzlement – after all, what the leader was demanding was
a radical change in their routinized ethos, posture and eschatological narrative – to a process of reflection and debate regarding how
to respond to Nunes's imposition and follow his directives. Several
different strategies were devised: active campaigning, a new communication strategy, the development of social aid actions, etc. In April

2010, a major breakthrough took place: a second 'Tokoist parish' was inaugurated in the Algarve (southern Portugal), and it was composed mainly of a small group of white, Portuguese believers (some of them *retornados* from Angola) who had been in contact with Tokoists living in the region and later worked with the head evangelist in the Lisbon parish. This fact was celebrated by the church in both Lisbon and Luanda, and was made possible through the contacts which some of the church leaders in Lisbon were establishing with *retornados* within the Christian circles in that region.[16]

These developments were also framed within a process of bureaucratic and identitary reorganization that simultaneously adapted the church to a transnational situation and reinforced Luanda as its focal point. As Bishop Nunes recently stated:

> Each member of the church should present, in the next five years, at least ten new members to the church. All provincial, national and parish leaders will have plenty of work. From this perspective, Portugal must be congratulated, but must keep working to bring everyone together, bringing to the church, if possible, all Europeans, Brazilians, Americans and Indians, to be converted to Tokoists, this will be a great blessing for Jesus beloved son of God. (*O País*, 29 December 2010)

From this moment on, the bishop's visits to Europe have become more and more regular, and the church in Portugal has become an official spearhead of Tokoist expansion in Europe.

The Globalization and Contestation of Charisma

Regardless of these ups and downs in the relationships between Luanda and Lisbon, the progressive installation and accumulation of the Tokoist nucleus in Lisbon spoke to the growing acknowledgement, on behalf of the Golfe leadership, of its role within the church's ideology of expansion. This was therefore an ad hoc appropriation on behalf of Nunes, and implied different conceptions of Tokoist territorial centrifugality. But a first confirmation that outreach was after all possible only took place in 2008, when a Japanese family converted to Tokoism after a visit from Bishop Nunes to Japan a few months earlier. This became a major event among the Tokoists in Luanda that year, and seemed to convince Nunes that a further leap was needed and possible. And indeed, the Direcção Universal later established a new church in Brazil (in 2011), while in the meantime several churches had been inaugurated in several southern African countries such as Namibia,

Zambia, Zimbabwe, South Africa, Mozambique and Madagascar (see *Angola Press*, 19 January 2009).

Nunes himself manifested these intentions in several public interventions in the Angolan media, where he inserted the church expansion within wider ideologies of 'African self-discovery' (*Angola Press*, 4 September 2011), 'Evangelical expansion' (*O País*, 29 December 2010) and Christian salvationism (ibid.):

> We want the African church to also be present in Europe, preaching just like the missionaries preached in before in our land, in difficult conditions. Our responsibility as African Christians is to salvage the Christian matrix, in a Europe invaded by religions that are contrary to our faith. The Christian matrix that guided the Europeans in the past is now disappearing. (*O País*, 29 December 2010)

This public proselytist display, explicitly resonant of 'reverse mission' theorizations, illustrates the novelty of the Direcção Universal's outward-looking stance, which overcame the 'traditional' national, Angolan frontiers and finally confirmed the inaugurational prophecy of a 'church in the world'. From this particular perspective, Nunes's renewed, new millennium proposals explicitly invoked a specific sense of 'charismatic power', in many ways resonant with Pentecostal and Evangelical practical modalities and discursive regimes – namely, in what concerns a conjugation of charisma as power, agency and dissuasion within 'belicist' phrasings of 'battle', 'conquest' and 'victory' (see e.g. Coleman 2000; Mafra 2002; Ojo 2006: Smit 2007; Swatowiski 2007; O'Neill 2010), etc. For instance, in one particular interview with Angolan media, Nunes mentioned the creation of 'an army of new servers in Christ' (*Angola Press*, 19 January 2009). This proactivity implied an important change regarding more classic proselytist policies within the church (see Blanes 2011b), which traditionally were not construed nor devised to speak to a non-African audience. On the other hand, it can be seen as part of a movement of extraversion (Thornton 1998b; Bayart 2000; Englund 2003) by which religious territorialities no longer are confined within frontiers (whether political or otherwise), but are inherently externalized, rhizomatic, branched (see Amselle 2001). There is, therefore, beyond the physical and demographic movement, a conscious political agency of extraversion (Bayart 2000) which has become progressively central within certain, prevailing Tokoist allegiances.

However, despite the progressive appropriation on behalf of the Direcção Universal, Lisbon also simultaneously became a territory of dispute, where some of the tensions observed in Luanda were reproduced in diasporic terrain. One such event was the inauguration of a second Tokoist church in northern Lisbon, associated with the Doze. This church first began to operate in the house of an elderly sister in Brandoa, also in northern Lisbon. They would gather in her living room every Sunday, and pray and sing throughout the day. In 2009, when I first met this small group, they were struggling to find a new space for their celebrations, and engaging in paperwork in order to become officially recognized in Portugal. I eventually lost contact with them, as my relationships and routines were already established in the Vale do Forno church, and I did not want to cause discomfort or promote any potential rivalry between the groups. However, some time later, while in Luanda, I came across a local Tokoist newspaper, *Jornal Evangélico Tokoista* (published by the Doze), which reported that the church in Brandoa was officially recognized as *the first* Tokoist church in Portugal – as the group in Vale do Forno was still, technically, a mere 'association'.

The sites of contestation, apart from the de-territorialization and extraversion, also reveal a culmination of the different 'moral circumscriptions' (Blanes 2009c, 2012a) that were – and are – active in the church. These moral circumscriptions refer to the idea of significant ascriptions that religious movements attribute to particular territories, either through the identification of its moral valence (Basso 1996; Smith 2000; Taylor 2007), historicity (Ashworth and Graham 2005), conceptual (Feld and Basso 1999) and ethical (Smith 2000) significance. From this perspective, more than the scapes or sceneries described by Appadurai in his theory of modernity and identity (1996), a different conception of territoriality and belonging arises – one that is determined by the *branchements* that assign 'variable geometries' to land and territory (Amselle 2001).

In what concerns Tokoism, the prophetic trajectory described in chapters 1 and 2 reveals none other than those processes of circumscription and contestation: if in the first decades of the movement's existence the significant borders were shaped around ideas of *kongolité*, Angolanity and African-ness, the leader's sojourn in the Azores and the posterior presence of Angolan Tokoists in Lisbon transformed this city into a site of political action and contestation – very much in the same way Paris and Brussels have become for the Kimbanguist Church, as has been explained by Anne Mélice and Ramon Sarró (2010, 2012), for instance. As we saw in chapter 4, these different processes reverted into dispute and debate. There is in this sense a dynamics of political and identitary enveloping defined by the narratives of prophetic trajectory that circulate within the church, the novelty being its extraversion. This enveloping circulates around a particular idea of charisma and place that, from an Angolan perspective, remains contested.

Double Presences: Mobility, Territory and Belonging

The configuration of Lisbon as a site of evangelical expansion and simultaneously an arena of political dispute is, as I am arguing here, the outcome of the evolving engagements between processes of mobility, territory and belonging experienced by the Tokoists, involved in a history of constant re-territorialization and identification. From this perspective, the relationship between church institutional expansion and ideas of belonging and agency is not necessarily equal or balanced. What I described in the previous chapters are processes of growth and conquest, but also of tension, misunderstanding and dispute, revealing the ambiguities behind the idea of a globalizing and globalized movement (Meyer and Geschiere 1999; Meyer 2010).

My reference here to 'double presences' is a direct pun to the post-humous book published by the Algerian sociologist Abdelmalek Sayad, *La Double Absence* (1999).[17] Sayad's work was fundamental in the development of an academic approach to migration that moved away from economicist and quantifying depictions of the migrant subject, often instrumentalized as a mere 'labour force', and in contrast highlighting the experiential dimension, considering the socio-psychological dimensions of the migratory process, where the subject engages in self-representation and adaptation to new life conditions – often in 'contradictory' and 'suffering' conditions (2004: 179).

His proposal of understanding migration as a production of 'absences' – absence from the life left behind in the home country, and the absence of 'becoming invisible' in the host country – that invokes an 'impossible ubiquity' is, from my point of view, composed of the same kind of consciousness and agency that produce particular senses of belonging among migrants, who engage in processes of reflection and debate regarding their previous and new conditions (Blanes 2007, 2008b). The paradox of the migrant, who is present 'despite being absent' in his homeland and absent 'despite being present' in his new address, is, despite the dangers and deprivations highlighted by Sayad, also a space of potential; migration, from the point of view of life experiences, worldviews and expectations, becomes a social dimension in itself – or what for many could be described as a 'transnational existence' that incorporates novel geographies (Mapril 2009), territorialities and boundaries (see Basch, Glick-Schiller and Szanton-Blanc 1994; Baumann 1999; Levitt 2001, 2007).

From a religious and political point of view, this invocation also connects to a previous discussion I established with Ramon Sarró, with whom we reflected upon the concept of 'prophetic presences' in terms of a dialectic that affected issues of leadership, mobility and generational transition. In other words, on how in the Tokoist Church the historical and experiential 'presence' or 'concealment' (be it physical or symbolic) of the leader among his followers geared different memory perceptions and political positioning, mediated by processes of succession and generational transition, and by the development of complex territorialities. In this regard, memory and belonging (and the current disputes regarding both factors in the Tokoist movement) are often mediated by this dialectics of presence and concealment, producing diversified experiences among believers of the same church (Engelke 2007). If in the previous chapter we saw different and opposing methods of making the prophet 'present', the concomitant process of extraversion and re-territorialization provoked new senses of absence and presence, mediated by a diasporic experience and generational transition.

Therefore my approach here builds on this dialectics and on Sayad's approach, which had already incorporated the need to look at migration as a dual phenomenon; but it also attempts to complexify its politico-identitary stance by suggesting that the migratory process also produces, apart from those tragic absences, particular senses of presence and belonging. By this I mean that through the process of mobility and circulation, the migrant often engages in multiple agencies and works in different planes of interaction, including the place of origin and the host society (Mapril 2009). Such is the case, I argue, of Angolan migrants in Portugal such as the Tokoists, who, as I explain above, dwell in permanent circulation. More often than not, ideas of centre and periphery come into play, producing tensions between centrifugal (universalizing) and centripetal (particularizing) tendencies of belonging (Sarró and Blanes 2009; Sarró and Mélice 2012).

However, the idea of a multiple engagement also refers to the way migrants politically participate in 'struggles for recognition', simultaneously as emigrants, as an idea of 'diaspora' that is construed within the homeland, and as immigrants, as foreigners in the process of externally imposed 'integration' in conditions of subordination (Sayad 2004: 118 and ff.). Elsewhere I argued that this multiple engagement often produces, among migrant religious communities, a 'third way':

the outcome of a dialectic process between heritages, constraints and expectations (Blanes 2007). The composition between an urge for a rhizomatic metaphor and the autonomic agency that characterized the installation of a Tokoist church in Lisbon is illustrative. In any case, migrants find themselves becoming socially relevant agents in two – or eventually more – planes of interaction and signification, from the place of origin to the place of destiny. From this perspective, trans-nationality becomes the very soil through which ideas of heritage and belonging are managed and reproduced – a 'diasporic culture', as it were (Eisenlohr 2007; Johnson 2007; Levitt 2007), where the relation-ship between territory and belonging becomes multifarious and com-plexified. In such religious contexts, the idea of presence also engages ideologically with ideas of universalism and belonging, and especially in what concerns classic ideas of Christian mission and contact – a topic that has been acutely discussed by anthropologists working in Africa (Comaroff and Comaroff 1991; Valverde 1997; Pels 1999) and elsewhere (e.g. Vilaça and Wright 2009). In cases such as the one de-scribed by Peter Pels in late colonial Tanganyika, 'presence' and 'pres-entation' were two inescapabilities in the processes ('microphysics') of missionary contact (Pels 1999: 4–5).

Here, the shifting discourses of missionization, migrant ordeals, conquest and moral dilemmas reveal novel processes of recognition that couple novel senses of territoriality and extraversion with theories of alterity (Vilaça 2010).

Notes

1. Research such as that of Esteves (1991), Bastos and Bastos (1999), Pires (2002) and, more recently, Rosales, Jesus and Parra (2009) show how Af-rican and in particular Angolan migration evolved from residual to demo-graphically significant after the Carnation revolution on 25 April 1974.
2. The anthropologist Cecilie Oien, who worked with the Angolan diaspora in Lisbon, showed figures from the SEF (Frontier and Foreigners Office): in 2004, there were over 26,000 Angolans living in Portugal. According to these figures, which obviously do not include people living in irregu-lar conditions, the Angolans would constitute the second-largest African-originated community in Portugal, after the Cape Verdeans (Oien 2008: 26). The National Institute of Statistics (INE) would later update the num-bers in 2006, counting 28,000 (INE 2007). See also Grassi (2007).
3. The CPLP (Community of Portuguese Language Countries, also referred to as PALOP in Portuguese) became in 1996 an official bloc involving seven countries that shared the Lusophone colonial past: Portugal, Brazil,

Angola, Cape Verde, Guinea-Bissau, Mozambique, São Tomé and Príncipe and, since, 2002, East Timor.

4. Regarding the last two points, I am thinking here about what migration studies researchers have called *push and pull factors* (factors motivating migration and/or return), but also on the social networks and regional contexts that favour the perpetuation of certain demographic movements. In the European case, I am referring to the specific idea of this continent alternating, since the constitution of the European Union, between an image of 'fortress' and of 'Eldorado' (King, Lazaridis and Tsardanidis 2000).

5. Dora Possidónio notes that the dimension of the number of Angolans in illegal or undocumented situations in Portugal became visible in their participation in the campaigns of extraordinary regularization of immigrants promoted by the Portuguese government in 1992–1993 and 1996, where Angolans were the nationality with more applications (2006: 97).

6. Here I am referring to the documentary *Outros Bairros* (Other Neighbourhoods, 1999), directed by Kiluanje Liberdade, Inês Gonçalves and Vasco Pimentel, that performs a portrait of the life of descendants of Cape Verdean migrants in Lisbon, namely in clandestine neighbourhoods in the city's periphery, away from the public gaze.

7. Here in turn I am thinking of the documentary *Lisboetas* (2004), directed by Sérgio Treffaut, an intimate portrait of how African, Brazilian and Eastern European migrants live and experience the Portuguese capital.

8. This plural setting requires the incorporation of a recent trend: the context of economic crisis experienced since 2008 in Portugal, which, associated with the recent transformations in Angolan society (the 2002 armistice, economic growth), seemed to have inverted the previous trends to the point that many Angolans expatriates are returning to their country, and a new wave of Portuguese emigration to Angola is developing (*O País*, 10 January 2010).

9. However, this wasn't the first time that such a notion appeared: already in the 1960s and 1970s there were references, in Simão Toko's correspondence, to Tokoists living in Portugal (e.g. letter by Simão Toko, 16 March 1973). My discussion here refers to an organized and institutionalizing presence.

10. Here I am referring to the controversial process of implantation of the Universal Church of the Kingdom of God in Portugal in the early 1990s. This motivated a strong public reaction and an almost unanimous rejection of so-called Christian sects (see Mafra 2002). In the long run, it also implied that many non-Catholic churches were placed under the same conceptual umbrella and seen with mistrust by many Portuguese.

11. Some church members estimate that there may be altogether around five hundred Tokoists in Portugal, and a few thousand throughout the European territory – many of which, due to lack of financial conditions or opportunity, rarely or never visited a Tokoist church.

12. It was in fact through these networks that I was able to visit other Tokoist churches in the European territory, namely in London and Rotterdam.

13. Obviously, such mobilities are not necessarily inaugurated in Lisbon or Europe. They are part of wider patterns of circulation within and through-

out Africa and beyond (see e.g. de Bruijn, van Dijk and Foeken 2001; Sarró 2009c; Schielke and Graw 2012).

14. Part of what follows was invoked and debated in Blanes (2011b).
15. He is referring to the period of exile in the Azores Islands. See chapter 2 on Toko's reflections regarding faith in Portugal.
16. After few months, however, the nucleus became dormant, because most of its members decided to migrate to Angola.
17. The book was later published in English under the title *The Suffering of the Immigrant* (2004).

Conclusion

It was September 2008 when I first met Ilda Toko, Simão's elder daughter. She was living in London, but had travelled to Portugal for her nephew's wedding, and was invited to visit the Tokoist church in Vale do Forno. Having spent most of her life in Europe, she was known, as was her sister Esmeralda and cousin João Sivi, for having renounced her part in the Tokoist movement and following other creeds. In her case, after her father returned to Angola in 1974, and after a brief attempt to live in Luanda, she stayed in Europe and lived, worked and married in Portugal until, after her divorce, she decided to move to London; in the meantime, she joined the Church of the Latter-Day-Saints in South Kensington, where she congregates to this day.

Therefore, at the time it was a special and rather unique occasion to have the *dirigente*'s daughter visiting the church for the first time. I had been tipped off the night before by Simão Vemba, and showed up at the service with great curiosity; after reading and hearing so much about Simão Toko, this was a chance to glimpse an intimate, direct account of the person, the man, the individual. As she was greeted by the church and handed the microphone to address the crowd, I remember sensing her discomfort, not necessarily for having to address an audience (or this audience in particular), but rather because her words invoked painful recollections. She explained that she could not say much because the mere act of remembering her relationship with the church was very painful for her:

> As you know, obviously I am part of the church, I was born in the church. It is with great pain that I can tell you that I saw my father suffering many times.… I really don't like to talk about this.… But we, as his sons, were part of that suffering. I cried so many times.… Many of you may ask why I am not in the church. It's only natural. Because I suffered so much. (7 September 2008).

I understood that what had pulled her away from Tokoism was the pain that the act of remembering a particular history – her own and that of her family's – provoked. The memory of suffering cultivated within the church was still very much painfully present and lingering in the bodies and hearts of many Tokoists, and especially in people like Ilda. The conflicts described in chapters 4 and 5 of this book can also be read in terms of how this memory of suffering is dealt with: either safeguarded as the very ethos of the church (as in the case of the Doze), or revised and set aside towards an onward perspective (as in the case of the Universal).

In the following months and years, I was able to meet and interact with Ilda quite a few times, both in London and Lisbon. In our conversations, I was able to gain a new perspective on the leader of Tokoism – an intimate, domestic portrait of a man who bore the responsibility of leading in exile a flock of dozens of thousands of people, while domestically raising his own children and taking care of his bedridden wife.

I was therefore confronted with a side I often overlooked in my study of this prophetic biography: the effects and consequences of Simão Toko's life of martyrdom on his family and descendants, the hardships provoked by his life of detention, exile and refuge, the family's progres-

Illustration 20. Simão Toko's personal belongings in Ponta Albina, 1957. *Source:* "Tocoismo no Povo Taia" PT/TT/PIDE-DA-C-1-154513. Image reproduction authorized by ANTT.

sive publicization and consequent loss of intimacy, and his wife's long-lasting illness. As Ilda herself told me, she was born in the fields of the Huíla region, while her father was moving towards his *desterro* (exile) in the south of Angola. She then spent her youth in remote locations like distant lighthouses in the southern African desert or the Atlantic islands with practically no social contacts, until she eventually began to interact with other people of her age in the Catholic boarding school at Ponta Delgada (the capital of São Miguel) her father sent her to. From the distance, she then observed how her father was again persecuted in Angola, and then how his legacy was disputed and disrupted after his death. So her pain and discomfort on the day she spoke at the church in Lisbon were expectable and comprehensible.

This personal account contrasts with – and is recurrently subalternized by – the more public registers displayed in both and Angola and Portugal, which insert Toko within particular 'imaginative horizons' (Crapanzano 2004) and expectations on behalf of those who followed or in turn persecuted him, or were just familiar with his notoriety, in negotiation with the public imprint and legacy (Fernandez 1973; Mac-Gaffey 1983: 102–120) of the religious leader Simão Toko. In this regard, there is a public, political history that I have described throughout this book, which inserts the movement in a central but rather ambiguous position within Angolan late-colonial and postcolonial ideological movements and expectations. In the first place, through its construction – both from an autochthon (Angolan) and imperial (Portuguese) perspective – as a resistant, revolutionary movement that fought for a societal, political change in its significant territorial circumscriptions – Bakongo territory, Angola, Africa and the world (Blanes 2012a). From this perspective, Simão Toko, despite certain stances of 'forgotten histories', inevitably became a public figure, subject to multiple recognitions.

In the second place, through its self-awareness as a politically autonomist, libertarian movement that preached a rejection of externally imposed politically repressive models and instead cultivated a solidary, pacifist, egalitarian movement that preached personal betterment and collective commitment in conjunction with a sense of a possible better future. The acts of resistance in the *colonatos*, Toko's recommendations for learning and instruction, their denial of participating in armed conflict – all these statements and postures reflected upon distinctive expressions of faith and belief that were made visible in the Angolan scenario and progressively incorporated certain political ontologies based on libertarianism and independency. In this regard, the resistance to both colonial and postcolonial repression, mediated by strong convictions and beliefs beheld by Toko and his followers, can be seen as a consequence of a particular messianic stance and proclamation. If, in the early 1950s, many Angolan natives were attracted by his discourse on the 'changing of things' ('c'est pas la fin du monde, mais le changement des choses'), his biography of suffering and martyrdom, as well as that of his immediate followers, acted simultaneously as a catalyst for the movement's social reproduction through its coupling with stances of resistance and endurance. These stances were ultimately guided by a conviction that change was inevitable, as was, in a way, to be confirmed soon after, in 1974. But the post-independence period simultaneously prolonged the history of suffering and postponed the prophetic expectations of the Tokoists, as Toko realized that the change had only occurred at a political – and not spiritual – level.

However, in truth, theologically and spiritually speaking, Toko was not a messianic preacher. He was, instead, an object of messianization, as performed in Pastor Melo's book (2002) and revelations, as well as in other accounts and prophetic statements displayed within the Tokoists' charismatic culture. But despite his personal interest and future-oriented theology and spiritualism, Toko's main theological stance was in fact an exercise in remembrance, through which the Tokoists built a particular timeline that connected biblical history to certain, spiritually revealed futures and updated configurations of the present. This exercise, as we saw in chapter 4, was also contested and subject to creative appropriations and epistemological operations.

But who was Simão Gonçalves Toko after all? Throughout this book, we have been confronted with several internal and external portrayals of a man who became notorious and 'public' through his religious ministry but whose subjectivity did not cease after his physical passing in 1984, creating what Joseph Tonda describes as a 'syndrome' (2001) in what concerns the precariousness of his image and classification. On the one hand, we have the opinions and memories of those who chose to follow him, mediated by different logics and vital forces: generation, territoriality and the dynamics of absence/presence. Here we distinguished between different 'methods of memory', which relied on different intellectual and experiential operations: testimoniality, hagiography and charismatic attribution, biographical extension and spiritual mediation.

On the other hand, we also have exogenous portraits of Simão Toko, in particular those produced from within the colonial apparatus and politically biased by its demeaning intentions. From this perspective, Toko was a farce, a naïve theologian, a liar, an ambitious, corrupt political leader, a conspirationist and, at his best, a revolutionary. It was

recurrently against these portraits that the logics of memory cultivated within Tokoism fed into a historiographical construction of his
prophetic biography/trajectory: the need to combat the wrongness of
these ideas or justify the righteousness of his path reverted in a sort of
'anxiety' through which the Tokoists engaged in intellectual produc-
tions such as the historiographical research and publication. But, as I
suggested in chapter 4, the anxiety was also provoked by the episodes
of internal crisis and dispute, and in fact many of the processes of
memory, reconstruction and heritagization observed within the movement were in fact exponentialized after the arrival of Bishop Afonso
Nunes, who engaged in a particular form of 'relating' – through spiritual coating, personification and biographical extension – to Simão
Toko. Nunes's arrival, in a way, pushed Tokoism into an intense spiritual and historiographical revisionism, seeking for sanction, confirmation and orthodoxy for the otherwise trepidant Tokoist existence in
the post-1984 period.

This brings us back to the definitional problems that are imposed
upon religious leaders such as Simão Toko. The forgotten history I
described in the introduction to this book was partly a consequence
of an academic and political imposition within certain theoretical
paradigms: Kongo prophetism, subversive anticolonial messianism,
Angolan political leadership, etc. One such straightjacket was Toko's
marginal insertion into a 'modern Kongo prophet' (MacGaffey 1983)
template, against which he was recurrently placed.[1] This was performed both as an intellectual exercise of comparison on behalf of the
European and North American academia, but also as a political, strategic placement on behalf of the colonial authorities. Both coincided
in a depiction of an offshoot of Kongo prophetism and simultaneously
a 'modern', anti-traditional movement. But, in fact, Simão Toko conjugated different expressions of leadership that, through time, escaped
the theoretical 'localizing strategies' (Fardon 1990) that were common-
place in late-colonial and post-independence Angola and Sub-Saharan
Africa. For instance, if, theologically speaking, prophecy (prediction,
acknowledgement, spiritual mediation) was a central aspect of Toko's
proposals, more so were the theories of remembrance and reformism
he constantly invoked. Furthermore, from a socio-political perspective Toko combined particular models of leadership that incorporated
other forms of charisma, temporalization and routinization, thus com-
plexifying the individual portrait and rendering the concept of prophetic leadership insufficient to grasp the whole scenario.

Toko's composite heritage, incorporating multiple sources, perspectives and materializations, resulted, as we saw in chapter 4, in 'plural-

izing pasts' (Ashworth et al. 2007); but it also resulted in ambiguous characterizations and appropriations. As a religious leader commented on the day of Toko's funeral,

> Brother Simão Toko is an extraordinary person; he is a man who committed his life to the Gospel and everything he achieved can be appreciated in his works. But one of the things he was not able to do was to remove the idea off his believers' head that he is not the reincarnation of Christ. Fortunately or unfortunately, he could not avoid this conception in his believers. (Pastor from the Evangelical Baptist Church of Luanda; quoted in Kisela 2004: 251; my translation)

From this perspective, Toko's ministry and leadership was in many ways publicly negotiated in terms of a 'charismatic enveloping' – and from a particular perspective continued after his death: in the first place, through a post-facto charismatic attribution that was produced by his following's remembrance; and secondly, through the attempts of making him 'present' after the process of succession.

This post-mortem charismatic attribution was, in part, a reflection of what is commonly defined as a process of generational succession, exponentialized in religious movements based on prophetic leadership: the sedimentation, through processes of hagiographization, heroicization, mythification, etc., of a particular prophetic biography. This sedimentation occurs through materializations and stylizations such as those described for the liturgical and experiential settings in chapter 3. From this perspective, in addition to the life of leadership certainly enhanced by Toko's psychological charismatic qualities, the development of prophetic biographies is in itself a materialization of the process of charismatic attribution, through which a poetic process of memory, realization and stabilization/destabilization occurs (Lambek 1998). Thus, there is an exchange between dynamics of leading and following, charisma and consciousness (Lindholm 1990; 2003) that does not necessarily cease after the disappearance of the leader and the installation of processes of transition. In fact, the stages of deterritorialization, processed through multiple 'involuntary mobilities', and culminating in the emergence of a 'Tokoist diaspora', enhanced this idea of continuation through the appearance of new senses of presence and belonging.

However, this process also incorporates other perceptions and configurations of charisma. I briefly return to the events of July 1949 to make this point: according to Toko's recollection of the Pentecostal event described in chapters 2 and 4, there was a charismatic profusion by which many of those present began to speak in tongues, be possessed by the Holy Spirit and perform miraculous forms of mediation, communication and healing. But Toko himself was not 'possessed', nor did he later become a medium or a *vate*. Instead, his charismatic gift was one of acknowledgement, later subject to a process of rationalization and routinization (see Coleman 2004) through the development of the prophetic-charismatic culture of the *vates* and the tabernacles. This had two implications: the inauguration of a charismatic 'repertoire' and 'aesthetics', as well as particular 'regimes of power' that affected spiritual practice and political culture. It also implied the inauguration of a spiritual temporality that would become linchpin in the Tokoist's theological, spiritual, experiential and political configurations. There was, therefore, an ontogenic process of 'making history' (Toren 1988, 2004) involved in the charismatic attribution.

From this perspective, the way the Tokoists look at their leader today is also revelatory of a wider epistemological and experiential production: the conceptions of time, the multiple temporalities that are conjugated in different planes: quotidian, political, spiritual, ideological, liturgical. This multiplicity reveals both an explicit concern regarding the past, the present and the future, and the recognition of its inherently unstable nature. Incorporating Simon Coleman's suggestion, Tokoists conjure different planes of historiopraxy or perceiving and 'acting out history' (2011). If one were to return to Matt Hodges's critique on 'time's arrow', or its linearization within a particular, fluid trajectory (2008), one could say that it was precisely a prophetic trajectory – that of Simão Gonçalves Toko – which developed a history of temporal multiplications, in which my own 'prophetic insertion', as the foreign researcher who will tell the world about the church, should be understood. And if we assume, as Johannes Fabian did, that time is constitutive of social reality (1983: 24), then we begin to question the possibility of co-constitution, and what are the typifications at stake at an intellectual level – from an anthropological (Munn 1992) or religious point of view. The focal point then becomes the very idea of 'trajectory' and its '-ialization', despite Pierre Bourdieu's critiques in his take on the 'biographical illusion' (1986).

The same point could thus be made regarding spatiality and memory. Toko's biography became a – not necessarily linear – trajectory of mobility and territorial experience that offered senses of 'walking' and 'belonging' to his movement's believers, who matched these sensibilities to their own paths of 'involuntary mobility'. However, they did not constitute sceneries or scapes (as Arjun Appadurai [1996] would have devised), but instead provoked divergent and complexified allegiances that more often than not became sensorially frictionate.

Notes

1. I must point out, however, that Wyatt MacGaffey was not suggesting an idea of 'prophetic modernity' against particular ideas of tradition, witchcraft. In fact, his description is one of continuities (1983: 2). From this perspective, 'modernity' appears as a complementary temporal categorization.

Primary Sources

Archives

Archives Africaines du SPF Affaires Etrangères, Brussels
Archives 'Affaires Indigènes', portfolio 4746

Arquivo Histórico Ultramarino, Lisbon
Ministério do Ultramar, Gabinete de Negócios Políticos, Process 020, Parts 1 to
    9, 'Seita Místico Religiosa Simão Gonçalves Toco'

Arquivo Nacional – Torre do Tombo, Lisbon
PIDE Archives
Direcção Geral de Segurança, Serviços Centrais, Process 1825, volumes 1 to
    11, 'Simão Gonçalves Toco'
Direcção Geral de Segurança, Serviços Centrais, CI(2), Process 6462, 'Toco-
    ismo, Religião da Estrela'
Delegação de Angola, Process 1-33746 'Seita Tocoismo Individuos Fichados'
Delegação de Angola, Process 54009 'Simão Gonçalves Toco'
Delegação de Angola, Process C-1-1545A 'Testemunhas de Jeová'
Delegação de Angola, Process C-1-1546A 'Tocoistas'
Delegação de Angola, Process C-1-154513 'Tocoismo no Povo Taia'
Delegação de Angola, Process C-3-731-1 to 9 'Simão Gonçalves Toco'
Delegação de Angola, Process P.INF-1544A-1 'Colonato do Vale do Loge'
Serviços Centrais, Process CI2-6462 'Tocoismo Religião da Estrela'
Serviços de Centralização e Coordenação de Informações de Angola -773100-
    A-cx262 'Tocoismo Estudos sobre a Seita'
Serviços de Centralização e Coordenação de Informações de Angola, Process
    773100, box 261, 'Pareceres sobre Proscrição'
Serviços de Centralização e Coordenação de Informações de Moçambique,
    Process A-9-149, 'Alberto Cossa'

Centro de Informação e Documentação Amílcar Cabral
H51-17 'Tocoismo e Kimbanguismo em Angola'

Instituto Português de Apoio ao Desenvolvimento, Lisbon
MU/DGE/RPAD/1415/06276 'Estudo e Planeamento do Núcleo do Vale do
  Loge, 1970–1974'

Media

Alfa & Omega
Angola Press
Angolense
Angonotícias
Folha 8
Jornal de Angola
Jornal Evangélico Tokoista
O País
Rádio Nacional de Angola
Televisão Pública de Angola

Bibliography

Agamben, G. 2002. 'The Time that is Left', *Epoché* 7(1): 1–14.

Agostinho, P. n.d. *Simão Gonçalves Toco e os Tocoistas no Mundo.* Luanda: Edição de Autor.

Akyeampong, E. 2000. 'Africans in the Diaspora: The Diaspora and Africa', *African Affairs* 99(395): 183–215.

Alexandre, V. (ed.). 2000. *O Império Africano: Séculos XIX e XX.* Lisbon: Colibrí.

———. 1979. *As Origens do Colonialismo Português Moderno (1822–1891).* Lisbon: Sá da Costa.

Allerton, C. 2009. 'Introduction: on Spiritual Landscapes', *Anthropological Forum* 19(3): 235–251.

Almeida, C. 2010. 'Entre 'gente áspera e dura' – advertências de um missionário no Kongo (1713–1723)', in Saraiva, C., J. Tavim and P. Havik (eds.), *Caminhos Cruzados em História e Antropologia. Ensaios de Homenagem a Jill Dias.* Lisbon: Imprensa de Ciências Sociais, 71–92.

Álvaro, A. N. 2011. *As Profecias de Mayamona.* Luanda: GCNET.

Amaral, I. 1968. *Luanda. Estudo de Geografia Urbana.* Lisbon: Junta de Investigação do Ultramar.

Amassari, S. 2005. *Migration and Development: New strategic outlooks and practical ways forward: The cases of Angola and Zambia.* Geneva: International Organization for Migration.

Amselle, J. L. 2001. *Branchements. Anthropologie de l'Universalité des Cultures.* Paris: Flammarion.

Anderson, A. 2005. 'New African Initiated Pentecostalism and Charismatics in South Africa', *Journal of Religion in Africa* 35(1): 66–92.

Andersson, E. 1968. *Churches at the Grass-roots: A Study in Congo-Brazzaville.* London: Lutterworth.

———. 1958. *Messianic Popular Movements in the Lower Congo.* Uppsala: Almquist & Wiksells.

Antze, P., and Lambek, M. (eds.). 1996. *Tense Past: Cultural Essays in Trauma and Memory.* London and New York: Routledge.

Appadurai, A. 1996. *Modernity at Large: Cultural Dimensions of Globalization.* Minneapolis: University of Minnesota Press.

Asad, T. 1993. *Genealogies of Religion: Discipline and Reasons of Power in Christianity and Islam.* Baltimore: Johns Hopkins Press.

Asamoah, J. K. 2005. *African Charismatics: Current Developments within Inde-pendent Indigenous Pentecostalism in Ghana.* Leiden: Brill.

Ashworth, G., and B. Graham (eds.). 2005. *Senses of Place, Senses of Time.* Bur-lington and Farnham: Ashgate.

Austin, J. 1963. *How to Do Things with Words.* Harvard: Harvard University Press.

Baganha, M. I., and P. Gois. 1999. 'Migrações Internacionais de e para Portu-gal: O que Sabemos e Para onde Vamos', *Revista Crítica de Ciências Sociais* 52–53: 229–280.

Balandier, G. 1999. 'Ce que j'ai appris de l'Afrique', *Journal des Africanistes* 69(1): 259–270.

———. 1971. 'Politique et Contestation en Afrique', *Canadian Journal of Afri-can Studies* 5(2): 131–134.

———. 1965. 'The Colonial Situation', in P. van den Berghe (ed.), *Africa: Social Problem of Change and Conflict.* San Francisco, CA: Chandler Publishing Co.

———. 1963 [1955]. *Sociologie Actuelle de l'Afrique Noire.* Paris: Presses Uni-versitaires de France.

———. 1953. 'Messianismes et Colonialismes en Afrique Noire', *Cahiers Inter-nationaux de Sociologie* 14: 41–65.

———. 1952. 'Approche Sociologique des Brazzavilles Noires: Études Prélimi-naires', *Africa* 22(1): 23–34.

Ball, J. 2006. 'I Escaped in a Coffin: Remembering Angolan Forced Labour from the 1940s', *Cadernos de Estudos Africanos* 9–10: 61–74.

———. 2005. 'Colonial Labor in Twentieth Century Angola', *History Compass* 3(1): 1–9.

Ballesteros, P., and C. Sánchez-Carretero. 2011. 'En Torno a las Ausencias y Presencias del Concepto de "Patrimonio". Prácticas y Discursos Patri-monializadores en el Camino de Santiago a Fisterra', paper presented at the XII Congreso de Antropología de la FAAEE, León, Spain, September 2011.

Barker, J. (ed.). 2007. *The Anthropology of Morality in Melanesia and Beyond.* Farnham and Burlington: Ashgate.

Barrett, D. 1967. *Schism and Renewal in Africa: An Analysis of Six Thousand Contemporary Religious Movements.* Oxford: Oxford University Press.

Basch, L., N. Glick-Schiller and C. Szanton-Blanc. 1994. *Nations Unbound: Transnational Projects, Postcolonial Predicaments and Deterritorialized Na-tion-States.* London: Gordon and Breach.

Basso, K. 1996. *Wisdom Sits in Places: Landscape and Language among the Western Apache.* Albuquerque: University of New Mexico Press.

Bastos, C., M. V. Almeida and B. Feldman-Bianco. 2002. *Trânsitos Coloniais. Diálogos Críticos Luso-Brasileiros.* Lisboa: Imprensa de Ciências Sociais.

Bastos, C. 2009. 'Maria Índia, ou a Fronteira da Colonização: Trabalho, Mi-gração e Política no Planalto Sul de Angola', *Horizontes Antropológicos* 15(31): 51–74.

———. 2004. 'Omulu em Lisboa. Etnografias para uma Teoria da Globaliza-ção', *Etnográfica* 5(2): 303–324.

Bastos, J., and S. Bastos. 1999. *Portugal Multicultural.* Lisboa: Fim de Século.

Baumann, G. 1999. *The Multicultural Riddle: Rethinking National, Ethnic, and Religious Identities.* London and New York: Routledge.

Bayart, J. F. 2000. 'Africa in the World: A History of Extraversion', *African Affairs* 99(395): 217–267.

———. 1989. 'Les Églises Chrétiennes et la Politique du Ventre: le partage du Gâteau Ecclésial', *Politique Africaine* 35: 3–26.

Bediako, K. 2000. 'Africa and Christianity on the Threshold of the Third Millennium: The Religious Dimension', *African Affairs* 99(395): 303–323.

———. 1985. *Christianity in Africa: The Renewall of a Non-Western Religion.* Edinburgh: Edinburgh University Press.

Beidelman, T. 1982. *Colonial Evangelism: A Socio-Historical Study of an East African Mission at the Grassroots.* Bloomington, IN: Indiana University Press.

Bender, G. 2009 [1978]. *Angola Under the Portuguese: The Myth and the Reality.* Berkeley and Los Angeles: University of California Press.

———. 1973. 'Planned Rural Settlements in Angola: 1900–1968', in F. W. Heimer (ed.), *Social Change in Angola.* Munich: Arnold Bergstrassen Institut.

Benjamin, W. 1968. 'Theses on the Philosophy of History', in *Illuminations.* New York: Schocken Books, 253–264.

Berliner, D. 2012. 'Multiple Nostalgias: The Fabric of Heritage in Luang Prabang (Lo PDR)', *Journal of the Royal Anthropological Institute* 18(4): 769–786.

———. 2010. 'Anthropologie et Transmission', *Terrain* 55: 4–19.

Berliner, D., and C. Bortolotto. 2012. *Patrimoine et Anthropologie: L'Unesco dans Tous ses États.* Paris: Gradhiva.

Berliner, D., and R. Sarró (eds.). 2008. *Learning Religion: Anthropological Perspectives.* New York and London: Berghahn Books.

Bernard, G. 1971. 'La Contestation et les Églises Nationales au Congo', *Canadian Journal of African Studies* 5(2): 145–156.

Beyer, P. 2003. 'De-Centring Religious Singularity: The Globalization of Christianity as a Case in Point', *Numen* 50(4): 357–386.

Bilger, V., and A. Kraler. 2005. 'Introduction: African migrations. Historical perspectives and contemporary dynamics', *Stichproben. Wiener Zeitschrift für kritische Afrikastudien* 8: 5–21.

Bird-David, N. 1999. 'Animism Revisited: Personhood, Environment, and Relational Epistemology', *Current Anthropology* 40(S1): S67–S91.

Birkeland, N. 2000. 'Forced Migration and Deslocados in the Huambo Province, Angola', *Norsk Geografisk Tidsskrift - Norwegian Journal of Geography* 54(3): 110–115.

Birmingham, D. 2006. *Empire in Africa: Angola and its Neighbors.* Athens: Ohio University Press.

———. 2004. *Portugal and Africa.* Athens: Ohio University Press.

———. 2000. *Trade and Empire in the Atlantic, 1400–1600.* London and New York: Routledge.

———. 1998. 'Merchants and Missionaries in Angola', *Lusotopie* 1998: 345–355.

Bittencourt, M. 2010. 'Angola. Tradição, Modernidade e Cultura Política', in D. Reis et al. (eds.), *Tradições e Modernidades.* Rio de Janeiro: FGV.

———. 2008. *Estamos Juntos! O MPLA e a luta anticolonial (1961–1974)*, 2 vols. Luanda: Kilombelombe.

———. 2000. 'A História Contemporânea de Angola: seus achados e suas armadilhas', in Comissão Nacional para as Comemorações dos Descobrimentos Portugueses, *Construindo o Passado Angolano: as fontes e a sua interpretação. Actas do II Seminário Internacional sobre a História de Angola (4 a 9 de Agosto de 1997)*. Luanda, 161–185.

———. 1997. 'A Criação do MPLA', *Estudos Afro-Asiáticos* 32: 185–208.

Blanes, R. 2013. 'Da Confusão à Ironia. Expectativas e Legados da PIDE em Angola', *Análise Social* XLVIII (1): 30–55.

———. 2012a. 'Moral Circumscriptions: Involuntary Mobility, Diaspora and Ideological Configurations in the Angolan Tokoist Church', *Canadian Journal of African Studies* 46(3): 367–380.

———. 2012b. 'O Tempo dos Inimigos: notas para uma antropologia da repressão no século XXI', *Horizontes Antropológicos* 37: 261–275.

———. 2011a. 'Unstable Biographies: The Ethnography of Memory and Historicity in an Angolan Prophetic Movement', *History and Anthropology* 22(1): 93–119.

———. 2011b. 'Double Presence: Proselytism and Belonging in an Angolan Prophetic Church's Diaspora', *Journal of Religion in Europe* 4(3): 409–428.

———. 2010. 'The Personification of a Prophet: Leadership, Charisma and the Globalization of the Angolan Tokoist Church', in S. Fancello and A. Mary (eds.), *Chrétiens Africains en Europe. Prophetismes, Pentecôtismes et Politique des Nations*. Paris: Karthala, 69–92.

———. 2009a. 'Remembering and Suffering: Memory and Shifting Allegiances in the Angolan Tokoist Church', *Exchange* 38(2): 161–181.

———. 2009b. 'O Messias Entretanto Já Chegou. Relendo Balandier e o Profetismo Africano na Pós-Colônia', *Campos – Revista de Antropologia Social* 10(2): 9–23.

———. 2009c. 'Circunscrição Moral. Mobilidade, diáspora e configurações doutrinais na Igreja Tokoista', in R. Carmo and J. Simões (eds.), *A Produção das Mobilidades. Redes, Espacialidades e Trajectos num Mundo em Globalização*. Lisbon: Imprensa de Ciências Sociais, 247–262.

———. 2009d. 'O Que se Passa Tabernáculo? Oração e Espacialização na Igreja Tokoista Angolana', *Religião e Sociedade* 29(2): 116–133.

———. 2008a. *Os Aleluias. Ciganos Evangélicos e Música*. Lisbon: Imprensa de Ciências Sociais.

———. 2008b. 'Um Cemitério chamado Europa: cristianismo, consciência global e identidades migratórias', in R. Carmo, D. Melo and R. Blanes (eds.), *A Globalização no Divã*. Lisbon: Tinta da China, 317–333.

———. 2007. 'Why Africans Do What They Do: Arguments, Discussions and Religious Transmission in Angolan Pentecostal Churches in Lisbon', *Quaderns del ICA* 23(7): 123–137.

Bloch, M. 1977. 'The Past and the Present in the Present', *Man (N.S.)* 12(2): 278–292.

Bourdieu, P. 1986. 'L'Illusion Biographique', *Actes de Recherches en Sciences Sociales* volume 62/63: 69–72.

Boylston, T. 2012. 'The Shade of the Divine: Orthodox Christian Time and History in Zege, Ethiopia', PhD thesis, Department of Anthropology, London School of Economics and Political Science.

Brinkman, I. 2008. 'Refugees on Routes. Congo/Zaire and the war in Northern Angola (1961–1974)', in B. Heintze and J. Von Oppen (eds.), *Angola on the Move: Transport Routes, Communications and History.* Frankfurt am Main: Verlag Otto Lembeck, 198–220.

———. 2004. 'Language, Names, and War: The Case of Angola', *African Studies Review* 47(3): 143–163.

———. 2003. 'War and Identity in Angola: Two Case-Studies', *Lusotopie* 2003: 195–221.

———. 2000. 'Ways of Death: Accounts of Terror from Angolan Refugees in Namibia', *Africa* 70(1): 1–24.

Cabral, J. 2013. 'The Two Faces of Mutuality: Contemporary Themes in Anthropology', *Anthropological Quarterly* 86(1): 257–275.

———. 2001. 'A Difusão do Limiar: margens, hegemonias e contradições', *Análise Social* 153: 865–892.

———. 1991. *Os Contextos da Antropologia.* Porto: Difel.

Cahen, M. 2006. 'Lutte d'Émancipation Anticoloniale ou Mouvement de Libération Nationale? Processus Historique et Discours Idéologique. Le Cas des Colonies Portugaises, et du Mozambique en Particulier', *Revue Historique* 2006(1): 113–138.

Cannell, F. 2006. *The Anthropology of Christianity.* Durham, NC: Duke University Press.

Carreira, A. 1977. *Angola: da Escravatura ao Trabalho Livre. Subsídios para a história demográfica do século XVI até à independência.* Lisbon: Arcádia.

Castelli, E. 2007. *Martyrdom and Memory: Early Christian Culture Making.* New York: Columbia University Press.

Castelo, C. 2007. *Passagens para África: O Povoamento de Angola e Moçambique com Naturais da Metrópole (1920–1974).* Porto: Afrontamento.

———. 1998. *O Modo Português de Estar no Mundo: o luso-tropicalismo e a ideologia colonial portuguesa (1933–1961).* Porto: Afrontamento.

Castro, E. V. 1998. 'Cosmological Deixis and Amerindian Perspectivism', *Journal of the Royal Anthropological Institute* 4(3): 469–488.

———. 1992. *From the Enemy's Point of View: Humanity and Divinity in an Amazonian Society.* Chicago, IL: University of Chicago Press.

Carvounas, D. 2002. *Diverging Time: The Politics of Modernity in Kant, Hegel and Marx.* Lanham, MA: Lexington Books.

Chabal, P., and N. Vidal. 2007. *Angola, The Weight of History.* New York: Columbia University Press.

Chabal, P. (ed.). 2002. *A History of Postcolonial Lusophone Africa.* London: Hurst & Co.

Christian Jr., W. 1989. *Local Religion in Sixteenth-Century Spain.* Princeton, NJ: Princeton University Press.

Clarence-Smith, W. 1985. 'Runaway Slaves and Social Bandits in Southern Angola, 1875–1913', *Slavery & Abolition* 6(3): 23–33.

Clastres, H. 1993 (1975). *La Tierra sin Mal. El Profetismo Tupí-Guaraní.* Buenos Aires: Ediciones Colihue.

Clastres, P. 1974. *La Société contre l'État. Recherches d'Anthropologie Politique.*
     Paris: Les Éditions de Minuit.
Cole, J. 2001. *Forget Colonialism? Sacrifice and the Art of Memory in Madagas-*
     car. Berkeley and Los Angeles: University of California Press.
Coleman, S. 2010. '"Right Now!": Historiopraxy and the Embodiment of Char-
     ismatic Temporalities', *Ethnos* 76(4): 426–447.
———. 2004. 'The Charismatic Gift', *Journal of the Royal Anthropological Insti-*
     tute (N.S.) 10: 421–442.
———. 2000. *The Globalisation of Charismatic Christianity: Spreading the Gos-*
     pel of Prosperity. Cambridge: Cambridge University Press.
Collingwood, R. 1994. *The Idea of History.* Oxford: Oxford University Press.
Comaroff, J. 1985. *Body of Power, Spirit of Resistance: The Culture and History*
     of a South African People. Chicago, IL: University of Chicago Press.
Comaroff, J., and J. Comaroff. 1997. *Of Revelation and Revolution, volume 2:*
     The Dialectics of Modernity on a South African Frontier. Chicago, IL: Uni-
     versity of Chicago Press.
———. 1992. *Ethnography and the Historical Imagination.* Boulder, CO: West-
     view Press.
———. 1991. *Of Revelation and Revolution, volume 1: Christianity, Colonialism*
     and Consciousness in Southern Africa. Chicago, IL: University of Chicago
     Press.
———. 1989. 'The Colonization of Consciousness in South Africa', *Economy*
     and Society 18: 267–296.
Comerford, M. 2003. 'Peace Agreements in Angola and Implications for Gover-
     nance', *Conflict Trends* 3: 14–18.
Connerton, P. 2009. *How Modernity Forgets.* Cambridge: Cambridge. Univer-
     sity Press.
Cox, J. 1998. *Rational Ancestors: Scientific Rationality and African Indigenous*
     Religions. Cardiff: Cardiff Academic Press.
Crapanzano, V. 2004. *Imaginative Horizons: An Essay in Literary-Philosophical*
     Anthropology. Chicago, IL: University of Chicago Press.
———. 2000. *Serving the Word: Literalism in America from the Pulpit to the*
     Bench. New York: New Press.
Csordas, T. 2009. 'Growing up Charismatic: Morality and Spirituality among
     Children in a Religious Community', *Ethos* 37(4): 414–440.
———. 1997. *Language, Charisma, and Creativity: The Ritual Life of a Religious*
     Movement. Berkeley: University of California Press.
———. 1994. *The Sacred Self: A cultural Phenomenology of Charismatic Heal-*
     ing. Berkeley: University of California Press.
Cunha, J. 1959. *Aspectos dos Movimentos Associativos na África Negra, Volume*
     II (Angola). Lisbon: Junta de Investigações do Ultramar.
De Craemer, W., J. Vansina and R. Fox. 1976. 'Religious Movements in Central
     Africa: A Theoretical Study', *Comparative Studies in Society and History*
     18(4): 458–475.
De Bruijn, M., R. Van Dijk and D. Foeken (eds.). 2001. *Mobile Africa: Changing*
     Patterns of Movement in Africa and Beyond. Leiden: Brill.
DeRogatis, A. 2003. *Moral Geography: Maps, Missionaries, and the American*
     Frontier. New York: Columbia University Press.

Derrida, J. 1995. *Archive Fever: A Freudian Impression.* Chicago, IL: University of Chicago Press.

Desjarlais, R. 2003. *Sensory Biographies: Lives and Deaths among Nepal's Yolmo Buddhists.* Berkeley and Los Angeles: University of California Press.

Domingos, N., and V. Pereira (eds.). 2010. *O Estado Novo em Questão.* Lisbon: Edições 70.

Douglas, M. 1999. *Leviticus as Literature.* Oxford: Oxford University Press.

Doutreloux, A. 1965. 'Prophetisme et Culture', in VV.AA., *African Systems of Thought.* London and Oxford: International African Institute & Oxford University Press.

Dozon, J. P. 2006. 'D'un Prophétisme à l'Autre ou une Histoire de Modernité à Contretemps', *Socio-Anthropologie* 17–18. Accessed online at http://socio-anthropologie.revues.org/index449.html.

———. 1974. 'Les Mouvements Politico-Religieux: Syncrétismes, Messianismes, Néo-traditionnalismes', in M. Augé (ed.), *La Construction du Monde: Religion, Représentations, Idéologie.* Paris: F. Maspero.

Droogers, A. 1980. 'Kimbanguism at the Grass Roots: Beliefs in a Local Kimbanguist Church, *Journal of Religion in Africa* 11(3): 188–211.

Dulley, I. 2010. *Deus é Feiticeiro. Prática e Disputa nas Missões Católicas em Angola Colonial.* São Paulo: Annablume.

Edgar, R., and H. Sapire. 2000. *African Apocalypse: The Story of Nontetha Nkwenkwe, a Twentieth-Century South African Prophet.* Athens: Ohio University Press.

Egan, K. 2011. 'I Want to Feel the Camino in my Legs: Trajectories of Walking on the Camino de Santiago', in A. Fedele and R. Blanes (eds.), *Encounters of Body and Soul in Contemporary Religious Practices.* Oxford and New York: Berghahn Books, 3–22.

Eisenlohr, P. 2009. 'Technologies of the Spirit: Devotional Islam, Sound Reproduction and the Dialectics of Mediation and Immediacy in Mauritius Patrick Eisenlohr', *Anthropological Theory* 9(3): 273–296.

———. 2007. *Little India: Diaspora, Time and Ethnolinguistic Belonging in Hindu Mauritius.* Berkeley and Los Angeles: University of California Press.

Eisenstadt, S. 1968. *Max Weber on Charisma and Institution Building: Selected Papers and with an Introduction.* Chicago, IL: University of Chicago Press.

Ellis, S., and G. ter Haar. 2004. *Worlds of Power: Religious Thought and Political Practice in Africa.* London: Hurst & Co.

Engelke, M. 2010. 'Past Pentecostalism: Notes on Rupture, Realignment, and Everyday Life in Pentecostal and African Independent Churches', *Africa* 80(2): 177–199.

———. 2009. 'Reading and Time: Two Approaches to the Materiality of Scripture', *Ethnos* 74(2): 151–174.

———. 2007. *A Problem of Presence: Beyond Scripture in an African Church.* Berkeley: University of California Press.

———. 2004. 'Discontinuity and the Discourse of Conversion', *Journal of Religion in Africa* 34(1–2): 82–109.

Engelke, M., and J. Robbins. 2010. 'Global Christianity, Global Critique', Special Issue, *South Atlantic Quarterly* 109(4).

Englund, H. 2003. 'Christian Independency and Global Membership: Pentecostal Extraversions in Malawi', *Journal of Religion in Africa* 33(1): 83–111.

Espírito Santo, D. 2010. 'Spiritist Boundary-Work and the Morality of Materiality in Afro-Cuban Religion', *Journal of Material Culture* 15(1): 64–82.

Espírito Santo, D., and R. Blanes (eds.). 2013. *The Social Life of Spirits*. Chicago, IL: University of Chicago Press.

Espírito Santo, D., and N. Tassi (eds.). 2012. *Making Spirits: Materiality and Transcendence in Contemporary Religions*. London: IB Tauris.

Estermann, C. 1983. *Etnografia de Angola (sudoeste e centro): colectânea de artigos dispersos*. Lisbon: Instituto de Investigação Ciêntífica Tropical.

———. 1965. 'O Tocoismo como Fenómeno Religioso', *Garcia de Orta* 13(3): 325–342.

Esteves, E. 2010. 'O Trabalho Forçado nas Companhias Ferroviárias de Angola (séculos XIX–XX)', in C. Saraiva, J. Tavim and P. Havik (eds.), *Caminhos Cruzados em História e Antropologia. Ensaios de Homenagem a Jill Dias*. Lisbon: Imprensa de Ciências Sociais.

Esteves, M. (ed.). 1991. *Portugal, País de Imigração*. Lisbon: Instituto de Estudos para o Desenvolvimento.

Fabian, J. 1995. 'Ethnographic Misunderstanding and the Perils of Context', *American Anthropologist* 97(1): 41–50.

———. 1983. *Time and the Other: How Anthropology Makes its Object*. New York: Columbia University Press.

———. 1969. 'Charisma and Cultural Change: The Case of the Jamaa Movement in Katanga (Congo Republic)', *Comparative Studies in Society and History* 11(2): 155–173.

Fardon, R. (ed.). 1990. *Localizing Strategies: Regional Traditions in Ethnographic Writing*. Edinburgh: Scottish Academic Press.

Fasholé-Luke, E., et al. 1978. *Christianity in Independent Africa*. London: R. Collings.

Faubion, J. 2001. *The Shadows and Lights of Waco: Millennialism Today*. Princeton, NJ: Princeton University Press.

———. 1993. 'History in Anthropology', *Annual Review of Anthropology* 22: 35–54.

Feld, S., and K. Basso (eds.). 1996. *Senses of Place*. Rochester, NY: Boydell & Brewer.

Ferguson, J. 2006. *Global Shadows: Africa in the Neoliberal World Order*. Durham, NC: Duke University Press.

———. 1999. *Expectations of Modernity: Myths and Meanings of Urban Life on the Zambian Copperbelt*. Berkeley: University of California Press.

Fernandez, J. 2003. 'Emergence and Convergence in some African Sacred Places', in S. Low and D. Lawrence-Zúñiga (eds.), *The Anthropology of Space and Place*. Oxford: Blackwell Publishing.

———. 1973. 'The Precincts of the Prophet: A Day with Johannes Galilee Shembe', *Journal of Religion in Africa* 5(1): 32–53.

———. 1970. 'Rededication and Prophetism in Ghana', *Cahiers d'Études Africaines* 10(38): 228–305.

Fernando, M. 2010. *As Religiões em Angola. A Realidade do Período Pós-Independência (1975–2010)*. Luanda: INAR.

Ferrão, A. 1957. *Colonato do Vale do Loge. Sete Anos de Actividade (1950–1956)*. Luanda: Junta de Exportação do Café / Delegação de Angola.

Ferreira, C. 2012. 'O Tokoismo como Elemento da Identidade Angolana (1950–1965)', MA thesis, African History, University of Lisbon.

Ferreira, E., C. Lopes and M. Mortágua. 2008. *A Diáspora Angolana em Portugal. Caminhos de Retorno*. Cascais: Principia.

Festinger, L., H. Riecken and S. Schachter 1956. *When Prophecy Fails: A Social and Psychological Study of a Modern Group that Predicted the Destruction of the World*. London: Harper Co.

Feuchtwang, S. 2008. 'Suggestions for a Redefinition of Charisma', *Nova Religio* 12(2): 90–105.

———. 2002. 'Remnants of Revolution in China', in C. Hann (ed.), *Postsocialism: Ideals, Ideologies, and Practices in Eurasia*. London: Routeldge.

———. 2001. *Popular Religion in China: The Imperial Metaphor*. Richmond: Curzon Press.

Feuchtwang, S., and M. Rowlands. 2010. 'Re-evaluating the Long Term: Civilisation and Temporalities', in D. Garrow and T. Yarrow (eds.), *Archaeology and Anthropology: Understanding Similarity, Exploring Difference*. Oxford: Oxbow Books.

Feuchtwang, S., and W. Mingming. 2001. *Grassroots Charisma: Four Local Leaders in China*. London and New York: Routledge.

Fonte, M. 2007. 'Urbanismo e Arquitectura em Angola. De Norton de Matos à Revolução', PhD thesis, Urban Planning, Technical University of Lisbon.

Formenti, A. 2011. 'Being Migrants and Missionaries: Guinean Evangelical Christians in Lisbon', working paper, Institute of Social Sciences, Lisbon.

Freston, P. 2005. 'The Universal Church of the Kingdom of God: A Brazilian Church finds Success in Southern Africa', *Journal of Religion in Africa* 35(1): 33–65.

———. 2001. *Evangelicals and Politics in Asia, Africa and Latin America*. Cambridge: Cambridge University Press.

Freudenthal, A. 2011. '50 Years, the 4th January 1961 Peasant Rebellion', paper presented at the international conference *The End of the Portuguese Empire in a Comparative Perspective*, Lisbon, June 2011.

———. 2005. *Arimos e Fazendas. A Transição Agrária em Angola*. Luanda: Chá de Caxinde.

Gabriel, M. 1978. *Angola, Cinco Séculos de Cristianismo*. Queluz: Literal.

Geertz, C. 1966. 'Religion as a Cultural Sysem', in M. Banton (ed.), *Anthropological Approaches to the Study of Religion*. London: Tavistock Publications, 1–46.

Gell, A. 1992. 'The Technology of Enchantment and the Enchantment of Technology', in J. Coote and A. Shelton (eds.), *Anthropology, Art and Aesthetics*. Oxford: Clarendon Press, 41–63.

Geschiere, P. 1997 [1995]. *The Modernity of Witchcraft: Politics and the Occult in Postcolonial Africa*. Charlottesville: University Press of Virginia.

Gifford, P. 1995. *Christian Churches and the Democratisation of Africa*. Leiden: Brill.

Gonçalves, A. 2003. *Tradição e Modernidade na (Re)Construção de Angola*. Porto: Afrontamento.

———. 1985. *Kongo: Le Lignage contre l'État: dynamique politique kongo du XVIème au XIIIème siècle*. Lisbon and Évora: Instituto de Investigação Científica Trropical, Universidade de Évora.

———. 1984. 'Analyse Sociologique du Tokoisme en Angola', *Anthropos* 79: 473–483.

Gonçalves, J. 1967. 'O Tocoismo Perante a Sociedade Angolana (Relatório de Material Escolhido)', *Bulletin de l'Institut Fondamentale de l'Afrique Noire* 29(3–4): 678–694.

———. 1960. *Protestantismo em África*, vols. 1–2. Lisbon: Junta de Investigações do Ultramar.

Goody, J. 2006. *The Theft of History*. Cambridge: Cambridge University Press.

Grassi, M. 2008. 'Mobilidade, Fronteiras e Capital Social na Angola Contemporânea', *Revista Angolana de Sociologia* 3.

———. 2007. 'Práticas, Formas e Solidariedades da Integração de Jovens de Origem Angolana no Mercado de Trabalho em Portugal', *Economia Global e Gestão* 12(3): 71–91.

Graw, K., and U. Schielke (eds.). 2011. *The Global Horizon: Migratory Expectations in Africa and the Middle East*. Leuven: Leuven University Press.

Gray, R. 1999. 'A Kongo Princess, the Kongo Ambassadors and the Papacy', *Journal of Religion in Africa* 29(2): 140–154.

———. 1983. '*Come Vero Principe Catolico*: the Capuchins and the Rulers of Soyo in the Late Seventeenth Century', *Africa* 53(3): 39–54.

Green, M. 2003. *Priests, Witches and Power: Popular Christianity after Mission in Southern Tanzania*. Cambridge: Cambridge University Press.

Grenfell, J. 1998. 'Simão Toco: An Angolan Prophet', *Journal of Religion in Africa* 28(2): 210–226.

———. 1996. 'The History of the Baptist Church in Angola, 1879–1975', unpublished manuscript.

Guyer, J. 2007. 'Prophecy and the Near Future: Thoughts on Macroeconomic, Evangelical and Punctuated Time', *American Ethnologist* 34(3): 409–421.

Hackett, R. 1998. 'Charismatic/Pentecostal Appropriation of Media Technologies in Nigeria and Ghana', *Journal of Religion in Africa* 28(3): 258–277.

Halbwachs, M. 1992. *On Collective Memory*. Chicago, IL: University of Chicago Press.

Halloy, A. 2010. 'Chez Nous, le Sang Règne! L'Apprentissage Religieux dans le Culte Xangô de Recife (Brésil)', *Terrain* 55: 40–53.

Hansen, A. 1979. 'Once the Running Stops: Assimilation of Angolan Refugees into Zambian Border Villages', *Disasters* 3(4): 369–374.

Hansen, A., and D. Tavares. 1999. 'Why Angolan Soldiers worry about Demobilisation and Reintegration', in R. Black and K. Koser (eds.), *The End of the Refugee Cycle? Refugee Repatriation and Reconstruction*. Oxford and New York: Berghahn Books, 198–209.

Hansen, M. 2006. '"God for Everyone – Everyone for Himself"? An Angolan Example of Civil Society Beyond the Blueprints', integrated thesis, International Development Studies, Roskilde University; Portuguese Studies, Copenhagen University.

Harding, S. 2000. *The Book of Jerry Falwell: Fundamentalist Language and Politics*. Princeton NJ: Princeton University Press.

Hastings, A. 1998. 'The Christianity of Pedro IV of the Kongo, "The Pacific" (1695–1718)', *Journal of Religion in Africa* 28(2): 145–159.

———. 1996. *The Church in Africa, 1450–1950*. Oxford: Oxford University Press.

———. 1996b. 'From Agbebi to Diangienda: Independency and Prophetism', in *The Church in Africa, 1450–1950*. Oxford: Oxford University Press, 493–540.

———. 1974. *A History of African Christianity 1950–1975*. Cambridge: Cambridge University Press.

Hastrup, K. (ed.). 1992. *Other Histories*. London and New York: Routledge.

Hefner, R. (ed.). 1993. *Conversion to Christianity: Historical and Anthropological Perspectives on a Great Transformation*. Berkeley: University of California Press.

Heimer, F. W. (ed.). 1973. *Social Change in Angola*. Munich: Arnold Bergstrassen Institut.

Heintze, B., and J. Von Oppen (eds.). 2008. *Angola on the Move: Transport Routes, Communications and History*. Frankfurt am Main: Verlag Otto Lembeck.

Henderson, L. 1990. *A Igreja em Angola. Um Rio com Várias Correntes*. Lisbon: Editorial Além-Mar.

———. 1971. 'Protestantism: A Tribal Religion', in R. Parsons (ed.), *Windows on Africa – A Symposium*. Leiden: Brill, 51–80.

Henriques, I. 2004. 'A Materialidade do Simbólico: Marcadores territoriais, marcadores identitários angolanos (1880–1950)', *Textos de História* 12(1–2): 9–41.

———. 1997. *Percursos da Modernidade em Angola: dinâmicas comerciais e transformações sociais no século XIX*. Lisbon: Instituto de Investigação Científica e Tropical.

Hess, D. 1990. 'Ghosts and Domestic Politics in Brazil: Some Parallels between Spirit Possession and Spirit Infestation', *Ethos* 18(4): 407–438.

Heywood, L. (ed.). 2002. *Central Africans and Cultural Transformations in the American Diaspora*. Cambridge: Cambridge University Press.

———. 1989. 'Unita and Ethnic Nationalism in Angola', *Journal of Modern African Studies* 27(1): 47–66.

Hill, J. (ed.). 1988. *Rethinking History and Myth: Indigenous South American Perspectives on the Past*. Urbana: University of Illinois Press.

Hilton, A. 1985. *The Kingdom of Kongo*. Oxford: Clarendon Press.

———. 1983. 'Family and Kinship among the Kongo South of the Zaire River from the Sixteenth to the Nineteenth Centuries', *Journal of African History* 24(2): 189–206.

Hirschkind, C. 2006. *The Ethical Soundscape: Cassette Sermons and Islamic Counterpublics*. New York: Columbia University Press.

Hodges, M. 2008. 'Rethinking Time's Arrow: Bergson, Deleuze and the Anthropology of Time', *Anthropological Theory* 8(4): 399–429.

———. *The Ethnography of Time: Living with History in Modern Rural France*. Lampeter: Edwin Mellen Press

Horton, R. 1976. *Patterns of Thought in Africa and the West: Essays on Magic, Religion and Science*. Cambridge: Cambridge University Press.

Hunt, S. 2005. 'The *Alpha* Program: Charismatic Evangelism for the Contemporary Age', *Pneuma* 27(1): 65–82.

Ingold. T. 2010. 'Footprints through the Weather-World: Walking, Breathing, Knowing', *Journal of the Royal Anthropological Institute* 16: S121–S139.

———. 1993. 'The Temporality of the Landscape', *World Archaeology* 25(2): 152–174.

Ingold, T., and J. Vergunst (eds.). 2008. *Ways of Walking: Ethnography and Practice on Foot.* Burlington and Farnham: Ashgate.

James, W., and D. Mills (eds.). 2005. *The Qualities of Time: Anthropological Approaches.* Oxford and New York: Berg.

James, W. (ed.). 1995. *The Pursuit of Certainty: Religious and Cultural Formulations.* London and New York: Routledge.

Jameson, F. 2005. *Archaeologies of the Future: The Desire Called Utopia and Other Science Fictions.* London: Verso.

Jenkins, P. 2007. *God's Continent: Christianity, Islam, and Europe's Religious Crisis.* Oxford: Oxford University Press.

———. 2006. *The New Faces of Christianity: Believing the Bible in the Global South.* Oxford: Oxford University Press.

———. 2002. *The Next Christendom: The Rise of Global Christianity.* Oxford: Oxford University Press.

Johnson, D. 1994. *Nuer Prophets: A History of Prophecy from the Upper Nile in the Nineteenth and Twentieth Centuries.* Oxford: Oxford University Press.

Johnson, D., and D. Anderson (eds.). 1995. *Revealing Prophets in Eastern African History.* London: James Currey.

Johnson, P. 2007. *Diaspora Conversions. Black Carib Religion and the Recovery of Africa.* Berkeley: University of California Press.

Jules-Rosette, B. (ed.). 1979. *The New Religions of Africa.* London: Ablex Publishing.

———. 1975. *African Apostles: Ritual and Conversion in the Church of John Maranke.* Ithaca, NY: Cornell University Press.

Kabongo-Mbaya, P. 1991. 'Protestantisme Zairois et Déclin du Mobutisme. Ajustement de Discours ou Rupture de Stratégie', *Politique Africaine* 41: 72–89.

Keane, W. 2008. 'The Evidence of the Senses and the Materiality of Religion', *Journal of the Royal Anthropological Institute (N.S.)* 14: S110–S127.

———. 2007. *Christian Moderns: Freedom and Fetish in the Mission Encounter.* Berkeley: University of California Press.

———. 2004. 'Language and Religion', in A. Duranti (ed.), *A Companion to Linguistic Anthropology.* Oxford: Blackwell.

———. 2003. 'Semiotics and the Social Analysis of Material Things', *Language and Communication* 23: 409–425.

———. 2002. 'Sincerity, Modernity and the Protestants', *Cultural Anthropology* 17(1): 65–92.

Keese, A. 2003. '"Proteger os Pretos": Havia uma Mentalidade Reformista na Administração Portuguesa na África Tropical (1926–1961)?' *Africana Studia* 6: 97–125.

Keller, E. 2005. *The Road to Clarity: Seventh-Day Adventism in Madagascar.* New York: Palgrave Macmillan.

Khalili, L. 2007. *Heroes and Martyrs of Palestine: The Politics of Historical Commemoration.* Cambridge: Cambridge University Press.

King, R., G. Lazaridis and T. Tsardanidis. 2000. *Eldorado or Fortress: Migration in Southern Europe.* New York: Macmillan.

Kirsch, T. 2008. *Spirits and Letters: Reading, Writing and Charisma in African Christianity.* Oxford: Berghahn.

———. 2007. 'Ways of Reading as Religious Power in Print Globalization', *American Ethnologist* 34(3): 509–520.

Kisela, J. 2004. *Simão Toco. A Trajectoria de um Homem de Paz.* Luanda: Editorial Nzila.

Klaver, M., and L. van de Kamp. 2011. 'Embodied Temporalities in Global Pentecostal Conversion', *Ethnos* 76(4): 421–425.

Knauft, B. (ed.). 2002a. *Critically Modern: Alternatives, Alterities, Anthropologies.* Bloomington, IN: Indiana University Press.

———. 2002b. 'Critically Modern: An Introduction', in B. Knauft (ed.), *Critically Modern: Alternatives, Alterities, Anthropologies.* Bloomington, IN: Indiana University Press, 1–55.

Koselleck, R. 2004. *Futures Past: On the Semantics of Historical Time.* New York: Columbia University Press.

———. 2002. *Aceleración, Prognoss y Secularización.* Valencia: Pre-Textos.

———. 1985. *The Practice of Conceptual History: Timing History, Spacing Concepts.* Stanford: Stanfod University Press.

Kuper, A. 1988. *The Invention of Primitive Society: Transformations of an Illusion.* London and New York: Routledge.

Lambek, M. 2007. 'Sacrifice and the Problem of Beginning: Meditations from Sakalava Mythopraxis', *Journal of the Royal Anthropological Institute (N.S.)* 13: 19–38.

———. 2002. *The Weight of the Past: Living with History in Mahajanga, Madagascar.* New York: Palgrave Macmillan.

———. 1998. 'The Sakalava Poiesis of History: Realizing the Past Through Spirit Possession in Madagascar', *American Ethnologist* 25(2): 106–127.

———. 1990. 'Certain Knowledge, Contestable Authority: Power and Practice on the Islamic Periphery', *American Ethnologist* 17(1): 23–40.

Lanternari, V. 1963. *The Religions of the Oppressed.* New York: Alfred Knopf.

Latour, B. 1991. *Nous n'Avons Jamais été Modernes: Essais d'Anthropologie Symmétrique.* Paris: La Découverte.

Lave, J. 1988. *Cognition in Practice: Mind, Mathematics and Culture in Everyday Life.* Cambridge: Cambridge University Press.

Lave, J., and E. Wenger. 1991. *Situated Learning: Legitimate Peripheral Participation.* Cambridge: Cambridge University Press.

Leach, J. 2004. *Creative Land: Place and Procreation on the Rai Coast of Papua New Guinea.* Oxford and New York: Berghahn Books.

Leenhardt, M. 1902. *Le Mouvement Éthiopien au Sud de l'Afrique de 1896 à 1899.* Paris: Couesland.

Legesse, A. 1994. 'Prophetism, Democharisma and Social Change', in T. Blakely, W. van Beek and D. Thompson (eds.), *Religion in Africa: Experience and Expression.* London: James Currey, 315–341.

Levitt, P. 2007. *God Needs No Passport: Immigrants and the Changing American Religious Landscape*. New York: New Press.
———. 2001. *The Transnational Villagers*. Berkeley: University of California Press.
Lindholm, C. 1990. *Charisma*. Oxford: Wiley & Sons.
Lopes, C. 2007. *Roque Santeiro - Entre a Ficção e a Realidade*. Lisboa: Principia.
Lowy, M. 2005. *Fire Alarm: Reading Walter Benjamin's 'On the Concept of History'*. London: Verso.
Luhrmann, T. 2007. 'How do You Learn to Know That it is God who Speaks?' in D. Berliner and R. Sarró (eds.), *Learning Religion: Anthropological Perspectives*. Oxford and New York: Berghahn.
Mabeko-Tali, J.-M. 1995. 'La Chasse aux Zairois a Luanda', *Politique Africaine* 57: 71–84.
MacGaffey, J., and R. Bazenguissa-Ganga. 2000. *Congo-Paris: Transnational Traders on the Margins of the Law*. Oxford: International African Isntitue & James Currey.
MacGaffey, W. 1986. *Religion and Society in Central Africa: The BaKongo of Lower Zaire*. Chicago, IL: University of Chicago Press.
———. 1983. *Modern Kongo Prophets: Religion in a Plural Society*. Bloomington, IN: Indiana University Press.
———. 1977. 'Cultural Roots of Kongo Prophetism', *History of Religions* 17(2): 177–193.
———. 1970. 'The Religious Commissions of the Bakongo', *Man (New Series)* 5(1): 27–38.
Mafra, C. 2002. *Na Posse da Palavra. Religião, Conversão e Liberdade Pessoal em Dois Contextos Nacionais*. Lisbon: Imprensa de Ciências Sociais.
Malaquias, A. 2006. *Rebels and Robbers: Violence in Post-Colonial Angola*. Uppsala: Nordiska Afrikainstitutet.
Malheiros, J., and F. Vala. 2004. 'A Problemática da Segregação Residencial de Base Étnica. Questões Conceptuais e Limites à Operacionalização: O Caso da Área Metropolitana de Lisboa', *Revista de Estudos Demográficos* 36: 89–110.
Manger, L., and M. Assal (eds.). 2006. *Diasporas Within and Without Africa: Dynamism, Heterogeneity, Variation*. Uppsala: Nordiska Afrikainstitutet.
Manzambi, V. 1995. 'A Trajectória de Simão Gonçalves Toko e o Tokoismo no Despertar da Consciência Nacional em Angola – Um Contributo para a Luta de Libertação Nacional', in VV.AA., *Angola. 40 anos de Guerra*. Gaia: Sociedade de Estudos e Intervenção Patrimonial, 22–33.
Mapril, J. 2009. 'Geografias da Virtude: "bons" muçulmanos e as políticas da oração entre os bangladeshis de Lisboa', *Religião e Sociedade* 29(2): 134–151.
———. 2007. 'Maulana says the Prophet is Human, Not God: Milads and Hierarchies among Bengali Muslims in Lisbon', *Lusotopie* 14(1): 255–270.
Marcum, J. 1978. *The Angolan Revolution: Exile Politics and Guerrilla Warfare (1962–1976)*. Boston, MA: MIT Press.
———. 1969. *The Angolan Revolution: The Anatomy of an Explosion (1950–1962)*. Boston, MA: MIT Press.

Margarido, A. 1972. 'The Tokoist Church and Portuguese Colonialism in Angola', in R. Chilcote (ed.), *Protest and Resistance in Angola and Brazil: Comparative Studies*. Berkeley: University of California Press, 29–52.
———. 1966. 'L'Église Toko et le Mouvement de Libération de l'Angola', *Le
Mois en Afrique* 5: 80–97.
Marques, J. 2010. 'Quiméricos e reservados: a África no Portugal de Oitocen-
tos', in P. Havik, C. Saraiva and J. Tavim (eds.), *Caminhos Cruzados em
História e Antropologia. Ensaios de Homenagem a Jill Dias*. Lisbon: Im-
prensa de Ciências Sociais, 93–107.
Marshall, R. 2009. *Political Spiritualities: The Pentecostal Revolution in Nigeria*.
Chicago, IL: University of Chicago Press.
Martin, M. L. 1975. *Kimbangu: An African Prophet and his Church*. Oxford:
Basil Blackwell.
Marwick, M. 1950. 'Another Modern Anti-Witchcraft Movement in East Cen-
tral Africa', *Africa* 20(2): 100–112.
Mary, A. 2005. 'Histoires d'Église: héros chrétiens et chefs rebelles des nations
célestes', in L. Fourchard, A. Mary and R. Otayek (eds.), *Entreprises Reli-
gieuses Transnationales en Afrique de l'Ouest*. Paris: Karthala.
———. 2002. 'Prophètes Pasteurs: La politique de la délivrance en Côte d'Ivoire',
Politique Africaine 87: 69–84.
Maskens, M. 2010. 'Semer des Graines Divines dans le Coeur des Prostituées à
Brxelles: Analyse d'une Entreprise Missionnaire Locale', in S. Fancello and
A. Mary (eds.), *Chrétiens Africains en Europe. Prophétismes, Pentecôtismes
et Politique des Nations*. Paris: Karthala, 327–350.
Mateus, D. 2004. *A PIDE/DGS na Guerra Colonial: 1961–1974*. Lisboa:
Terramar.
Matory, J. L. 2005. *Black Atlantic Religion: Tradition, Transnationalism and Ma-
triarchy in the Afro-Brazilian Candomblé*. Princeton, NJ: Princeton Univer-
sity Press.
Matos, P. 2006. *As Côres do Império. Representações Raciais no Império Colo-
nial Português*. Lisbon: Imprensa de Ciências Sociais.
Matumona, M. 2009. 'Messianismo Bantu como Ponto de Partida da Teologia
Africana: Referências Particulares ao Profetismo Bakongo', *Revista Ango-
lana de Sociologia* 4: 103–117.
Mauss, M., and H. Hubert. 2003 [1899]. *On Prayer*. Oxford and New York:
Berghahn Books.
Maxwell, D. 2005. 'The Durawall of Faith: Pentecostal Spirituality in Neo-Lib-
eral Zimbabwe', *Journal of Religion in Africa* 35(1): 4–32.
Mazrui, A. (ed.). 2010. *História Geral da África, vo. VIII. África desde 1935*.
Brasília: UNESCO.
Mboukou, S. 2010. *Messianisme et Modernité: Dona Béatrice Kimpa Vita et le
Mouvement des Antoniens*. Paris: L'Harmattan.
McIntosh, J. 2009. *The Edge of Islam: Power, Personhood and Ethnoreligious
Boundaries on the Kenya Coast*. Durham, NC: Duke University Press.
Mélice, A. 2011. 'La Cité Sainte de Nkamba: Anthropologie d'un Espace Théo-
logico-Politique', paper presented at the Anthropology Seminar, ICS, Lis-
bon, February 2011.

———. 2006. 'Un Terrain Fragmenté. Le kimbanguisme et ses ramifications', *Civilisations* 54(1–2): 67–76.

———. 2001. 'Le Kimbanguisme: un millenarisme dynamique de la terre aux cieux', *Bulletin des Seances* 47 (supplement): 35–54.

Melo, J. 2002. *Jesus L'Africain, Le Vrai Grand Secret de Fatima*. Paris: NeKongo Press.

Melo, R. 2005. '*Nyaneka-Nkhumbi*: uma *carapuça* que não serve aos Handa, nem aos Nyaneka, nem aos Nkhumbi', *Caderno de Estudos Africanos* 7–8: 157–178.

Messiant, C. 2008. *L'Angola Postcolonial*, vols. 1–2. Paris: Karthala.

———. 2006. *1961. L'Angola Colonial, Histoire et Société. Les Prémises du Mouvement Nationaliste*. Bâle: P. Schlettwein.

———. 1998. 'Protestantismes en Situation Coloniale. Quelles Marges?' *Lusotopie* 1998: 245–256.

———. 1995. 'Avant-propos. L'Angola dans la Guerre', *Politique Africaine* 57: 3–10.

———. 1994. 'Angola, les Voies de l'Ethnisation et de la Décomposition I. De la guerre a la paix (1975–1991): le conflit armé, les interventions internationales et le peuple angolais', *Lusotopie* 1–2: 155–210.

Meyer, B. 2010. 'Aesthetics of Persuasion: Global Christianity and Pentecostalism's Sensational Forms', *South Atlantic Quarterly* 109(4): 741–763.

———. 2006. 'Impossible Representations: Pentecostalism, Vision and Video Technology in Ghana', in B. Meyer and A. Moors (eds.), *Religion, Media and the Public Sphere*. Bloomington, IN: Indiana University Press, 290–312.

———. 2003. 'Visions of Blood, Sex and Money: Fantasy Spaces in Popular Ghanaian Cinema', *Visual Anthropology* 16: 15–41.

———. 1999. 'Commodities and the Power of Prayer: Pentecostalist Attitudes Towards Consumption in Contemporary Ghana', in B. Meyer and P. Geschiere (eds.), *Globalization and Identity. Dialectics of Flow and Closure*. Oxford: Wiley-Blackwell, 151–176.

———. 1998. 'Make a Complete Break with the Past: Memory and Post-Colonial Modernity in Ghanaian Pentecostalist Discourse', *Journal of Religion in Africa* 28(3): 316–349.

Meyer, B., and P. Geschiere (eds.). 1999. *Globalization and Identity: Dialectics of Flow and Closure*. Oxford: Wiley-Blackwell.

Meyer, B., and P. Pels (eds.). 2003. *Magic and Modernity: Interfaces of Revelation and Concealment*. Stanford, CA: Stanford University Press.

Middleton, J. 1999. 'Preface', in H. Behrend, *Alice Lakwena and the Holy Spirits: War in Northern Uganda, 1986–97*. Oxford: James Currey.

Miller, D. 2008. *The Comfort of Things*. Oxford: Polity Press.

Mittermaier, A. 2011. *Dreams that Matter: Egyptian Landscapes of the Imagination*. Berkeley: University of California Press.

Miyazaki, H. 2006. 'Economy of Dreams: Hope in Global Capitalism and Its Critiques', *Cultural Anthropology* 21(2): 147–172.

———. 2004. *The Method of Hope: Anthropology, Philosophy and Fijian Knowledge*. Stanford, CA: Stanford University Press.

———. 2003. 'The Temporalities of the Market', *American Anthropologist* 105(2): 255–265.

———. 2000. 'Faith and its Fulfillment: Agency, Exchange and the Fijian Aesthetics of Completion', *American Ethnologist* 27(1): 31–51.

Mourão, F. 2005. 'O Espaço Urbano no Contexto Colonial: o caso de Luanda', *África: Revista do Centro de Estudos Africanos USP* 24-25-26: 175–192.

Mudimbe, v. 1988. *The Invention of Africa: Gnosis, Philosophy and the Order of Knowledge*. London and Bloomington, IN: James Currey and Indiana University Press.

Munn, O. 1992. 'The Cultural Anthropology of Time: A Critical Essay', *Annual Review of Anthropology* 21: 93–123.

Musumeci, L. (ed.). 2002. *Antes do Fim do Mundo: Milenarismo e Messianismos no Brasil e na Argentina*. Rio de Janeiro: UFRJ.

Nashif, E. 2008. *Palestinian Political Prisoners: Identity and Community*. London and New York: Routledge.

Naumescu, V. 2011. 'The Case for Religious Transmission: Time and Transmission in the Anthropology of Christianity', *Advances in Research: Religion and Society* 2: 54–71.

———. 2010. 'Le vieil Homme et le Livre. La Crise de la Transmission chez les Vieux-croyants (Roumanie)', *Terrain* 55: 72–89.

Ndiokwere, N. 1981. *Prophecy and Revolution: The Role of Prophets in the Independent African Churches and in Biblical Tradition*. London: SPCK.

Neto, M. 2011. 'The Catholic Paradox: Supporting Colonialism and Producing Anti-colonialists', paper presented at the international conference *The End of the Portuguese Empire in a Comparative Perspective*, Lisbon, June 2011.

Neves, J. 2008. *Comunismo e Nacionalismo em Portugal. Política, Cultura e História no Século XX*. Lisbon: Tinta-da-China.

———. 2006. 'On Communism and the Nation: Notes on the History of the Colonial Question in the Portuguese Communist Party', *E-JPH* 4(1): 1–11.

Newitt, M. 1981. *Portugal in Africa: The Last Hundred Years*. London: Longman.

Nora, P. 1989. 'Between Memory and History: Les Lieux de Memoire', *Representations* 26: 7–24.

Nordstrom, C., and A. Robben (eds.). 1995. *Fieldwork under Fire: Contemporary Studies of Violence and Survival*. Berkeley: University of California Press.

Nzila, V. 2006. *Introdução ao Tocoísmo*. Luanda: GCNET.

Oien, C. 2008. 'The Angolan Diaspora in Lisbon: An Introduction', *Economia Global e Gestão* 12(3): 23–33.

———. 2007. 'Pathways of Migration: Perceptions of Home and Belonging among Angolan Women in Portugal', PhD thesis, Faculty of Humanities, University of Manchester.

———. 2006. 'Transnational Networks of Care: Angolan Children in Fosterage in Portugal', *Ethnic and Racial Studies* 29(6): 1104–1117.

Ojo, M. 2006. *The End-Time Army: Charismatic Movements in Modern Nigeria*. Trenton, NJ: Africa World Press.

———. 1988. 'The Contextual Significance of the Charismatic Movements Independent Nigeria', *Africa* 58: 175–92.

O'Neill, K. 2010. *City of God: Christian Citizenship in Post-War Guatemala*. Berkeley: University of California Press.

Orsi, R. 2008. 'Abundant History: Marian Apparitions as Alternative Modernity', *Historically Speaking* September/October: 12–26.

Palmié, S. 2011. 'The Ejamba on North Fairmount Avenue, the Wizard of Menlo Park and the Dialectics of Ensoniment: As Episode in the History of an Acoustic Mask', paper presented at Yale University, 1 November.

———. 2007. 'Introduction: Out of Africa?' *Journal of Religion in Africa* 37(2): 159–173.

———. 2002. *Wizards and Scientists: Explorations in Afro-Cuban Modernity and Tradition*. Durham, NC: Duke University Press.

Paxe, A. 2009. 'Dinâmicas de Resiliência Social nos Dircursos e Práticas Tokoistas no Icolo e Bengo', MA thesis, African Studies, ISCTE-IUL, Lisbon.

Péclard, D. 1998. '*Eu sou americano.* Dynamiques du champ missionnaire dans le planalto central angolais au XXe siècle', *Lusotopie* 1998: 357–376.

———. 1998b. 'Religion and Politics in Angola: The Church, the Colonial state and the emergence of Angolan Nationalism, 1940–1961', *Journal of Religion in Africa* 28(2): 160–186.

———. 1995. *Ethos Missionaire et Esprit du Capitalisme. La Mission Philafricaine en Angola, 1897–1907*. Bern: Le Fait Missionaire (Cahier Occasional nº 1).

Pedro, F. 2008. *O Vaticínio na Igreja de Cristo*. Luanda: GCNET.

Peel, J. D. Y. 2003. *Religious Encounters and the Making of the Yoruba*. Bloomington, IN: Indiana University Press.

Pélissier, R. 1978. 'A la Recherche d'un Dieu Anti-Colonialiste', in *La Colonie du Minotaure. Nationalismes et Révoltes en Angola (1926–1961)*. Orgeval: Éditions Pélissier, 159–188.

Pels, P. 1999. *A Politics of Presence: Contacts Between Missionaries and Walugru in Late Colonial Tanganyika*. Amsterdam: Harwood Academic Publishers.

Pereira, L. 2004. 'Os Bakongo de Angola: Religião, Política e Parentesco num Bairro de Luanda', PhD thesis, Department of Anthropology, University of São Paulo.

Pereira, A. 1994. 'The Neglected Tragedy: The Return to War in Angola, 1992–3', *Journal of Modern African Studies* 32(1): 1–28.

Pimentel, I. 2007. *A História da PIDE*. Lisbon: Temas e Debates.

Pinto, Pedro. 2012. 'A Implantação das Testemunhas de Jeová em Portugal e no Ultramar Português (1925–1974)', *Lusitania Sacra* 25: 127–179.

Pires, R. 2002. 'Mudanças na Imigração. Uma análise das estatísticas sobre a população estrangeira em Portugal, 1998–2001', *Sociologia Problemas e Práticas* 39: 151–166.

———. 1987. *Os Retornados: um Estudo Sociográfico*. Lisbon: IED.

Porto, N. 1999. *Angola a Preto e Branco. Fotografia e Ciência no Museu do Dundo*. Coimbra: Museu Antropológico da Universidade de Coimbra.

Possidónio, D. 2006. *Descendentes de Angolanos e de Luso-Angolanos na Área Metropolitana de Lisboa. Inserção Geográfica e Social*. Lisbon: ACIME.

Pype, K. 2012. *The Making of the Pentecostal Melodrama: Religion, Media and Gender in Kinshasa*. Oxford and New York: Berghahn Books.

Queiroz, M. 1965. *O Messianismo no Brasil e no Mundo*. São Paulo: Dominus & Editora da Universidade de São Paulo.

Quibeta, S. n.d. *Simão Tôco. O Profeta Africano em Angola. Vida e Obra*. Luanda: Edição de Autor.

Ranger, T. (ed.). 2008. *Evangelical Christianity and Democracy in Africa.* Oxford: Oxford University Press.

———. 1986. 'Religious Movements and Politics in Sub-Saharan Africa', *African Studies Review* 29(2): 1–69.

———. 1968. 'Connexions between "Primary Resistance" Movements and Modern Mass Nationalism in East and Central Africa. Part I', *Journal of African History* 9(3): 437–453.

Rego, A. 1970. 'Syncretic Movements in Angola', *Luso-Brazilian Review* 7(2): 25–43.

Reis, F. 2010. 'Das Políticas de Classificação às Classificações Políticas (1950–1996). A Configuração do Campo Político Angolano. Contributo para o Estudo das Relações Raciais em Angola', PhD thesis, Modern and Contemporary History, ISCTE-IUL, Lisbon.

Richards, A. 1935. 'A Modern Movement of Witch-Finders', *Africa* 8: 448–461.

Robbins, J. 2010. 'Anthropology, Pentecostalism, and the New Paul: Conversion, Event and Social Transformation', *The South Atlantic Quarterly* 109(4): 633–654.

———. 2007. 'Continuity Thinking and the Problem of Christian Culture', *Current Anthropology* 48(1): 5–38.

———. 2004. *Becoming Sinners: Christianity and Moral Torment in a Papua New Guinea Society.* Berkeley: University of California Press.

———. 2001. 'Secrecy and the Sense of an Ending: Narrative, Time, and Everyday Millenarianism in Papua New Guinea and in Christian Fundamentalism', *Comparative Studies in Society and History* 43(3): 525–551.

Robbins, J., and M. Engelke. 2010. 'Introduction: Global Christianity, Global Critique', *The South Atlantic Quarterly* 109(4): 623–632.

Rocha, E. 2003. *Contribuição ao Estudo da Génese do Nacionalismo Moderno Angolano: período de 1950–1964: testemunho e estudo documental.* Luanda: Kilombelombe.

Rodrigues, C. 2007. 'From Family Solidarity to Social Classes: Urban Stratification in Angola (Luanda and Ondjiva)', *Journal of Southern African Studies* 33(2): 235–250.

Rosales, M., V. Jesus and S. Parra. 2009. *Crescer Fora da Água? Expressividades, Posicionamentos e Negociações Identitárias de Jovens de Origem Africana na Região Metropolitana de Lisboa.* Lisbon: Observatório da Imigração.

Rowland, R. 1987. *Antropologia, História e Diferença. Alguns Aspectos.* Porto: Afrontamento.

Rowlands, M. 1993. 'The Role of Memory in the Transmission of Culture', *World Archaeology* 25(2): 141–151.

Sahlins, M. 2004. *Apologies to Thucydides: Understanding History and Culture and Vice Versa.* Chicago, IL: University of Chicago Press.

———. 1985. *Islands of History.* Chicago, IL: University of Chicago Press.

———. 1981. *Historical Metaphors and Mythical Realities: Structure in the Early History of the Sandwich Islands Kingdom.* Ann Arbor, MI: University of Michigan Press.

Salazar, C. 2008. 'Prayer and Symbolisation in an Irish Catholic Community', *Etnográfica* 12(2): 387–402.

Samarin, W. 1986. 'Protestant Missions and the History of Lingala', *Journal of Religion in Africa* 16(2): 138–163.

Sánchez-Carretero, C. (ed.). 2011. *El Archivo del Duelo*. Madrid: CSIC.

Sánchez-Carretero, C., and P. J. Margry (eds.). 2011. *Grassroots Memorials: The Politics of Memorializing Traumatic Death*. Oxford and New York: Berghahn Books.

Sanneh, L., and J. Carpenter (eds.). 2005. *The Changing Face of Christianity: Africa, the West and the World*. Oxford: Oxford University Press.

Sansi-Roca, R. 2007. *Fetishes and Monuments: Afro-Brazillian Art and Culture in the 20th Century*. Oxford and New York: Berghahn Books.

Santos, B. S., and P. Meneses (eds.). 2009. *Epistemologias do Sul*. Coimbra: Almedina.

Santos, E. 1969. *Religiões de Angola*. Lisbon: Junta de Investigações do Ultramar.

Santos, M. 2000. 'Angola', in C. Azevedo (ed.), *Dicionário de História Religiosa de Portugal*. Lisbon: Círculo de Leitores.

Santos, M., and M. Torrão. 1993. *Missões Religiosas e Poder Colonial no Século XIX*. Lisbon: Instituto de Investigação Científica e Tropical.

Sarró, R. 2009a. 'Kongo en Lisboa: un ensayo sobre la reubicación y extraversión religiosa', in Y. Aixelá et al. (eds.), *Introducción a los Estudios Africanos*. Barcelona: CEIBA, 115–129.

———. 2009b. 'O Sofrimento como Modelo Cultural: uma Reflexão Antropológica sobre a Memória Religiosa na Diáspora Africana', in L. Pereira and C. Pussetti (eds.), *Os Saberes da Cura*. Lisbon: ISPA.

———. 2009c. 'La Aventura como Categoría Cultural: apuntes simmelianos sobre la emigración subsahariana', *Revista de Ciências Humanas* 43(2): 501–521.

———. 2008a. *The Politics of Religious Change on the Upper Guinea Coast: Iconoclasm Done and Undone*. Edinburgh: International African Library.

———. 2008b. 'Arrodíllate y Creerás: Reflexiones sobre la Postura Religiosa', in M. Cornejo, M. Cantón and R. Blanes (eds.), *Teorías y Prácticas Emergentes en Antropología de la Religión*. San Sebastián: FAAEE, 273–292.

———. 2007. 'Demystified Memories: The Politics of Heritage in Post-Socialist Guinea', in F. De Jong and M. Rowlands (eds.), *Reclaiming Heritage: Alternative Imaginaries of Memory in West Africa*. Walnut Creek, CA: Left Coast Press, 215–229.

———. 2009. 'Prophetic Diasporas. Moving Religion Across the Lusophone Atlantic', *African Diaspora* 2(1): 52–72.

Sarró, R., R. Blanes and F. Viegas. 2008. 'La Guerre en temps de Paix. Ethnicité et Angolanité dans l'Église Kimbanguiste de Luanda', *Politique Africaine* 110: 84–101.

Sarró, R., and A. Mélice. 2012. 'Kongo–Lisbonne: la dialectique du centre et de la périphérie dans l'Église kimbanguiste', *Canadian Journal of African Studies* 46(3): 411–427.

———. 2010. 'Kongo and Lisbon: The Dialectics of Center and Periphery in the Kimbanguist Church', in S. Fancello and A. Mary (eds.), *Chrétiens Africains en Europe: Prophétismes, Pentecôtismes et Politique des Nations*. Paris: Karthala, 43–68.

Sayad, A. 2004 (1999). *The Suffering of the Immigrant.* Cambridge: Cambridge University Press.

Scheper-Hughes, N. 1994. 'Embodied Knowledge: Thinking with the Body in Critical Medical Anthropology,' in R. Borovski (ed.), *Assessing Cultural Anthropology.* New York: McGraw-Hill, 229–242.

Schielke, U., and K. Graw (eds.). 2012. *The Global Horizon: Expectations of Migration in Africa and the Middle East.* Leuven: Leuven University Press.

Schoffeleers, M. 1991. 'Ritual Healing and Political Acquiescence: The Case of the Zionist Churches in Southern Africa', *Africa: Journal of the International African Institute* 61(1): 1–25.

Schubert, B. 2000. *A Guerra e as Igrejas: Angola, 1961–1991.* Bern: P. Schlettwein Publishing.

———. 1999. 'Os protestantes na guerra angolana depois da independência', *Lusotopie* 1999: 405–413.

Schubert, J. 2010. 'Democratisation and the Consolidation of Political Authority in Post-War Angola', *Journal of Southern African Studies* 36(3): 657–672.

Scott, J. 2009. *The Art of Not Being Governed: An Anarchist History of Upland Southeast Asia.* New Haven, CT: Yale University Press.

———. 1990. *Domination and the Arts of Resistance: Hidden Transcripts.* New Haven, CT: Yale University Press.

———. 1985. *Weapons of the Weak: Everyday Forms of Peasant Resistance.* New Haven, CT: Yale University Press.

Scott, M. 2007. *The Severed Snake: Matrilineages, Making Place, and a Melanesian Christianity in Southeast Solomon Islands.* Durham, NC: Carolina Academic Press.

———. 2005. 'I Was Like Abraham: Notes on the Anthropology of Christianity from the Solomon Islands', *Ethnos* 70(1): 101–125.

Seesemann, R., and B. Soares. 2009. 'Being as Good Muslims as Frenchmen: On Marabouts, Colonial Modernity, and the Islamic Sphere in French West Africa', *Journal of Religion in Africa* 39(1): 91–120.

Serrano, C. 2008. *Angola. Nascimento de uma Nação. Um Estudo sobre a Construção da Identidade Nacional.* Luanda: Kilombelombe.

Shepperson, G. 1953. 'Ethiopianism and African Nationalism', in I. Wallerstein (ed.), *Social Change: The Colonial Situation.* New York: John Wiley and Sons, 478–488.

Shils, E. 1965. 'Charisma, Order, and Status', *American Sociological Review* 30(2): 199–213.

Sinda, M. 1972. *Le Messianisme Congolais et ses Incidences Politiques. Kimbanguisme, Matsouanisme, Autres Mouvements.* Paris: Payot.

Smit, R. 2007. 'The Power of the Word: How Angolan Pentecostal Christians in Rotterdam Experience Power in an Uncertain World', paper presented at conference *International migration, multi-local livelihoods and human security: Perspectives from Europe, Asia and Africa,* Institute of Social Studies, Netherlands, August.

Smith, D. 2000. *Moral Geographies: Ethics in a World of Difference.* Edinburgh: Edinburgh University Press.

Smith, J. 1982. *Imagining Religion: From Babylon to Jonestown*. Chicago, IL: University of Chicago Press.

———. 1978. *Map is not Territory: Studies in the History of Religions*. Leiden: Brill.

St. Clair, G. 2011. 'Religious Reform: Different Options for Acting in the World', paper presented at the *Christianities Workshop*, LSE, 4–5 May.

Strenski, I. 2003. *Theology and the First Theory of Sacrifice*. Leiden: Brill.

Stromberg, P. 1993. *Language and Self-Transformation: A Study of the Christian Conversion Narrative*. Cambridge: Cambridge University Press.

Sundkler, B. 1948. *Bantu Prophets in South Africa*. Oxford: Oxford University Press.

Swatowiski, C. 2010. 'Igreja Universal em Portugal: Tentativas de Superação de um Estigma', *Revista Intratextos* 1: 169–192.

———. 2007. 'Texto e Contextos da Fé: O Discurso Mediado de Edir Macedo', *Religião e Sociedade* 27(1): 114–131.

Tambiah, S. 1985. 'Form and Meaning of Magical Acts', in *Culture, Thought, and Social Action: An Anthropological Perspective*. Cambridge, MA: Harvard University Press, 60–86.

Taussig, M. 1987. *Shamanism, Colonialism and the Wild Man: A Study in Terror and Healing*. Chicago, IL: University of Chicago Press.

Taylor, L. 2007. 'Centre and Edge: Pilgrimage and the Moral Geography of the US/Mexico Border', *Mobilities* 2(3): 383–393.

Ter Haar, G. 1992. *Spirit of Africa: The Healing Ministry of Archbishop Milingo of Zambia*. London: Hurst & Co.

Thornton, J. 1998. *The Kongolese Saint Anthony: Dona Beatriz Kimpa Vita and the Antonian Movement, 1684–1706*. Cambridge: Cambridge University Press.

———. 1998b. *Africa and the Africans in the Making of the Atlantic World, 1400–1800*. Cambridge: Cambridge University Press.

———. 1991. 'Precolonial African Industry and the Atlantic Trade, 1500–1800', *African Economic History* 19(1): 1–19.

———. 1981. 'Early Kongo-Portuguese Relations: A New Interpretation', *History in Africa* 8: 183–204.

Thornton, J., and L. Heywood. 2007. *Central Africans, Atlantic Creoles, and the Foundation of the Americas, 1585–1660*. Cambridge: Cambridge University Press.

Tomlinson, M. 2009. *In God's Image: The Metaculture of Fijian Christianity*. Berkeley: University of California Press.

Tonda, J. 2005. *Le Souverain Moderne. Le Corps du Pouvoir en Afrique Centrale (Congo, Gabon)*. Paris: Karthala.

———. 2001. 'Le Syndrome du Prophete. Médécines Africaines et Précarités Identitaires', *Cahiers d'Études Africaines* 161: 139–162.

Toren, C. 2004. 'Becoming a Christian in Fiji: an Ethnographic Study in Ontogeny', *Journal of the Royal Anthropological Institute* (N.S.) 9: 709–727.

———. 1988. 'Making the Present, Revealing the Past: The Mutability and Continuity of Tradition as a Process', *Man* (N.S.) 23: 696–717.

Torgal, L., et al. 2008. *Comunidades Imaginadas: Nação e nacionalismos em África*. Coimbra: Imprensa da Universidade de Coimbra.

Torres, A. 1986. 'Le Processus d'Urbanisation de l'Angola dans la Période Coloniale (années 1940–1970)', *Revista Estudos de Economia* 7(1): 47–67.

Trouillot, M. 1995. *Silencing the Past: Power and the Production of History*. Boston, MA: Beacon Press.

Tumminia, D. 2005. *When Prophecy Never Fails: Myth and Reality in a Flying-Saucer Group*. New York and Oxford: Oxford University Press.

Turner, H. W. 1969. 'The Place of Independent Religious Movements in the Modernization of Africa', *Journal of Religion in Africa* 2(1): 43–63.

———. 1967. 'A Typology for African Religious Movements', *Journal of Religion in Africa* 1(1): 1–34.

Valverde, P. 1997. 'O Corpo e a Busca de Lugares da Perfeição: escritas missionárias da África colonial portuguesa', *Etnográfica* 1(1): 73–96.

Van der Veer, P. (ed.). 1996. *Conversion to Modernities: The Globalization of Christianity*. London and New York: Routledge.

Van Wijk, J. 2010. 'Luanda – Holanda: Irregular Migration from Angola to the Netherlands', *International Migration* 48(2): 1–30.

———. 2005. 'Forces to migrate from Angola to the Netherlands', SOCIUS Working Papers nº7, accessed May 2010 at http://pascal.iseg.utl.pt/~socius/index.htm.

Van Wing, J. 1959. *Études Bakongo. Sociologie – Religion et Magie*. Brussels: Desclee du Brower.

———. 1958. 'Le Kimbanguisme vu par un Temoin', *Zaire* 12: 563–618.

Vansina, J. 1962. 'Long-distance Trade Routes in Central Africa', *Journal of African History* 3(3): 375–390.

Varanda, J. 2011. 'A asa protectora de Outros: As relações transcoloniais do Serviço de Saúde da Diamang', in C. Bastos and R. Barreto (eds.), *Circulação do Conhecimento Médico*. Lisbon: Imprensa de Ciências Sociais, 339–374.

———. 2004. 'A Saúde e a Companhia de Diamantes de Angola', *História, Ciências Saúde Manguinhos* 11: 261–268.

Vasconcelos, J. 2008. 'Homeless Spirits: Modern Spiritualism, Psychical Research and the Anthropology of Religion in the Late Nineteenth and Early Twentieth Centuries', in F. Pine and J. P. Cabral (eds.), *On the Margins of Religion*. Oxford and New York: Berghahn Books, 13–38.

Vellut, J. 1989. 'The Congo Basin and Angola', in VV.AA., *General History of Africa, VI, Africa in the Nineteenth Century until the 1880s*. London: James Currey & UNESCO.

Vidal, N. 2007. 'Social Neglect and the Emergence of Civil Society', in P. Chabal and N. Vidal (eds.), *Angola: The Weight of History*. London: Hurst & Co, 224–232.

Viegas, F. 2008. *Panorama das Religiões em Angola Independente (1975 – 2008)*. Luanda: Ministério da Cultura/Instituto Nacional para os Assuntos Religiosos.

———. 2007. *Panorama das Religiões em Angola. Dados Estatísticos 2007*. Luanda: Instituto Nacional para os Assuntos Religiosos.

———. 1999. *Angola e as Religiões*. Luanda: Edição de Autor.

Vilaça, A. 2010. *Strange Enemies: Indigenous Agency and Scenes of Encounters in Amazonia*. Durham, NC: Duke University Press.

Vilaça, A., and R. Wright (eds.). 2009. *Native Christians: Modes and Effects of Christianity among Indigenous Peoples of the Americas*. Farnham and Burlington: Ashgate.

Vilaça, H. 2006. *Da Torre de Babel às Terras Prometidas. Pluralismo Religioso em Portugal*. Porto: Afrontamento.

Vines, A. 1995. 'La Troisième Guerre Angolaise', *Politique Africaine* 57: 27–39.

Wauthier, C. 2007. *Sectes et Prophètes d'Afrique Noire*. Paris: Éditions du Seuil.

Weber, M. 2006. *Sociologia da Religião*. Lisbon: Relógio d'Água.

———. 1947. *The Theory of Social and Economic Organization*. Glencoe, IL: Free Press.

Werbner, R. 2011. *Holy Hustlers, Schism and Prophecy: Apostolic Reformation in Botswana*. Berkeley: University of California Press.

West, H. 2005. *Kupilikula: Governance and the Invisible Realm in Mozambique*. Chicago, IL: University of Chicago Press.

Westphal, M. 2005. 'Prayer as the Posture of the Decentered Self', in B. Benson and N. Wirzba (eds.), *The Phenomenology of Prayer*. New York: Fordham University Press, 13–31.

Wheeler, D. 1971. 'Discovering Angola, 1926–1961', in D. Wheeler and R. Pélissier, *Angola*. London: Pall Mall Press, 165–189.

———. 1969. 'The Portuguese Army in Angola', *Journal of Modern African Studies* 7(3): 425–439.

———. 1968. 'Nineteenth-Century African Protest in Angola: Prince Nicolas of Kongo (1830?–1860)', *African Historical Studies* 1(1): 40–59.

Wheeler, D., and R. Pélissier. 1971. *Angola*. London: Pall Mall Press.

Witte, M. de. 2003. 'Altar Media's *Living Word:* Televised Charismatic Christianity in Ghana', *Journal of Religion in Africa* 33(2): 172–202.

Wolf, E. 1982. *Europe and the People Without History*. Berkeley: University of California Press.

Worsley, P. 1957. *The Trumpet Shall Sound: A Study of Cargo Cults in Melanesia*. London: McGibbon and Kee.

Young, J. 2007. *Rituals of Resistance: African Atlantic Religion in Kongo and The Lowcountry South in the Era of Slavery*. Baton Rouge: Lousiana State University Press.

Index

agency, 21, 31–33, 45, 59, 115, 145,
    153, 165, 174–75, 188, 190, 192,
    194
    political, 9, 28, 180, 190
    spiritual (*see* spirits)
Amselle, Jean-Loup, 190–91
Atlantic, 11, 25, 84, 97, 174
    history, 174, 179–80
Autochthony, 9
Azores Islands, 83–91

Bakongo. *See* ethnicity
Balandier, Georges, 6, 13–15, 27, 45,
    83, 90, 98, 144
belonging, x, 9, 17, 24–25, 32, 40, 74,
    123, 147, 174–75, 178, 183, 188,
    191–94, 202–3
    ideologies of, 74, 123
    movement and, 25, 32, 185, 188
    territorial, 24, 40, 147, 174–75,
        178, 188, 191, 192–94
Benjamin, Walter, 20
biography
    as method, 31, 42–45
    biographical illusion, 44, 203
    prophetic, x, 16–18, 25, 28, 32,
        42, 45, 107, 116, 138–39, 145,
        154–55, 161–62, 165–66, 185,
        198, 200–203
    sensory, 31
    spatialized, 31, 139
Bourdieu, Pierre, 44–45, 203

Casa de Oração, xiii, 170n6
Catete, 67–68, 117, 134, 149, 161

charisma, 17–18, 26–33, 68, 132–33,
    135, 137, 145, 152–53, 169, 180,
    192, 200–203
    and bureaucracy, 145
    charismatic gifts, 29, 101n22,
        111, 137, 152–53, 155, 202
    and leadership, 26–33, 45, 140,
        168, 189
    and time, 28, 68, 98, 101n14,
        165, 201–2
Comaroff, John and Jean, 9, 21,
    44–45, 101n21, 174, 194

diaspora, xii, 174, 193
    Angolan, 8, 11, 176, 194n2
    prophetic, 25
    Tokoist, 33, 172–96, 202
Direcção Mundial, 149, 150, 152, 156
Direcção Universal, x, xiii, 35n24,
    131, 141n9, 155–62, 169, 171n12,
    189–90, 198
Doze Mais Velhos, x, xii, 35n24, 55,
    57–58, 63n17, 98, 114, 148–51,
    163–66, 169, 170n4, 170n6, 191,
    198
Dozon. Jean-Pierre, 26, 28

Engelke, Matthew, 9, 21–24, 108,
    111, 113, 121, 145, 169, 174–75,
    193
eschatology, 19, 23, 48, 59, 127,
    135–36, 183, 188
ethnicity, 64, 89, 147, 162, 174
    in Angola, 7–8, 72, 93, 96, 99,
        170n3

Bakongo, 1–5, 7, 13–15, 24,
49–50, 60, 63n22, 71, 74,
96–97, 101n17, 103n34, 147,
162, 199
ethno-nationalism, 25, 97–98,
174
ethno-politics, 7, 103n37, 99,
162
ethno-theology, 18, 24, 60
multi-ethnicity, 72–73, 97, 147
expectation, 18–20, 29, 36n26,
40, 42, 122, 126, 134, 139, 145,
163–65, 192, 194, 199–200

Feuchtwang, Stephan, 20–21, 29,
31, 145
FNLA, 7, 34n8, 10, 11, 76, 86, 92,
|98, 102n32
forgetfulness, 12, 15–16, 22, 24, 27,
169
future, 20–21, 23, 42, 74, 80, 98–99,
108, 125, 127, 134–35, 199–200,
203
archaeology of, 20

geography, 24–26, 73, 176, 178,
1983, 192
moral, 4, 32, 39–40

historicity, 21, 25, 45, 140, 191
abundant history, 23–25, 107
autochthonous history, 24
conceptual, 20–21, 25, 114
end of, 24
historical linearity, 20–21
historiography, 4, 7, 16, 20,
28, 73, 132, 138, 154, 161,
166–67, 201
multiple, 21, 107
Hodges, Matt, 20, 203
hope, 19–20, 29, 76, 108, 127, 164,
166
hymns, 18, 49, 51–52, 62n7, 62n11,
74–75, 79, 85, 114–15, 117–18,
123–30, 132, 138, 141n5, 141n8,
185, 187
as history, 123–30

Kimbangu, Simon, 12–13, 15, 25,
27, 58–59, 167
Kimbanguism, x, xii, 5–6, 8, 12–13,
25, 34n14, 35n20, 39, 58, 60,
62n13, 63n19, 65, 83, 170n7, 173,
179, 191
Kimpa Vita (Dona Beatrice), 35n17,
60
Kirsch, Thomas, 101n21, 111–13,
141n12
Kongo, Kingdom of, 5, 15, 63n23
Koselleck, Reinhardt, 19–20, 114

Lambek, Michael, 18, 107, 140, 133,
155, 165, 169
leadership, 7–8, 13, 17–18, 26–31,
45, 58, 60, 76, 81, 83, 86–87, 98,
140, 144–45, 147, 150, 161–66,
171n18, 193, 201–202
and charisma (see charisma:
and leadership)
postal (see under letters)
prophetic, 17, 32, 58, 147, 201
remote, 81, 83–84, 87, 108, 145
and succession, 27, 144, 146–51,
176, 202
Leopoldville, 3, 5, 13, 32, 34n9,
49–60, 61n5, 62n6, 63n19, 64, 66,
71–72, 77, 82, 89, 96, 116, 124–25,
132, 142n16, 162
letters, 32, 61n3, 69, 86–87, 89–90,
102, 108, 110–13
and postal leadership, 86–87,
108–13
liberation, 71, 74, 76, 82–83, 125,
129, 141n9
African, 59, 71, 98
movements in Angola, 7, 15, 74,
76, 82–83, 97, 102n32
spiritual, 71, 74, 76, 83, 125,
129, 141n9
wars of, 7–8, 94, 97–98, 100n4,
102n33
Lindholm, Charles, 29, 145, 202
Lisbon, ix–xiii, 12, 16, 40, 42,
84–85, 92, 94, 112, 116–17, 123,
128, 130, 134, 157, 166, 168,

172–73, 176, 178–194, 195n6, 195n13, 198–99

Luanda, xii, 1–3, 8, 33n4, 47, 60, 66, 69–70, 72–73, 75, 79, 84–96, 101n12, 108, 113 122, 124, 128, 133–34, 137, 143–44, 146–49, 151–52, 154–57, 161–62, 170n4, 170n6, 186, 189–91, 198
   Bairro Indígena, 70, 72, 79, 96, 100n10, 164, 170n6
   Palanca, 3, 124, 126, 162

Lusophony, 11–12, 97, 174, 177, 179, 194n3

MacGaffey, Wyatt, 5, 13, 24, 27, 35n17, 50, 58–60, 144, 201, 204n1

martyrdom, 19, 41–42, 45, 98–99, 139, 145, 164–65, 185, 198, 200

Mbanza Kongo, xiii, 35n18, 61n4

Mboma, 103n34, 144, 148–49, 156

Mélice, Anne, 25, 40, 173, 191, 193

memory, x, 5, 17–20, 22–23, 25–26, 28–32, 39–42, 44–45, 58, 95, 108, 117, 125, 139–40, 145, 158, 160, 164–65, 168–70, 193, 198, 201–202
   art of, 44
   lieux de mémoire, 24
   methods of, 18, 42, 45, 200
   prophetic, 138, 166
   relembramento (re-remembering), 18–19, 33n1
   remembrance, 16, 18–20, 23, 28–9, 40, 43, 83, 94, 117, 125, 130, 136, 140, 164–67, 201–202

Messianism, 13–4, 19, 23, 26–27, 145, 201
   Bakongo, 14, 27, 35n17, 174
   (see also *Kongo prophetism*)

Meyer, Birgit, 9, 21–22, 101n14, 145, 192

millennialism, 9, 19–20, 23, 26, 36n27, 134, 156–57, 163, 169, 190
   everyday, 23

Miyazaki, Hirokazu, 19–20, 108, 127

mobility, ix, 24–25, 32, 40, 108, 147, 174, 176, 180, 184, 192–93, 203
   involuntary, 32, 40, 203

modernity, 21–24, 191, 204n1
   African, 9, 97, 204n1
   and amnesia, 24
   conversion and, 21–22
   forgetfulness and, 22
   omnibus, 21

Mpadi, Simon-Pierre, 6, 12, 15, 35n18, 59, 75

MPLA, 7–8, 10, 34n10–11, 76, 94, 96, 98, 102n32, 146, 150, 159

Mythopraxis, 18

Namibe (Angola), 32, 42, 66, 68

Neto, Agostinho, 8, 10, 35n16, 47, 94–97, 150

Nora, Pierre, 18, 22, 24, 31

Ntaia (or Taia), 2, 39, 45, 51, 72, 81, 89–90, 102n23–24, 103n34, 143, 146–48, 162

Nunes, Bishop Afonso, xiii, 3, 33n2, 131, 134, 146, 154–69, 171n16, 175, 187–90, 201

ontology, 20–21, 24, 152, 155–56, 163, 168–69
   ontogeny, 47, 203
   multiple or poly-ontologies, 20, 147, 169

Orsi, Robert, 23–25, 107, 169

Poiesis, 18, 202

prayer, 18, 51, 54–55, 71, 83, 114, 117–23, 128, 132, 135, 137, 149, 154, 156, 170n6, 182

presence, 26, 107–8, 113, 122, 169, 185, 188, 193–94, 195n9, 202
   double, 192–94
   versus absence, 32, 107, 200

prophetism, x, 9, 13, 24–27, 49
   Kongo prophetism, x, 12, 14, 24, 26–28, 35n17, 58, 201 (*see also* Bakongo messianism)
   prophecy, 25, 32, 98, 134, 145, 190, 201

prophetic biography (*see* biography)
prophetic *contretemps*, 28
prophetic leadership (*see* leadership)
prophetic temporality, 20, 35n24, 138, 166
providence, 19–20, 99, 145, 164, 167, 169

Robbins, Joel, 21–24, 174–75

sacrifice, 19–20, 42, 134, 139, 145, 155, 164–65, 167
Santos, José Eduardo dos, 11, 97, 103n38, 150, 159
Sarró, Ramon, 5, 9, 11–12, 18, 25, 27–28, 36n26, 40, 58, 107, 114, 116, 121, 139, 144–45, 157, 171n19, 173–74, 177, 180, 187, 191, 193
Scott, Michael W., 18, 20, 22, 24, 29, 147, 175
spirits, 96, 135–36, 138, 141n12, 143, 148, 151, 153–54, 168, 171n10
    spiritual agency, 24, 33, 151–54
    spiritual inhabitation, 135–37, 165
    spiritual warfare, 75, 153, 169
suffering, 8, 19, 40, 42, 90–91, 95, 97, 100, 134, 139, 151, 157, 161, 192, 196n17, 197–98, 200

tabernacle, 18, 44, 54–55, 60, 96, 114–15, 118, 121, 128, 130–33, 136–38, 141n12, 142n16, 155–56, 163, 166, 181–82, 203
temporality, 9, 19, 20, 24, 35n24, 101n14, 108, 123, 132, 136, 140, 169, 203
    beginnings and ends, 165
    calendar, 114–15, 118, 123, 138, 156, 171n12, 181
    non-linear, 20–22, 169, 203
    prophetic (*see under* prophetism)
    time's arrow, 20, 203
territoriality, 24, 26, 174, 191, 194, 200
    prophetic, 24
Thornton, John, 5, 10, 35n17, 58, 174, 190
Toko, Simão Gonçalves
    biography, 39–106
    heritage, 107–96
Topogony, 24
transmission, 20, 32, 108, 114–15, 129, 139

Uíge, 3, 39, 42, 45, 60, 61n4, 66, 72, 76, 79, 81, 89, 127, 147, 154, 163
UNITA, 7, 23, 34n10–11, 76, 95, 102n32, 159
universalism, 33, 175, 187, 193–94
Utopia, 19–20, 29, 71, 98
    and heterotopia, 19

Vale do Loge, 39, 42, 66–68, 72, 80–82, 89, 124, 136, 147, 162
vate (or *corpo vate*), 114, 137–38, 142n16, 152, 154–55, 203